WHITE HEAT

ALSO BY WAYNE JOHNSON

The Snake Game

Don't Think Twice

Six Crooked Highways

The Devil You Know

WHITE HEAT

THE EXTREME SKIING LIFE

WAYNE JOHNSON

ATRIA BOOKS   New York   London   Toronto   Sydney

ATRIA BOOKS

A Division of Simon & Schuster, Inc.
1230 Avenue of the Americas
New York, NY 10020

First Atria Books trade paperback edition November 2008

ATRIA BOOKS and colophon are trademarks of Simon & Schuster, Inc.

For information about special discounts for bulk purchases,
please contact Simon & Schuster Special Sales at
1-800-456-6798 or business@simonandschuster.com.

Designed by Jaime Putorti
Moutain photograph © istockphoto/Mike Morley

Manufactured in the United States of America

10   9   8   7   6   5   4   3   2   1

The Library of Congress has cataloged the hardcover edition as follows:

Johnson, Wayne.
    White heat : the extreme skiing life / Wayne Johnson.
        p.   cm.
    1. Skis and skiing. 2. Snowboarding. 3. Extreme sports. I. Title.
GV854.J544 2007
796.93—dc22   2007025811

ISBN-13: 978-0-7432-8733-3
ISBN-10:   0-7432-8733-9
ISBN-13: 978-0-7432-8734-0 (pbk)
ISBN-10:   0-7432-8734-7 (pbk)

AS ALWAYS, FOR KAREN

CONTENTS

White Heat: The Extreme Skiing Life is not meant to be a definitive work on the world of skiing and snowboarding. Rather, here I have attempted to give the reader a bona fide experience of "extreme skiing," how it is done, what it feels like, while also addressing the broader aspects of the sport—who lives it, where, and how. All the procedures in this book, from ski tuning and racing technique to rescue on the mountain and current snowboarding tricks, are accurate to the smallest detail, and are as I myself have experienced them. Some details may be idiosyncratic to my present geographical locale, that being Park City, Utah: for example, numerical radio protocol (radioing "we have a 10-50 on" as opposed to "we have an accident on") has been dispensed with in certain National Ski Patrol teams elsewhere.

This book is intended to put the reader on the mountain—which is a fantastic place to be. If you feel the need to get out there after reading White Heat, all the better.

Open the pages here and fly, dipsy-doodle, and rip down snowy mountainsides; take a run off the 140-meter jump in

Michigan, the famous Suicide Hill. Get a glimpse of racers and stars.

Enjoy the ride. If you can, get out there and live some of it yourself.

The mountains are waiting.

WAYNE JOHNSON

WHITE
HEAT

INTRODUCTION

Seventy miles per hour? That's nothing. My Civic will do 110, you say.

Yes, purring like a kitten, and the centerline comfortably blurring by to your left. You might, at that speed, even lift your coffee mug from the conveniently engineered dash holder to sip at your Starbucks Mocha Latte.

But imagine now you are driving down a mountain road with no guardrails. The maximum grade of any highway in the United States is 6 percent or less, usually 3 percent. That means, at the most, for every hundred feet you travel forward, you drop no more than three feet—or, at seventy miles per hour, a drop of three to six feet every second, roughly. But now, change the pitch of the road to a 40-percent slope. Every second now, and every one hundred feet you travel forward, you are dropping forty feet. Realize, you are nearly halfway to freefall.

Imagine now, too, that you have no brakes. Your only braking power is to turn sharply, which reduces your speed, but which also sends you veering toward the thousand-foot drop-off to your right, or toward the trees to your left. Remove the body of the car, all of it. The wind is howling in your ears. The wind is so powerful at this speed that it makes the jacket on your chest ruffle and flap. You are no longer holding a steering wheel. You are steering with your legs. Your four wheels have become two long-ish, flat-bottomed skates, say, a pair of Nordica Dobermann K12 GS. You had them race prepped this morning, and are hoping that the shop did an ace job for you—if not, if the edges at the shovel of the ski are too sharp, they might grab when you initiate a right turn and toss you over the precipice, or if you turn left, hurl you into the trees. Add to this now that the road is bumpy, very bumpy, and at times the ice under you, not pavement, sends shock waves up your legs. Bolts up under you and drops away tens of feet, leaving you airborne. Here that old equation, force equals mass times acceleration, is hammered into every cell of your body. At this speed, when the race course under you rises over a short distance, it creates forces equivalent to having a Steinway grand piano strapped to your back—but only for a fraction of a second. Just now, and fresh up near the top, your legs absorb every last bit of this shock, though your lower back is complaining. You ignore it.

You approach an S section in the course. You are moving at one hundred feet a second now. That boring seventy miles per hour. You need to clear the next gate, hook left around it. You want your left ski to be riding inches from the outside pole of the gate as you pass it, your right ski bearing the bulk of the centripetal force and in the precise cambered arc to carry you beyond the gate where you will step onto your uphill, left ski, to set up for your next gate. But you aren't past the gate yet. Moving at one hundred feet per second, this means as you approach the gate, you must be accurate to hundredths of a second—which means, literally, that you are skiing out of your mind. You cannot make decisions at this speed. No, it's your fifteen years of racing speaking from deep within you, every turn you ever made, every time you fell, those mornings up at five and out to the mountain to ski innumerable gates, bombing down runs as a ten-year-old, jumping from cornices, wind-formed crests of snow, into canyon runs, all of that is stamped into your feet, legs, spine, and head. You set your edges a half second from the gate, angulate, steer with the carving ski knee, the outside ski, ride the carving ski in a deliberate arc, one that only your body understands, that exact amount of knee steering, edge set, and weight on the ski. If you miss your mark, cut wide, you lose hundredths of a second, which, gate to gate, accumulates, adding up to a losing time. But you are not a loser. You're a winner, by God. So you cut it as close to the inside as possible. But if you are too far to the inside, the tip of your left ski will catch the gate, the ski hooking through the outside gate pole, the pole tearing your leg back—at exactly your present speed, one hundred feet per second. In the first hundredth of a second, your leg—and the tendons in your groin, in particular—will stretch (if the tendons don't simply tear). But already your motion, which was down the hill, is being converted into combined linear and rotational motion. If you are lucky, the rotation will free the ski, and you will land—at seventy miles per hour—somewhere in the region of your backside, hopefully down by your hips, where the impact may only break your pelvis or a femur, or a tibia or a fibula. If you are not so lucky, you will contact the ice/snow around the region of your thoracic or cervical spine. Or worse yet, your head. Remember, you are still traveling roughly one hundred feet per second. If, at this point, you go off into those trees to your left, mentioned earlier, the forces of deformation from striking those trees will exact a terrible price for your speed. Those trees may kill you. Or they may just break every bone in your body as you ricochet through them. At the least you will have broken arms and legs, compound fractures. A broken femur, midshaft, can cause bleeding so severe that a skier injured in this way can bleed out in as little as three to five minutes. But you don't go into the trees. No. There is the safety net to your right—and having caught your left ski, this is the direction the fall pitches you, if this happens.

But, like Bode Miller in the 2002 Olympics, you don't go into the net, you only catch an edge, and in a fraction of a second you right yourself, and point your skis into the next gate, a right-hander, knowing the course is rutted.

You are breathing deeply now, and the burning in your legs is fierce. The lactic acid buildup is beating you, slowly, but will it beat you before you reach the bottom?

The gates flash by you like torn colored silk. There is no time, no world now, only the sweet, sweet arc around the gate going by your shoulder at one hundred feet per second, the hammering of the blood in your head, the burning in your legs, your thighs beginning to weaken, that voice in your head telling you focus, focus, focus—just the gate in front of you, the signs of danger, darker snow here—RUTS RUTS RUTS! Play it safe? Or go inside anyway?

Inside. It's all or nothing for you. You catch air going over a rise, tuck to gain speed, rather than open up to scratch speed off. You are nearly doing eighty now. Gaining precious hundredths of seconds, you fall 150 feet onto the steepest section, risking coming hot (fast) into a more closely set group of technical gates, which you navigate, your legs getting sloppy, and dangerous. Even the slightest error in an edge set can kill you, or injure you for life—but you are only thinking about the sharpest, fastest, cleanest line down the remaining gates. The least bit of skidding—slowing, which you are sorely tempted to do because your legs feel like rubber now, and you worry about catching a gate and injuring yourself—will lose this race for you, and all that luck up top will be for nothing.

When the last gate is torn behind you, you tuck, skis squirreling crazily under you, in this last drop the snow packed so hard it is really just ruts and ice, and you flash by the finish line, skidding sideways in a spray of ice and snow to a stop, where you pull your goggles and helmet from your head. You watch the clock for your time and ranking in the tournament.

A minute and a half to two minutes have passed. Your time? Not fast enough.

But then it is never fast enough. Not even for Franz Klammer or Hermann Maier (known in skiing circles as the Hermanator).

There is *always* a cleaner run, a faster line, better luck.

You'll get it *just* right next time, you think, exhilarated. You'll go faster yet. You won't chicken out on the technical section, play it safe. (Though, God knows, you almost ate it on the upper section, pulled a yard sale on that left sweeper.) No, next time you'll burn that goddamned sweeper section down. You'll show the whole damned course who's boss.

But then again, it might show you.

The mountain shows skiers and riders (snowboarders) every day. And not just racers. We who love extreme winter sports, love the rush and run of it, the feeling of flying and darting down mountains, love that compressed, arced turning, push the envelope every day. On groomed runs and courses, and through trees and down chutes and bowls.

There are an infinite number of ways to "shred" the mountain. There's riding down terrain parks and halfpipes and over tabletops. There's jumping of all sorts, Nordic jumping, as seen in the Olympics, and freestyle jumping. There's competition bump skiing, and Steep and Deep, powdery slopes so severe they can only be reached by helicopter. Each variation on extreme winter sport has its own special thrill, its own special rewards, and each its dangers. And there is always, in heavy snowfall country, the possibility of avalanches.

Avalanches can be deadly.

Patrolling from Jupiter Peak at Park City, you are required to wear a Pieps, or Skadie—an avalanche beacon. So if you are buried in an avalanche, while aiding an injured skier or rider, your fellow rescuers can triangulate your position and, with the help of rescue dogs, dig you out.

In minutes.

Minutes count. In all of it. Each second can count.

I know. At Park City Mountain Resort, where I am on Mountain Patrol, we rescue the injured every day. Racers suffering high-speed injuries, kids turning aerials and inverts on the terrain parks, pow hounds poaching out-of-bounds caches. And there are the beginners: skiers who suffer lower body injuries, boot-top fractures, spiral fractures of the tibia or fibula from general tumbles, and clavicle fractures from low-speed falls (the skier puts his hand out to cushion the fall and—pop!—the clavicle breaks). And there are the snowboarder injuries, a higher percentage of them to the upper body and head than there are with skiers, given the physics of snowboarding—when a board catches an edge, it tends to catapult the rider from the waist into the hardpack. We see a fair number of these injuries, given the white-hot phenomenon snowboarding has become.

Snowboarders presently account for a *quarter* of all traffic on the slopes, and at certain resorts that have become meccas for riders, such as Brighton and Breckenridge, they account for *half*. Riders are *everywhere* on the mountain, though they tend to concentrate around terrain parks, built specifically for them, which, oddly enough, have recently been co-opted by "twin-tip" skiers.

And, for skiers and riders alike, there are injuries from collisions with trees.

Up at the Summit Patrol hut, at nearly ten thousand feet, or at the King Consolidated hut, Payday, Jupiter Peak, or Jupiter Bowl Patrol huts, we play it cool. At any moment the radio strapped to our chest might spit out a 10-50. That's radio protocol for an accident. Each patroller has a number. The Sunday patrol, which I'm on, has the prefix 12. My number is 12-28.

Waiting, we patrollers work the mountain. All mundane but pleasant enough labor: we raise safety pads to the proper height around lift towers; we police kids who are ripping down slopes recklessly; we offer directions to guests. We erect signs that warn of dangers, drop-offs, or jumps that are built where the jumpers, upon landing, will intersect with traffic. We move gear, oxygen tanks and backboards and toboggans, from Summit or Base Patrol huts to, say, Jupiter or Payday huts.

We try to take it easy.

The Summit Patrol hut, at the top of the mountain, is a beehive, perhaps five thousand square feet. Summit has a radio desk manned by two operators, while ten to fifteen patrollers circulate in and out of the building. There's running water, a microwave, a stove, two gurneys for guests with AMS—acute mountain sickness, or altitude sickness. Usually we run these guests with AMS down to base on toboggans. Patrollers take hut assignments on rotation with teams, four to six patrollers in each team. (A number of the patrollers work on snowboards now, though the bulk do so on skis.) The other huts are simply six-by-eight shacks with heaters in them and good-sized windows in the walls so they are light, keeping us on our toes. In the huts we talk shop—new gear, racing news, and rescue techniques (for a broken clavicle, should you use an airplane splint, a "figure eight," or a sling and swath? By the book, we'd all use the sling and swath, but sometimes, with this kind of injury, the guest is in less pain if the arm is positioned other than across her chest). We also talk about our "other" lives.

But then the call comes. (They usually start around ten, and intensify into the afternoon.)

"Summit Patrol to Payday. We've got a 10-50 on Homerun where it meets Crescent."

Today I'm a first responder at Payday.

I take the call. "Twelve twenty-eight to Summit. I'm on it," I radio back.

I stride from the warm hut and the other patrollers. I know a few things already. You can do sixty, if you want, on Crescent. So this could be serious. Not just a knee injury or a collarbone. This could be the real deal—so you don't waste time. I'm carrying nearly twenty pounds of gear. In my head, skiing fast, but not recklessly toward Homerun, I worry I won't be able to see the injured guest (the generic term we use for skiers and riders). There are over a hundred named runs at Park City. But I trust my—sometimes lousy—sense of direction to get me there. In my fanny pack, I have six blood stoppers, four plastic airways, scissors for cutting through clothing. I think through protocol: "Hello, I'm Wayne with the Park City Patrol. Can I help you?" Getting consent puts the Good Samaritan law in effect. I wonder what I'll see down there. Injured guests I've worked on, and gotten to the bottom, have had fatal or near-fatal injuries. In my fanny pack I also have bandages, a mask for CPR, tape for securing an injured guest's head to a backboard (if it is needed in addition to the gear we get in a trauma pack). Skiing, I'm thinking, MOI—mechanism of injury. Or it could be illness, some guy up from Florida having a coronary. Then OPQRST: onset, provocation, quality, radiation, severity, time. In my fanny pack I have rubber gloves for BSI—body substance isolation, for the bleeders. I have carabiners for attaching a toboggan towline to a snowmobile, if we have to go that route. I know the nearest helicopter landing pad is Base Patrol, so if it's a life-threatening injury we need to take him down, all the way. Here, I am navigating moguls and my head is alight with information. In my fanny pack I have glucose, in case I have a diabetic. I have a flashlight to check the skier's eyes, which should have PEARRL—pupils equal and round, regular in size, reactive to light. I have a portable pump to suck vomitus from the skier's mouth, if he or she has broken a bone, has fallen supine and inhaled vomit.

But I always return to the first thing: ABC—airway, breathing, circulation.

Taking a hard, carving arc and cutting over a rise, I see the guest, a skier, his boot in his lap, a number of bystanders a short distance from him. A very bad sign. Minor injuries attract other skiers and their sympathy. They get in close then. Serious injuries repel.

Through my head runs this: Goddammit! Sonofabitch! And, Shut up! Get focused. This is going to be UGLY.

And it is. I do a scene survey. Skis off in two different directions. So, a high-speed fall. Significant MOI. Vomitus on the snow. Blood on the snow. But a little blood will color an enormous amount of it.

I slide to a stop twenty or so feet above the skier. Kick out of my skis. Everyone recognizes my uniform, crayon red and black, white crosses on the chest, back, and arms.

I set my skis in an X above the injured guest, indicating traffic coming down the run should steer clear.

I can see I've got a femur fracture, but from this distance I can't tell where it is on the leg. Possible head injury. Possible loss of consciousness.

"Mountain Patrol," I tell the bystanders around him. "Move back, please."

I press the call button on my radio. "Twelve twenty-eight to Payday Patrol," I say. "I need a backboard, O_2, traction splint, and a toboggan. We'll need AirMed or Life Flight." A midshaft femur fracture is an automatic copter ride.

"Payday to twelve twenty-eight, we copy. ETA five minutes."

That gives me five minutes alone with this severely injured skier. This one could be fatal. No fucking around up here.

I point to a woman across from me. "Can you help?"

"Sure," she says, kicking out of her snowboard. I hand her a spare pair of gloves, glove up myself.

I stoop beside the skier. Here's the big moment. Is he breathing? Yes. Okay. How responsive is he?

"I'm Wayne, from the Park City Mountain Patrol," I say in a loud voice. "Can I help you?"

The skier, a boy of about twenty, only blinks. Not good. I pinch his earlobe and he flinches. Okay. Then he blinks and opens his eyes.

"How long has he been out?" I ask the group off to my side.

"A few minutes," a woman in a green outfit replies.

"Who are you?" the boy says. "What are you doing?" But as soon as he says it, he becomes aware of the pain in his leg. Still, I think, great. Airway. Breathing. He's conscious.

I instruct the woman I've asked over to hold his head. But even as I do that, he lurches up, bellowing.

"Oh, Jesus! Fuck! It hurts! It hurts goddammit Jesus Christ!"

"Hold him down," I tell the woman. I motion another of the

watching riders to her side. Skiers and riders are more than generous in these situations. Any one of us might at some time need this sort of help—asked for or not.

"What's your name?" I ask the boy.

"Cody!"

"Cody," I tell him, "don't sit up. I want you to stay put."

But he tries to sit up anyway, to see what's wrong with his leg. Blood. Shit. The last of the ABCs to deal with—circulation. Here, bleeding. I dig into my fanny pack for my blood stoppers, tear the packages open. I get out my scissors, cut through his ski pants. Open wound. Bone through the thigh, ivory white. I apply the sterile blood stoppers, press down on them. We haven't hit the artery, so it's not so critical, but it's bad. It could go critical. But I see from the pressure the bleeding has slowed and I bandage the leg and go to his boot, and, while he is literally screaming, apply traction.

Cody sighs, relieved.

"Jesus, what did you do?"

"I'm applying traction," I tell him. "As long as you don't move, the pain won't come back, all right?"

"I think I'm gonna be sick," he says.

"You!" I shout to yet another bystander. "Please. Over here." To the woman holding his head, I shout, "Okay, we're gonna log-roll him on the count of three! Hold his head in that position to his body when we roll him, got it?!" To the two riders alongside him now, I say, "You, grab his shoulder; you, take his pants. One, two, and *three!*" And we roll Cody, and he vomits into the snow. Then vomits again, and a third time. Usually it is three times.

Had he inhaled the vomit, I might be doing CPR on him now, the whole situation gone critical.

We roll him back on three, and I apply traction again.

I am relieved to see Walt, a onetime pro football player for the Philly Eagles coming down Homerun with a toboggan, two other seasoned patrollers with him, Jared and Moose, on his snowboard.

"Oooookay," Moose says, swinging around the group of us and popping off his board. Jared and Walt are out of their skis, too.

"You get his vitals?" Moose says, marching to Cody's side.

"No," I tell him. "I just got him in traction and he got sick."

"Yokay," Jared says. They're both down on top of Cody. Walt's got the toboggan set and secured, has the burrito out of it.

A burrito is a blanket, quick splint, pillow, and padding wrapped in a green canvas tarp. The toboggan is a Sun Valley, heavy and with a removable litter, one that can be directly lifted into a helicopter or ambulance.

Walt has the O_2 pack off the toboggan now, kelly green and stuffed with gear. In it are plastic airways, non-rebreather masks and hose, a Bag Valve Mask, and a little D cylinder of medical oxygen. Moose swings the trauma pack around, zipping it open, rifling through the cervical collars, one of which he hands to Jared.

Jared takes Cody's head and fixes the No-Neck plastic cervical collar on Cody.

"*Don't* nod, just blink," Jared says, then asks, "How's that? Can you breathe all right?"

Cody blinks.

"You want to use the BVM or the non-rebreather?" Walt asks.

"What're your vitals, Jared?"

Jared glances up at me. Shit again.

"Pulse one forty. Resp forty."

Moose, who does EMT work with the fire department, says, "Let's go with the BVM, this thing's midshaft."

Okay. We've gone from stable to unstable. Cody's going into shock. Not unusual with the midshaft femur fracture.

I reach for my radio. My call. "Twelve twenty-eight to Base Patrol."

"Base Patrol here."

I give Base the air ambulance protocol info on Cody—gender, age, and the vitals from Jared.

"What's your ETA?"

"Eight minutes."

"We copy that."

I bend down over Cody again.

"Jared," I say, "how about you get a blood pressure."

"Gotcha," he tells me.

Walt's come in from the side with the hare traction splint. Now's the ugly part for me.

"Cody, this is gonna hurt like hell, so hang on, okay?"

When we straighten out his leg, Cody screams. But then I crank down the traction and he whimpers.

"You fucker!" he says, relieved, looking at me, and I see he's joking. Injured skiers often joke. We joke with them, too. It helps.

"That's the spirit," I say, touching his shoulder. "Just a bad hair day."

"Asshole."

"You or me, pal?"

"What do you think?!"

Five minutes have gone by since our last set of vitals.

"What you got, Jared?"

"Pulse one thirty," Jared tells me. "BP's one hundred over seventy."

The pulse is good. One fifty, the opposite direction, would be a nightmare. But the blood pressure's questionable.

"Let's get him on the backboard," Moose says.

Again, on the count of three, we roll Cody on his side, and Walt slips the body-length backboard under him.

On three, we roll him back.

There's a procedure for securing the injured skier to the board. First, we position him by sliding him down, then back up, centering him. The straps are fixed in this order: nipples, nuts, then knees. When he's solid on the board, he won't move if we roll him; if he vomits on the way down again, we fix his head to the board. Walt does that. We can hear the helicopter chuttering down to Base, then see it bank sharply to land.

Just when I think this is as good as over, Jared says, "He's out."

"Got a BP?"

"Ninety systolic and holding, just that."

"Get him in the toboggan!" Moose says. We lift Cody, on the backboard, set it in the toboggan so his head is in the rear.

Moose straddles Cody with the BVM, pumping oxygen into him at 100 percent. He forces his knees into the space between Cody's waist and the litter, prepared to ride down.

"I got the toboggan," Walt says. He's six-four, 220, the right guy for the job with two on for the ride. "You just keep everybody out of the way, okay?"

"We good to go?" Moose says.

I call it. The O_2 cylinder is between Cody's legs. Hare splint set. Cody on the backboard and head immobilized. Chopper's at Base Patrol.

"Let's roll."

We have a rough section to travel, called Waterfall. Walt is big and a strong skier, but I take the safety rope at the rear, prepared to brake the motion of the toboggan for all I'm worth.

Walt pushes off. We pick up speed: ten, fifteen, twenty miles per hour. The toboggan, with Moose and Cody in it, weighs at least six hundred pounds. When we hit the Waterfall section, I swing braking turns behind the toboggan, Walt pressing down on the handles to use the braking chains.

"YO! STOP!" Moose shouts.

Walt and I skid to a stop with the toboggan. Moose leaps off, and we all three race to the side, and swing it up, Cody vomiting into the snow again.

As soon as that's over, we right the toboggan, and Moose leaps on with the BVM, giving Cody pure O_2.

"Ready?" Walt calls back.

"Go!" I shout, and we're off.

Now down Homerun, fifteen, twenty miles per hour. Jared is in front blowing his whistle, then shouting, "Coming through! Out of the way, coming through!"

Base is just blocks from us. My legs are aching from slowing the toboggan. The chopper, AirMed, is in the Base lot. When we slide into the lot, the med techs rush out. Jared gives them the vitals. We detach the litter from the toboggan, and carry Cody over. He is looking around again, but is unable to move his head. The med techs secure the litter in the chopper, and the pilot gets it started. The chopper lifts, hovers, its rotor only ten feet clear of the Base Patrol roof. The chopper lifts, even with the roof; if a side draft hit the chopper, the chopper would veer into the patrol station, kill all of us standing there watching.

But that doesn't happen. The chopper, as if magically, rises higher, then higher, then banks away, headed for the hospital downtown. The rotor wash blows dead brush in insane circles in the lot. Then it is quiet.

Moose holds up his hand. He's been on the patrol the longest, seventeen years.

We high-five each other.

Fifteen minutes have passed from the time I left the hut. I feel thrilled, exhausted, empty, happy that we got it done right, worried for Cody, happy to have people like Walt and Moose and Jared to work with.

We all do this for *free*, every Sunday. All day.

Midweek, when we can, most of us ski, out of uniform and happy to do whatever.

But Sundays are the big days. It's something that got wired into us, somewhere back in our childhoods.

Just skiing, unless it is racing, isn't enough anymore.

AVALANCHE CONTROL

ON DUTY WITH
DYNAMITE GIRL

It is shortly before 6:00 a.m., and you are sitting in the Park City Summit Patrol hut, waiting for Jackie, the Dynamite Girl.

All you've been told is, you won't forget her, which is really no help, you think, given the skiers crossing the hut are wearing bulky red and black Patrol outfits, gear festooned all over those outfits, rope, carabiners, first-aid tape, Pieps, shovels, and, on their backs, packs stuffed with yet more gear to near bursting. You settle in on the bench against the wall, angling your recently blown-out ski boots—which, already, have begun to torment your feet again—toward the fireplace, warming them.

Here at Summit the hut is the size of a lodge, really, and is a swarm of morning activity.

There's been a heavy snowfall, over three feet, a stiff wind from the south, and, being an unseasonably warm January, the temperature over the week has risen above and fallen below freezing umpteen times, creating sheets of snow in varying layers of density and composition. It has even rained briefly.

Perfect conditions for avalanches.

"You my Dynamite Donkey?" a tall, blond woman says, strutting in your direction, her face the kind you see in television ads, those making even lawn chairs or white bread seem sexy.

"*Jackie?*" you ask, not getting what she's just said, having been . . . distracted. *Dynamite Donkey?*

"*Are* you my *shadow?*" she says, in a cutting voice, as though you might be a little deaf, or, perhaps of diminished mental capacity (which is presently true), and something clicks in your head: *Right*, you're here to *shadow* an expert on an avalanche route after your Blaster's Clinic. You're glad now that even though you only got four hours of sleep, you stayed up to read the Patrol text on avalanche rescues, all that swimming to the frontal lobes of your brain, which you haven't been using for the last good ten seconds, watching—

"Jackovitch," she says, "but call me *Jackie*," you standing to shake her hand, thinking, Oh, *I get it*, but she's already moving away from you, and you follow her, admiring, from the back, that leonine strut of hers.

What a . . . *character*, you're thinking. And you're not wrong about that, either.

●

"This is the part I like," Jackie says, in the basement of the hut, a pile of gear at your feet.

"What part is that?"

"Getting out there with the explosives."

You've had to go through about a gazillion safety measures to be on for this gig (including a full FBI security check), and now Jackie is rigging a pack around your back, in it eight, two-pound pentolite charges, each equivalent to a stick of dynamite.

You feel bloated, all that firepower sitting right over your kidneys—even a little anxious. Could all of that explosive . . . kind of . . . just . . . *go off* somehow? (And what would you look like if it did?)

"Can't be short," she says, lifting four more charges. She gets three of them in the pack—twenty-two pounds now of explosive, on top of everything that's already jammed in there—hefting the last charge in her hand.

"Well?" you say.

"I like throwing these things," she tells you, something suggestive and warning in it, her eyes lighting up. Teasing.

She motions for you to turn again, and while she's getting that last charge in your pack, you don't feel so much like a donkey, but a camel—the proverbial one broken by that last straw.

Jackie starts hanging and clipping yet more things on you. First, a belt with a plastic gadget the size of a fist on it, your avalanche beacon, state of the art and the new frequency, 457 kHz, the international standard.

"*Never* use recharged batteries on a beacon," Jackie tells you.

Why, you ask.

"They'll test fine and then they'll drop dead on the mountain." Jackie takes a step back from you. "What's wrong with it?"

You crane your head down to check out the belt, which is clipped roughly over your navel. "Wrong with *what?*"

Jackie sighs, gives you a sharp rap alongside the head, as if this is her idea of some joke.

"Knot the belt, so if you get involved, your beacon won't get torn off." She gives you a level look. *Involved?* "One guy got dug out," she said, "was under for almost thirty minutes. The snowpack pressed so hard on him, when he peed later, it was like root beer. Pressure forced protein from his bloodstream into his kidneys and bladder."

Jackie now hangs a short-handled shovel to your pack and bungies it in place. The aluminum blade *upright*, "so the metal won't interfere with the beacon's signal, *if you're caught and tumbled under.*" Then avalanche probes, like tent poles, for finding victims. A snow saw. A forty-foot length of nylon rope. And last, she hands you a "crystal card" on a lanyard, which she tells you to hang from your neck. The "card" is really a thick, clear-plastic device with gadgets in it for measuring snow crystal size and types, and for gauging slope angles.

She winks at you, says, "Enough gear there?"

You flex your knees, give yourself a little shake. Were you just to, say, try this stuff on and stand in a nice, clean, temperature-controlled environment like this one, why, it would still feel ungainly, because . . .

You're also carrying, in addition to the twenty-four pounds of explosive, a two-way radio on a chest harness; carabiners, spring-locking and screw-locking, which hang from your beacon belt; in your fanny pack, you've got first-aid tape, gauze, triangular bandages, six blood stoppers, glucose, a multifunction pliers/cutter, latex gloves, an extra pair of leather gloves for rough work, and plastic airways in three sizes. From your neck are hanging, with the crystal card, your quick reference cards, Park City Helicopter landing sites, a Glasgow Coma Score, vital signs ranges, radio codes, and a quick assessment card.

And add to that what you're wearing, from inside to outside, bottom to top: a pair of wicking Cascade socks; a Duofold union suit (wicking and two-layered, cotton against the skin, wool off, and in one piece so snow will never get down your backside and onto bare skin); Mountain Hardwear ski pants made of double-strength Gore-Tex; a wicking Cascade turtleneck shirt, a wool U.S. Olympic Team sweater you got from a friend nearly thirty years ago (which is a talisman for good luck), a Mountain Hardwear vest, and a Mountain Hardwear double-lined ski jacket. And strapped over *that*, over your shoulders, is your sixteen-pocket Olympic three-quarters pack. Cocooning your hands are Cascade double-lined gloves.

On your head is the (required) Park City Patrol hat (wicking wool), and over that a pair of battery-powered, fan-driven Smith goggles (antifogging).

On your feet are Tecnica Diablos—racing boots that, off skis, are so rigid even with the upper cuffs unbuckled, that they make you walk like Frankenstein's monster. You are tempted to do that now, as Jackie, of the oiled hips, marches out the hut door with her mountaineering skis to the waiting snowcats.

Avalanche control workers, almost without exception, use *skis*, Alpine or mountaineering, as they need to climb and maneuver in their gear, something not possible on snowboards, given the rider's feet are fixed to a single surface.

RRRRR. RRRRRR, you growl behind Jackie, lifting your arms like some sleepwalker, or like Boris Karloff, laughing to yourself. (You've been a cutup all your life, this gag track running through your life, unstoppable—a good portion of the time—and you just have to live with it.)

Outside, though, you *do* stop all that.

"Oh, baby," you say, in it a kind of total dread, but with it . . . *excitement*.

And it has nothing to do with Jackie. "Come on," she says and, with an eagerness beyond explanation, you follow her out into the blizzard, to stand a block from the hut, taking it in.

A damn near, bona fide whiteout.

The mountains, in all that snow, are phantasmagorical blue-black and white teeth.

Standing just behind Jackie, the snow burning your face, you hear a sound in the distance not unlike what someone would make leaping face down onto a feather bed. A *whoooomphf!*

(And that's where that dreading part of you wants to be: back in bed, the sun not even up yet.)

"Avalanche, and no skier trigger," Jackie says, grinning. "It's gonna be a big day."

A *big day?*

And this is just for starters, recognizing the danger inherent in avalanche conditions.

Realize that avalanches in the United States alone kill on the average twenty-eight people a year. In the 2002–2003 season, in the United States, avalanches killed fifty-eight people: five climbers; twenty-five backcountry skiers; four snowboarders; twenty-three snowmobilers; and one hiker. Figures such as these, though, become even more significant when one works in a *continental* or *transitional* climate, such as that in Idaho, Colorado, or Utah, where most fatal avalanches occur.

Here they become a real and present danger that must be dealt with.

In Utah, in 2005, for example, eight people were killed in avalanches, among them, in the Salt Lake City area, twenty-three-year-old Zachary Eastman, thirty-seven-year-old Melvin Denis, and the snowboarder your life will become indelibly connected to on this avalanche training day, twenty-seven-year-old Shane Maixner, caught in an avalanche at the Canyons.

It was feared, initially, that as many as fifteen skiers and snowboarders were caught in the Canyons avalanche, the most deadly kind, a "slab avalanche," where a sheet breaks off from the slope underneath and hurls down the slope, in seconds the "slab" reaching speeds of 60 to 80 miles per hour, and sometimes, where not impeded, speeds as high as 120 miles per hour.

If you are standing off to the side of such an avalanche, the very compressed air generated from it can knock you off your feet.

When the snowpack collapses, again with that characteristic *whoooomphf!*, Jackie warns, "You hear and feel that under you out on some steep slope, you check your shorts and get ready for a fast ride to the bottom."

"So, how do we *not* do that—ride to the bottom?"

"Read the slope."

"But we're out here, patrolling, in the middle of it."

Strutting to the first waiting cat, its headlights cutting cones of boiling white in the falling snow, Jackie glances back at you over her shoulder.

"In conditions like this," she tells you, *"the wise only travel for the rescue of fools."*

And with that said, you get into the cat.

Which you sit in the back of, engine roaring, the cat pitching from side to side, the driver dropping off the AC team members at their assignment sites. Finally, it's just you and Jackie, and the cat is climbing from Peak, up the saddle to Pinecone.

You've got minutes here before you're back out in the driving snow, where you might be (a) shitting in your shorts and being carried at sixty miles per hour down a mountainside in a slab slide, or (b) screwing up the lighting of the dynamite—no, pento-lite—thereby blowing yourself up instead, or yet (c) having an exciting time and remaining safe, at least in part.

You opt for the latter, so you ask . . .

"What's the first thing I should know? I mean, beyond all that I had to read. What can *you* tell me?"

Jackie considers this. Every second the cat climbs you are closer to stepping out onto the most avalanche-prone slope at Park City. It is so avalanche prone that it is only open for weeks of the year.

"When it comes to judging slope stability, the rule of thumb is . . . there are no rules of thumb," Jackie tells you.

When you don't answer, she adds, "A disaster is triggered by someone's assumption that a slope is stable."

"So," you say, "I shouldn't trust the guidelines in Ed's book."

You've read *The ABCs of Avalanche Safety*, by Utah's longtime expert on avalanches, Ed LaChapelle, among other texts.

"When crossing an avalanche slope, he who hesitates is lost," she says, and laughs, the cat grinding to a halt.

Jackie's out first. Climbing from the cat after her, with that enormous, explosive-festooned pack on your back, you are put in mind of parachuting. Out you go, toward Pinecone Ridge, into that near whiteout. The cat, the second you are out, turns, and in seconds is swallowed up in the heavily falling snow.

Jackie is already moving away from you in the direction opposite the cat, cutting a high line across Pinecone, dragging behind her what appear to be three children's toboggans. But they can't be, can they?

Following her, your skis, mid-fats, barely keep you on the surface,

Jackie stops, and in all that falling snow, you very nearly bump into her. Nearly stumble on those damn toboggans. She holds your eyes in that near dark and snow, so close you can feel her warm breath on your face.

"Carry a probe as you would have others carry a probe for you, got it?"

"Right," you say.

"I know I can do right for you, but can you do right for me if it goes to shit?"

"Show me," you tell her.

"*That's* the right answer for a first timer," she shoots back, and pats you on the shoulder. "Just don't fuck up, all right?"

WHAT AVALANCHES ARE

Reading conditions for avalanches is a science, but even then, avalanche behavior is unpredictable. Yearly, around a million avalanches occur worldwide. They're just a way for the snow on steep slopes to adjust to gravity. Most of these avalanches are in and of themselves no great danger. Avalanches such as *loose snow avalanches*, sometimes called "sluffs," which occur at the surface in new snow or wet spring snow, seldom accumulate enough bulk to do more than push a skier over; *ice fall avalanches*, which occur when a glacier encounters a steep drop and a portion of the glacier breaks off or "calfs," don't usually involve hikers or skiers; *roof avalanches* can be eliminated by shoveling snow from roofs; and *cornice fall avalanches*, which occur when cornices break loose from the lee side of a mountain ridge, can be avoided by staying back from the peak of such ridges. All of these can be dealt with in relative safety.

But it is the *slab avalanche*—think of a dinner plate perched on a mountainside—that is the killer. And, even more important is this to consider: of all slab avalanches that kill, *over 95 percent are set off by the victim*, or a member of the victim's skiing or touring party—which makes the study of snow imperative for people working in avalanche country.

But snow is simple enough. Cut down through an accumulation of it, and it's just that old white stuff all the way down, right?

Wrong.

Snow is a complex, growing, changing, morphing potential killer.

Yes, in a slab avalanche a mass of snow, or *snowpack*, is released as a unit. But in a *continental* or *transitional* block, as found at most resorts, this dry snow is the most complex substance found in nature. Never the same from the time it falls from the clouds to the time it melts, this snowpack is in a perpetual state of flux. It creeps and glides down slopes, grows stronger or weaker over vast areas, and comes to adhere more firmly to mountainsides or hang tenuously—requiring only the slightest trigger to set tons of it free.

A trigger such as yourself, a skier.

And, consider, snow is the *only* environment on earth that life has been unable to find a home in. *Nothing* lives primarily in snow.

Yet snow is, in this way, a living thing in and of itself.

BLASTING

All of these snowpack characteristics are running through your head now, hiking up Pinecone Ridge, half blinded by the snow, which is freezing/burning the exposed portion of your face. And Jackie, you've been assured, will teach you more.

"Hey!" you call up to Jackie, who is methodically leading the way, her back to you. "Gimme a second here!"

At the top of Pinecone Ridge you are at ten thousand feet.

Given the size of the mountain, the altitude, the cloth ice mask you've donned, and the goggles you've got on over it, the hood over all that, your hands encased in double-thickness gloves, your jacket, vest, undergear, and all the gear on your back, and these GD Diablos you're skiing/traversing the slope in (the boots rigid and your feet so encased in them that you can barely feel your feet), you could be some NASA astronaut on a mission to another planet—that's how otherworldly this mountain ridge feels now.

And where it was around freezing down in Park City, here it is—according to your watch, which records not just time, but temperature—eight degrees Fahrenheit, which only adds to that otherworldliness you feel.

The air is so cold, so rarefied, you feel that if you were to leap from the ridge, you would fall thousands of feet.

Holding Jackie up a moment longer, looking around you in awe, you realize this is a strange kind of extreme *pleasure*, being here, the kind that writes itself on your mind and on your body.

It occurs to you, just now, that you love this place, but hope it doesn't reward that love by killing you, this ridge you are climbing, Pinecone, its face a carnival of snow arabesques, snow-laden pines, ledges, chutes, and at the very top now, since the snow came in from the north, a heavy cornice of snow, rolling the length of the ridge like a windblown wave in arrested motion.

You take note of the snow in the pine boughs, so, not settled elsewhere, either. Never travel in avalanche country immediately after a big snow—unless you must. And here, this morning, are all the dangers: Gradient. Formation of squared snow crystals (loose snow under a crust). Radical temperature drop. Earlier heavy snow. A heavier snow over that.

You stop seeing the beauty in the slope in front of you and begin to tally up the signs of avalanche danger.

You see that danger in the accumulated snow on the face's convexities; in the crack in the snow down the face of the slope (is that a *stress fracture*, or the result of a *glide* when it was warmer?). Your mind is racing, calculating, trying to get a hold on things.

At midnight, it was thirty-six degrees.

"Ah, whatever," Jackie says, beaming at you.

You're amazed that you can even be aware, out here, that

Jackie is attractive. It seems absurd, like some irritating remnant from a life you lived eons ago. So, it's just there, like the painful burning of your neuromas in your Diablos.

"'What do you mean, 'Whatever'?"

She tosses her shovel at you. "Dig," she says, and you are put in mind of *The Sopranos*.

You are going to get across the entire ridge, then return up it. On a good day, without all the gear on your back, and with some mountaineering skis with skins on them, it would take you an hour or more. And now you are sweating, which will be bad if you stop moving.

"Snow pit," Jackie says. "Seeing *is* believing."

Okay, you tell her. And you dig. (An AC worker digs a snowpit to reveal aspects of snowpack structure that are not visible from the surface.)

"How deep?"

"Six feet."

You don't ask her why six feet, it was just that you were hoping that she might just want say three or four, which would be easier. No, you don't go below six feet, because at that depth a skier's and a snowmobile's weight effect is essentially the same: zero effect. The snow, from the surface downward, so distributes the weight that at six feet the impact is negligible. And slabs triggered by humans are rarely thicker than six feet.

You, though, would be the first to set off a ten-footer, and *this* morning if you're not careful, so you take digging a snow pit seriously, and when you toss the last shovelful to your right, you and Jackie look at what you have.

"Here," Jackie says, and she cuts blocks out from the mountain side of the pit. The top layer of snow, this last night's layer, slides off the lower layer easily, which Jackie shakes her head at.

"Well, that sucks," she says, an odd cheer in her voice.

The whole snow face in front of you, this new three feet of snow, is perched on a snow crust caused by rain, which froze so quickly that the new snow after the rain didn't entirely bond with the icy snow under it.

And the next few layers down are various strengths, too, as evidenced by how easily, or not easily, they can be crushed with the backside of the shovel, or slid free of each other—even six feet under.

"So," you ask, "what do we do?"

"*Dynamite,*" Jackie says, grinning, "and *lots* of it."

Where? you ask. I mean, you're standing on a mountain.

She points to the most distant and steep aspect of the ridge. Not far from where you can see signs from the avalanche you heard at the hut. "Right at that curler, see it?" she says, and then adds, pointing lower, "We can cross there. The sign is all good, can you read it?"

"Not in a way I'd trust it."

"Good," she tells you, and after you have bungeed the shovel to her pack again, she angles across the slope in front of you, dragging those toboggans.

"And anyway, she says, "if the slope were unstable here, it would avalanche behind us, not under us."

This, you think, is less than reassuring. Like being told, at a sushi bar, that the blowfish you are eating is *extra special today,* as first chef come to work drunk, left blowfish out, and new blowfish brought right from Cessna flies from Seattle, so, no waiting! Prepared fast, fast, fast! Extra fresh!

Eat, enjoy!

●

Out on the slope, pins of electricity running the length of your spine, you absorb what Jackie can tell you about avalanche sign, imagining, every moment, that *whuuuump!* of the very ground breaking out from under you, that horrified moment. Falling, forever, crushed in snow. Trying to breathe and—

"Stay on the high line," Jackie says.

Crossing here, Jackie tells you, is not roulette. Oh, there's risk, sure, but right here it's *minimal*.

Compared to what? you ask yourself.

For one thing, the slope is only thirty-five degrees, Jackie points out. You check it with your crystal card. Sure enough.

Snow, since it is a granular substance, behaves like sand, you know. Sand, if you have ever noticed it in an hourglass, or played with it as a child, pouring it into piles on a beach, will not form in steep-sided masses. This is because the steepest surface angle a granular substance can maintain without collapsing due to the pull of gravity is thirty-eight degrees, this angle is called the *angle of repose*.

Snow, though, is *not* really a granular substance, especially in the case of snowpack composed of stellar crystals, which interlock.

So avalanches *start* in the range of twenty-five to fifty-five degrees, though most *occur* in the thirty-five to forty-five degree range.

(If you were thinking fifty-five degrees is not a steep slope, consider this: if you were to try skiing down such a slope, your uphill ski in any turn would be so close to the snow face that it would tear at your uphill boot's buckles. A fifty-five-degree slope is a wicked steep slope, a Double Black Diamond for experts—extreme skiers and nuts—only.)

So why is this thirty-five-degree slope you are on *mostly* safe?

First, the cornice begins a good distance ahead, even though you are on the leeward side of the mountain here. What wind pillows (compacted mounds of snow) have formed, have also formed *down* from the cornice. And you don't have to worry about a wet snow avalanche, which can be triggered on mild slopes—it is far too cold, and anyway there are signs of relative stability everywhere.

You didn't see them, though. But with Jackie pointing them out, you gain confidence.

For example, the specific areas on the ridge where avalanches *have* happened in the past, where there are obvious runouts, are below you and to the east. This you can tell by the willows and alders growing through the snow there, which are a sign of regular avalanche activity—*yearly* activity. You stand now, though, observing all this, in a broad growth of young aspen, which indicate slides *do* occur where you're standing, but only once every ten to fifteen years. However, the evergreens above the aspen you're in indicate that slides higher on this west end of the ridge occur only every fifty years or so—if even that. (When traversing what seem to be stable, low slopes, skiers have to consider that higher-elevation avalanches can be triggered from below, as well from above. So the evergreens above you now are a very good sign.)

And the ridgeline Jackie is using to get near the cornice is moderately *concave*, not convex, so it will support more snow.

Here, even the smaller pines in your path are not *flagged* as those are a distance ahead. Flagging is caused by snow slabs tearing off branches on the uphill side of evergreens.

Also, where scrub oak pokes through the pack, snow cones have formed, a sign of the snow settling. Which means more stability.

And, too, the slope is *south facing*, which promotes rounding of snow crystals and as a result strengthening in any snowpack; here the degree of slope under your feet now and ahead, while steep, never severely so, most southern slopes being "mild." North-facing slopes, on the other hand, are typically extremely steep, having been carved by glaciers, instead of being created by ridge lift and erosion, and these north-facing, more-shaded slopes, will also tend to cover anchors.

Of which there are many on this slope you're on now—rock outcroppings, the trees, and the pines that you are climbing (with some degree of relief) into.

Especially given the altitude you are at, which ultimately leads to the growth of continental pack with largely faceted crystal growth, or weakening—which is what you're seeing *ahead of you*, and what will be your job this morning.

Bringing that fragile, steeper slope snow down.

Jackie has stopped. In the now lightly falling snow, she's pouring herself a coffee from a slender thermos.

"Coffee?" you say, incredulous.

"No, it's whiskey," she says. She downs what is in it, smiling, then refills the cap and holds it out to you. "Ethiopian, with some decaf French roast thrown in for body."

She watches you drink.

"I give this back, you might get hoof and mouth," you tease. Jackie only raises an eyebrow. "You?" she says.

It might be the best coffee you've ever had in your life. Or is it drinking it with Jackie on this ridge that makes it so?

The coffee is complex, dark, and very sweet. It is nearly syrup, but this, the sugar in it, you know is just to help you charge up the much steeper slope back of that massive cornice.

It'll be a bitch, but you've warmed to it. Your heart's running like an old Dodge Power Wagon slant 6. It ain't Lance Armstrong's heart, but it'll take you right up the side of this bugger, and up Everest, if you were crazy enough to climb it. (Which, out here, in this weather, you wonder if you might like to try. It's only the money that saves you from seriously considering it. Which you do anyway, as there is this peculiar joy percolating in your blood again, out like this, and your resistance to it—high, remote, and dangerous—temporarily anyway, evaporated. You love it out here.)

You toss Jackie the cap, and she expertly catches it in her gloved hands.

"Why don't you lead now," she says.

Fortified, you head up. Climbing, you have this inane music running in your head, like Bill Murray in *Groundhog Day*, waking every morning to "I Got You Babe," only here it is AC/DC's "Highway to Hell," a song you never liked, you climbing mindlessly, using rock handholds, until Jackie says, behind you, in a very even and threatening voice, *"What's a terrain trap?"*

Which freezes you where you stand, slightly crouched over, and this buzzing hush in your head.

You glance down at your feet, which, in those Frankenstein-boot-like Diablos are pitched steeply upward. Did you fuck up somehow? You were simply getting into the additional incline, in the way you do when you run, which you've been doing for over twenty-five years. It's so automatic you didn't even think about it, the way you'd changed your balance and drew your arms into your sides for more power, but here you are standing on something that looks not unlike a crazed branch in the snowpack, on a hillock on a steep slope.

You are standing, you realize, on the downside of a bulge, or convexity, part of a larger mass of snow, leading uphill and above you to a very large, menacing lee-side snow pillow.

Jackie, you realize with shame, has directed you right into it.

And, she has stopped you here. Just short.

Before you wandered out onto what you know is, from your required reading, a *sweet spot*.

"Don't ever, ever trust someone in your group to send you out onto something, to see for you. Keep your eyes open, read all the terrain. *Don't* be a space case."

Your shame is so intense that for the moment, even as pumped as you are from climbing, you break out in a cold sweat.

"What are you seeing here?" Jackie asks.

You tell her, and add, in addition to the convexity and the snow pillows, there's brush down and to the east of you, just three hundred or so feet, *willow*—so, this is a *common avalanche area*. You crossed from a safe area into a dangerous one, without so much as noticing.

"What else?"

"Out there?"

"No, down at the hut! What did you *think* I meant?"

"There's a gully just ahead."

"And?"

"Even though we're on the lee side, the snow up there looks like it's wind packed."

"It is. And?"

You don't see anything else.

"Kick your boot into the snow."

You do, and the snow breaks up, on the top, a two-inch crust, under it sugar snow. And an elk has come down the ridge, no doubt to chew the bark off the willows ahead and below you.

"Elk sign," you say. Where there are elk, there're willow. And avalanche danger.

"Chocolate chips on vanilla icing, right?"

"Sugar snow."

"*Now* you're talkin'," Jackie says, though she has doffed her pack and is digging through it.

"Need help there?" you ask.

No, she tells you, she doesn't need your help, nor *can* you help her. You are not qualified, as her shadow, to make the radio calls. But you can watch, which you do. Jackie, her gear around her, thumbs the talk button.

It is still bitter cold out, and when she speaks into the radio, her breath comes out in a plume.

"Four eighty to Summit. Ten ninety-seven Pinecone Ridge. Early avalanche sign on Constellation, Half Moon, and Sam's Knob. I'm placing charges at Sam's Knob now."

The radio crackles.

"Ten four. We have you at Sam's Knob. *Hold.*"

"'Hold'?"

"That's ten four. HOLD. You have a snowmobile coming up Thayne's Canyon."

"Four eighty clear."

Jackie takes her thermos from her pack again, has a cup, refills it, and passes it to you. Sweet, bitter, hot.

"God, it's beautiful out here, isn't it?" she says.

You agree. Beautiful doesn't do this place justice. In the quiet, it is awesome out here; you are only a visitor, and a brief one at that. The cosmic proportion, in mountains like the Wasatch, is humbling.

Time yawns wide. Jackie passes you another cup of coffee.

"So, Jackie," you ask, enjoying this moment, this reprieve. "What do you do in your other life?"

Jackie glances over at you. "Guess."

And when you shake your head—you have no idea—she tells you.

GRAPPLER

"I got into wrestling after my divorce," Jackie tells you. "I needed some kind of outlet, you know, for what I was feeling, and—"

"*Wrestling?*"

"I'm a professional wrestler."

This piques your interest. It's one of those gold-star days, you think, as well as, So *that's* where that strut comes from! Not only are you sitting on the ridge of one of the most avalanche-prone slopes in the continental United States, you're talking to a lady pro wrestler who just happens to like throwing dynamite. Neat.

"No, really," you say, a second later, disappointed. And a bit surprised at yourself; you were slow at getting the joke.

"Really."

"You mean, where they jump off the ropes and do slam takedowns and all that? Like in the WWF?"

"It isn't the WWF anymore."

Jackie grins. You feel this happiness, the kind you feel when you meet people living *out of the box*. The way you felt meeting Jean-Claude Killy and his then pal Andre Arnold in Sun Valley. The way you felt meeting Clint Eastwood, Slim Pickens, and David Soul making a movie, *Swan Song*, on Bald Mountain, a lifetime ago. The way you felt meeting Dag Aabye, up at Silver Star in British Columbia, Dag the first of a generation of extreme skiers, still crazy as ever.

And it occurs to you what is so attractive about this woman, Jackie: she's bursting with this . . . *untamed* life. This wry, but engaged, sense of adventure in her.

"You fly around and all that?" you ask.

Jackie fills the coffee cup and you sip at it.

"I want all the gritty details."

"Really?" she says.

You motion with your hands toward Thayne's Canyon, where the snowmobile will appear.

You have time.

●

It had been Jackie's father who saw the ad, tacked up in a grocery store in Orem, just south of Salt Lake City: GATOR'S PRO WRESTLING SCHOOL "TRAIN IN A REAL WRESTLING RING" CALL TOLL-FREE 1-877-657-7029 FOR MORE INFO.

Jackie called. Gator's Professional Wrestling school, it turned out, was run by a Steve Ketcher, of Florida, who was a full-blood Cherokee Indian. His Cherokee name, Joustwiteet, means "Gator Wolf." Hence his World Wrestling Federation name, Gatorwolf. As Gatorwolf, Ketcher'd had stellar success, wrestling among the likes of Hulk Hogan and Ultimate Warrior, in the tradition of WWF Indian wrestlers.

Ketcher, three hundred pounds, moved quickly for his size and used moves he claimed he'd learned from his grandfather—particularly the *Cherokee Deathlock.* And for pupils of his school, he had connections.

His school wasn't cheap: $2,000 would buy you ninety days of instruction, which covered all the basic moves, videotaped workouts, advice on getting your boots and wrestling costume together, and "anything else needed to get you started in the Professional Wrestling Entertainment Business." Five hundred dollars would buy you ten lessons, $250, six basic workouts.

Jackie went for the whole deal. By that time, she was already co-owner, with her brother, of an auto shop.

Her dream was to "make it big" as a wrestler in two years.

Gatorwolf agreed; from the first, he saw Jackie as his gold

mine, someone special, even though she was his wrestling school's only "girl." She began training in earnest. To prove how tough she was, intially, she had to launch herself from the high rope of the ring with her hands behind her back—to smack face and chest flat on the mat, something that was *not* soft.

She got nosebleeds and was bruised so badly she'd wake mornings wondering if she could get herself out of bed.

Then the call came, only four weeks into her training. The American Wrestling Federation needed a "Baby Face" for an exhibition at March Air Force Base in Riverside, California. A "Baby Face" is a good guy in the "entertainment" of the sport, a "Heel" being the bad guy she would wrestle, this time a professional named Wildfire.

Jackie entered the ring as Sierra! Her promo eighty-by-ten glossy read, "I MAKE BOYS CRY."

Here was dark-haired villain (Wildfire) versus blond good guy (Sierra).

By then Sierra had her signature moves, the *Sidewinder* and the *Hang 'em High*. The Sidewinder was a "lucha" move, from Mexican wrestling, where the wrestler "throwing" the move comes off the ropes, jumps, and catches the opponent around the waist—or neck—then drops to the floor, taking the opponent with her. In the Hang 'em High, it is the opponent who is thrown into the ropes, the wrestler catching the opponent coming off the ropes by the hand and slinging the opponent over her shoulders, then dropping the opponent on her back.

Jackie also used sunset flips, body slams, and arm drags.

The crowd loved her. So much so that a promoter picked her up, booking fights for her in West Virginia, Ohio, North Carolina, and Kentucky, among others. By the time she was on avalanche control, she'd wrestled over a hundred matches, had suffered six concussions (which, she said, were not treated in wrestling the way the Mountain Patrol treated them: you simply got up and went back at it).

As she did.

"Wrestling is a very evil business," she said, "*if* you lower your standards."

There were, for example, the "Ring Rats," girls who gave favors for promotions and fights and who did porn.

Jackie wouldn't have it. She perfected more moves instead, like the *flying scissors*; learned how to chain wrestle; found out what a "Potato" was (pressing your opponent's hand when you were really knocked senseless and needed a minute to get back up to speed).

She met The Rock, Dwayne Johnson.

Got a personalized license plate for her car: JABRONI. Which means, in professional wrestling, your partner.

Her career was taking off, like a rocket.

But at home, Jackie was suffering the impending death of her much-loved grandfather, who was terminally ill and needed help. Watching EMT workers revive him one evening, she was impressed, and decided to get an EMT certification herself, which she did, then moved her grandfather into her three-bedroom home in Spanish Fork, just south of Salt Lake City.

She was working long hours at her auto shop, and even longer hours at home, caring for her grandfather.

Sometimes Jackie's grandfather went into a coma, and Jackie worked on him herself, reviving him, more than a little of the pioneer spirit in her.

Then, at a job fair—the wrestling matches came at such intervals that she flew out to them a few days a month—she met the director of Mountain Patrol at Park City Mountain Resort. Jackie and he talked. About her wrestling and EMT work, her auto shop, her love of skiing.

Here, the director of PCMR Patrol decided, was someone who could handle dynamite. Smart, focused, sometimes fierce, but, in a person like this, also an unusual warmth—the director of Mountain Patrol seeing in Jackie what Gatorwolf had: here was an altogether *singular* woman. (And she was more than nice to look at, not something you can say for most of the bearded roughneck characters who do AC work.)

Would she like to be on avalanche control?

Jackie agreed, and began training—while still flying out to wrestling matches. Three years of it on crews, blasting, setting up "woodies" (a device for installing fuses on the explosives), learning the ABCs of avalanche work, before she was given her own routes.

Which she took on with an especial verve.

●

"And here I am!" she says, beaming at you, self-mocking, but friendly. "And it's the WWE, now," she tells you. "World Wrestling Entertainment."

You are surprised she's such a cream puff (in a way), that she has this so-sunny something about her.

You hear that characteristic whine of a snowmobile engine in the distance, and now see a headlight, the light jerking and swooping, the snowmobile going by in the canyon below you—a thousand feet or so. The snowmobile roars up the length of the canyon to the east, then takes a cat track, climbing the canyon wall opposite you, up Single Jack to Summit.

The snowmobile's roar thins to a whine again and is gone.

Jackie thumbs her radio. "Four eighty to Summit. Ready to proceed at Sam's Knob."

"Ten twenty-three," the radio responds.

Jackie cocks her head, her hand on her hip. You wait what seems minutes, this vague sense of procedure happening elsewhere, like distant gears meshing.

"Summit to Four eighty," the radio crackles. "You have an all clear. Proceed. Do you copy?"

"Four eighty to Summit. That's a go."

"Ten four."

"Four eighty clear."

Jackie strides over to her bag, that strut in her again.

"Now we get to the good part," she says. And while she's digging through her gear, she tells you about the Principle of the *Three Red Flags.*

Which in effect states that most avalanche accidents are not the result of unavoidable, hit-by-a-meteor-coincidence, but are the predictable outcome of a series of related events. The best policy concerning avalanches being *not to get into them in the first place.*

Any three markers for danger, such as "shooting cracks," soft slab formation, or radical changes in temperature, since snowpack can't adjust to rapid change, constitute either a no-go for skiing or travel, or a green light for AC teams to trigger instabilities to make slopes safe. Especially for the extreme skiers who would be on such slopes. And there were the avalanche-country commandments: *Always* travel in avalanche paths *one at a time* on windward sides. *Never* enter the slope *above your pard. Always* have *an escape route.*

"And if you *are* caught on a slab," Jackie tells you, "one breaking away from the mountainside, try to ski off it at a forty-five-degree angle. If it breaks up, you have to *swim* to stay near the surface. Grab for trees, or anything that's stationary. If that doesn't work, before the snow hardens around you, create a breathing space."

"Right," you reply, even out in that vast space feeling suddenly suffocated. "Then what?"

Now Jackie really smiles—it's a forty-thousand kilowatt smile. "Your pards dig you out—or you die."

"Sweet."

"Price of a ticket out here—sometimes."

You glance up the ridge ahead of you, then out at the mountains you can just see through the falling snow.

"Anything else?"

"Watch out for *hangfire* snow."

Which is snow that didn't release on a first slide, an issue when you're a member of a rescue party—you don't want to trigger a second slide, taking down a whole team. So you might have to put off a rescue, Jackie tells you.

"Put it off?"

"If it's a possibility of five going down or onc?" Jackie shrugs. "But don't worry, only the director of AC makes those kinds of calls."

"That puts me at ease."

"Yeah," Jackie says, pulling one of the kids' toboggans toward her. "And if you're on a team rescue, out on the site, don't so much as think to take a pee—even if you've gotta go like a race horse."

"Why?"

"They'll be bringing in the rescue dogs, if they're not there already, and that'll throw off the scent. And no spitting tobacco, or pouring out coffee, or any of that. Nothing that'd throw off the dogs."

"What about the probes?" (You've got two in your pack, presently folded triple—ten feet long when locked open. You've read all about coarse probing, working up the mountainside, and fine probing. Being careful and exact in their use is critical, looking for clues, like a glove, and working in "high-probability-catchment" areas, probing in a pattern, even using a specific stepping motion to create a grid, probing in front of both toes as well as in between.)

"If the vic isn't wearing a beacon, get ready for a long, miserable recovery."

"You mean rescue?"

"No, *recovery*—it's usually popsicles then."

Popsicles.

You pat your jacket to feel your beacon, though you know it is there, its hard little fist-shape reassuring you.

Beacon rescues, you know, *do* work—as you saw during your training at mountain survival camp. There, your trainers buried a—nonclaustrophobic—guy with the unfortunate last name of Paine under three feet of snow. Your team had to, in under fifteen minutes, locate and dig him out, on a slope two football fields wide and three long, on this slope a slide marked for your team by the trainers.

Basically, in a beacon search, you find the victim's signal, then narrow the search area and decide where to dig.

Easier said than done, of course.

In Phase One of a beacon search you identify the *slide zone*, out of those thousands of square feet of terrain. Then, traversing the slope, each member of your team spreads out, the distance between them less than two-thirds of the standard beacon range. Beacon searchers stop every ten meters and orient their beacons, trying to pick up the signal. You move as quickly as possible, in a corduroy pattern toward the bottom. In Phase Two, you start at the spot where the victim's signal is first detected. Here you orient your beacon for the loudest received signal. You turn your volume as low as possible (your receiver has audio, a whining sound) while still clearly hearing the signal. You traverse the hill perpendicular to the fall line, keeping the beacon orientation constant until you find a fade point. Now you traverse 180 degrees back across the hill and find the fade point in the opposite direction. The straight line across the slope between these two points is your *first bracket*. You go to the middle of this line you've created, and turn 90 degrees to it, and repeat this process, again searching for a fade point, thus creating a second bracket.

You'd like, by the time you find your second bracket, just to have it over. You are in a cold sweat and have used up ten minutes.

You, in a near frenzy, work within this square you have created.

Realize the trainers have left you no sign whatsoever. No glove. No disturbed snow. You have to, basically, find a pin in this quarter acre of snow.

Your victim under the snow is dying. (Not really, as Paine has done this before, but he is by no means comfortable, either—and you don't want to appear incompetent.)

You and your three *pards* bracket like crazy, until—you bloody well hope—you've got your brackets down to a length of six feet.

Coffin length.

You've hit your time limit, for location—you, in Phase Three, now scrabbling on your hands and knees, holding your beacon inches from the snow and trying to pinpoint your victim's beacon, all sorts of rescue gear having slid to your side.

Now, though, something's interfering with your signal.

One of your pards runs to you, helps you get off your pack and aluminum shovel, which is the culprit.

Thirteen minutes and counting.

You bracket again, down to three feet, and your pards rush in with their probes.

Bracket length is two times the burial depth now.

One of your pards tosses you a probe.

"Sixty seconds!" a trainer calls, and you have it, your victim's location, and in a total but careful frenzy you dig, yanking a very relieved Mr. Paine from his would-be snowy grave.

"Time!" shouts the trainer, your rescue a success.

But even given that, you know your training exercise and its happy result are far from guaranteed in the real world. Where you are now on this ridge, if you were to be caught in a slide, there would only be Jackie here for you, or you for her, until others could rush to the scene.

Minutes, in this kind of environment, you realize, become very dear. Every second counts.

It makes you a little breathless.

"So, any of you AC guys ever get caught in a slide?" you ask, Jackie wrestling with one of those kids' sleds.

You are expecting to hear, Nope, we're too careful. But what she says, over the hush of the falling snow is, "Yup. That guy Cal? Bearded guy?"

You nod.

"He wrapped himself around a tree, got through it that way. Only broke a few of his ribs. Pretty good, considering."

"I suppose so," you tell her, then add, "What are you doing over there?"

"An air blast is more effective than having the pentolite go right into the snow, see, since the snow cushions it. So we put the charges on the toboggans and lower them down. Beats howitzers every time."

At many resorts, firing shells into avalanche areas is the preferred method. Jackie glances up from what she's doing, anticipating your line of thinking: So why not here?

"Having crews place the explosives is more accurate," she tells you. "*And* you don't have charges going over mountain ranges into people's backyards."

This was something you heard about, a howitzer crew in Provo Canyon doing AC work, firing an overcharged shell (it came loaded with seven, two of which should have been removed) over their target area, the shell clearing an entire ridge and landing in the backyard of a Pleasant Grove home, blowing out the windows of that home and others nearby, as well as damaging a car. The blast occurred just minutes before a school bus dropped students off in the neighborhood. The Utah DOT, responsible for the crew making the error, suspended howitzer use in Provo Canyon.

Jackie swings her arm around, your radiant pard.

"Come on over—we're gettin' to the part where we get to blow things up."

Jackie has formed a makeshift workspace out of her pack and a sheet of red Gore-Tex.

Using the woodie, she forces two fuses into the backside of a pentolite charge (about the size of a can of Coke), then tosses you a roll of electrical tape.

"Get that going, will you?" she asks.

You ask what you're using the tape for. She stands, holding the pentolite charge against her hip, points up the ridge, where that large lee-side cornice now seems to loom over you. It is beautiful, a thing of nature, but it is the most unstable feature on the entire snow-covered ridge.

"Lucky us," Jackie says.

You ask why so.

"Big one like that needs a triple charge."

When you follow, she directs you to the charges, tells you how to tape the two-pounders together. Your hands shake. To your relief, she doesn't sneak up behind you and shout, *"BOOM!"* Yet your hands feel oddly distant, you having, as a boy, experimented with explosives with near-disastrous results.

"What do we get on these fuses?" you ask.

"Ninety seconds."

Jackie hands you a ziplock plastic bag, in it what appear to be eight or ten cardboard capped pens. That's right, cardboard capped pens. Which of course they are not, but then, *what* are they?

"Blasting cap pull wires," Jackie tells you. "Don't put them on those fuses now."

You give her a flat, bovine stare.

"All right, you didn't deserve that."

"What's the biggest charge you've seen?" you ask.

"Eight two-pounders."

"That kinda shake the earth for you?"

"Wouldn't you like to know!" Jackie says, setting her hands on her hips.

Here, you remind yourself, is a woman you don't want to piss off.

"Next?" you say.

You attach the skins Jackie hands you to the bases of your skis, don all of your gear, and, like that, feeling yet again like Frankenstein's monster, head out toward the cornice, your heart ticking over like it's got molasses pumping through it.

Jackie stops on a high, natural formation of stone, just back of and under the cornice, trees here—pines, you're happy to see.

"Pull wires," she tells you, and you hand her two.

She squats over the small toboggan, attaching the pull wires to the pentolite charges you've taped together and bound to the toboggan.

She stands, then reaches into her jacket, thumbing the talk button on her radio.

"Four eighty to AC."

"AC," her radio crackles.

"We're ten seventeen on Pinecone."

"All clear?"

"All clear."

Jackie grasps the nylon rope she's tied to the toboggan, two coils at her feet, and glancing over her shoulder at you, says, "I'll let you do the honors."

She thumbs her radio again.

"FIRE IN THE HOLE!"

There's some kind of radio affirmation, which you barely make out through the static and high-pitched hum in your head. Jackie gives you that look. This time, probably, you do deserve it. The fuses are side by side, and, holding the fuses tightly in your left hand—as if they might electrocute you—you pull the caps back with your right and . . .

SNAP!

They're burning. Jackie lowers the toboggan with the pentolite charges on it with the rope, the rope whirring roughly through her hands, the toboggan coming to rest right beneath the cornice.

What seems an eternity, but is only seconds, passes. Then, under your feet, the ground gives a shake, this shock wave coming through the ground first, a sound following it so loud it literally thumps you in the chest, hits you like a fist, the whole wall of snow ahead of you falling, and with it comes this roaring that you don't just hear, it is *in* everything, the very air, blurring your vision.

There is something awesome about the fall of millions of tons of snow, you standing just a hundred yards back of it.

The fall goes on for what seems forever, the ground thrumming under your feet, this a big fall, but when it is over, less than a minute has passed.

Astounding. But more so is this:

"Okay," you say, in a voice seemingly tiny in the vacuum left by the avalanche, your ears ringing. *"Now* what?"

"Now?"

"Yeah, *now.*"

"We get to ski the slope. Since it's safe."

"Ski the slope?"

She points to the area the slide has cleared.

"There?" you ask.

"Yes, there," Jackie replies.

You strip the skins from your skis. You are so revved up you can't feel the pack or gear on you.

"Ladies first," you tell her.

"I'll let you do the honors."

You wonder, for just a second, if you are doing something so stupid that you will curse yourself for it shortly, in what might become the last few minutes of your life. But you won't be shown thin.

"Fuck it," you say. And leap from the rock face onto what you couldn't have imagined—sugar snow.

Snow like heavy water.

Like . . . *nothing* you've ever skied, anywhere, or will ever again. Heavenly, just you and Jackie here, in the whole world, cutting zippers down the entire uninterrupted, terrifying, and blissful length of it.

●

An hour later, further up Pinecone Ridge where AC snowmobiles have dropped you off, you repeat the process. But now, already, you are becoming a seasoned hand.

You know the ritual.

You love the CRUMP! of the explosions. Handling the gear.

With a certain triumph, you set up this second site, now all that faster since Jackie doesn't need to explain it to you.

"You wanna toss it this time?" Jackie asks.

You don't hesitate. With the fuse hissing, you rear back with this two-pounder, give it a pitch Sandy Koufax would have been proud of. When the second charge goes off, like a kick to your chest, you are thrilled, all over again. And you don your skis, anticipating one last run in this impossibly fluid snow.

"Last run?" you say, grinning at Jackie. It is after ten, and the snow is still coming down hard.

"Last run?"

"No?"

"Sweetheart," she says, in this Mae West sort of voice, amused at you, "We have just gotten *started.*"

●

Three o'clock, and you trudge, skis slung over your shoulder, from C.B.'s, a north side run, toward the locker room. Jackie is whistling something rap rock or hip-hop, swinging with her skis, happy with the day.

You are, too, but you are bone tired, your legs twitching. When you approach the Base Patrol hut, where assessments on injured skiers are done, and, too, where most critically injured skiers are put on AirMed or Life Flight helicopters, you see a flurry of activity, patrollers running in all directions in the parking area, getting the ambulances started. One patroller you recognize, Walt, bolts out the door.

"Big slide over at the Canyons," he says.

"They say what *kind?*" Jackie asks.

"Slab. Might be as many as fifteen people buried."

Something heavy as a stone sits in your stomach. You sense it coming.

"We just talked to the county sheriff's office," Walt adds. "They could use a couple fine probers. If they wanted us to send you two over, could you go?"

Jackie tosses that thick, blond hair of hers.

"Yeah," she says, just like that.

Which leaves you.

"I'm in," you tell him, and even as Walt marches back into Base Patrol, you turn your face to the falling snow. What is usually flat-out beautiful, something you love, has taken on yet another dimension in your life of skiing.

"Coffee?" Walt calls over his shoulder, at the door, and Jackie shrugs.

You're to wait in the lot, it'll be fifteen minutes until they know if they need you. Walt's back out with the coffees, full of sugar, and you take yours.

There's that KAAAAARUMP! of another pentolite charge going off in the distance. In front of you, on Payday Ridge, and on Silver Skis, Silver Queen, and on the Men's Slalom and Women's Slalom courses, people are skiing.

Now there's an ironic something to the laughter of the children loading at the First Time lift, having fun.

"Well," you say to Jackie, sipping your coffee. "I suppose this is a kind of vacation from the wrestling life, right?"

Jackie's got her sunglasses on, big-lensed, glamorous things, like no one else on patrol wears, but they look just right on her.

"This is my twenty-first day," she tells you.

"Of what?"

"On AC or patrol."

This you cannot have heard right.

"You mean this *winter*," you say. It is only the end of January, after all.

"*In a row*," Jackie tells you, sipping calmly at her coffee.

And when the county sheriff's Blazer pulls into the lot, you watch her calmly stride from you toward the rear doors that have been flung open, with that selfsame strut, though more liquid now, that calm, no-nonsense something there. Hers is the job no one sees, not the recreational skier, or the snowboarder, or the instructor; not the wife with a cup of cocoa on the plaza, or the children throwing snowballs at the base of First Time, or even the oh-so-focused racers on Silver Skis, or the extreme skiers out on Pinecone, but is critical for the safety of all.

She gets partially into the Blazer, then turns, to look for you.

You standing there in the falling snow.

"Hey," she says, cocking her head in her direction. "What are you waiting for?" And you cross the lot to her. Jackie, dynamite girl.

RACING

MONEY, MAGIC, AND
A WHOLE LOTTA MOXIE

Three turns into the race your heart is beating two hundred times a minute. You are as alive and in the moment as you have ever been. You are not thinking, you are inside this moment, aimed at the next gate, taking the straightest line to it, which will buy you time, but will also necessitate applying the greatest turning force once there. In the back of your mind is the possibility of scrubbing off a bit of speed by skidding your skis the slightest fraction, but you will not do that. In fact, you squat further, tighter, your body rocketing ahead, even though you have never skied this course, have only been permitted to examine it before the race.

Pitch, the steepness of the hill, complicates each gate, as turning around one at forty-five degrees is far different from navigating one on a pitch of thirty.

Rocketing directly at the gate, you hold your glide into that dangerous red zone, and at the last nanosecond, you roll your skis on edge, and at that moment there is this exquisite veering around the axis of your skis' designed arc, you applying greater energy to the outside ski, the skis in reverse camber, but particularly the outside ski, both skis holding on the snow—your skis cutting lines in the snow on two-millimeter strips of honed steel—this in itself an act of faith, as your body now is literally stretched out over *not* the skis, but the snow that is traveling under your right hip at sixty feet a second.

At the apex of the turn, you are—fluidly—making a kind of bent spoke of your legs, the bulk of the force on the outside ski.

Three g. The equivalent of doing a five-hundred-pound squat. Your legs are not burning yet, but they will be soon.

On this giant slalom course, Alpine racing's gold standard, you have fifty such gates to get around, and here you are, eating up energy like a fighter jet on turn three.

And time. You're eating up time.

Time is the enemy here, and the straightest line is the Holy Grail. The problem with it, though, is this: the course is rutted, and in this arc you are turning around even now, the ski encounters irregularities, cutting through them, over them, and being deflected by them, so there is, at times, the equivalent of a 4 g jackhammer pounding at your legs.

Your skis, because they are stiff to accommodate cutting clean turns, send this energy right up your legs, for the most part into your thighs, but also into the small of your back and into your neck. If you let it, your head would bounce like one on those bobble characters people put on the rear decks of their cars—which would cause you terrible disorientation. But your head doesn't bobble.

Your entire body is this superintelligent spring steel, your eyes set in your head as if monitors for some out-of-body intelligence. All seeing.

Splitting hairs, here in giant slalom, is what it is all about. You will cut as closely as possible to each gate, but doing so will necessitate the use of larger turning forces and will greatly increase the possibility of straddling the gate, which would disqualify your run and end your race.

And cutting this close to the gates will exhaust you far more quickly. But that's what this is all about.

Spending it all.

At each gate you smack the outside pole, resistant fiberglass with a spring-loaded base.

If you are heavier than your fellow racers, you have a distinct advantage; if lighter, a disadvantage.

And, here, as you turn past the apex, you are already subtly shifting back over your skis exactly at the rate the g forces that are holding you up disappear, the skis having turned their designed arc, and you exiting the gate and aiming for the next.

All this in a fraction of a second, but these moves so ingrained, so studied and honed and practiced on a thousand runs like this one, that a kind of magic is produced, some quiet *other* skiing.

That is, until the course nearly hammers a ski out from under you, and you have to do damage control.

Which *always* happens. And it happens anywhere. Turn one to turn fifty. Which has you lit up like a pinball machine on each run. The surprise is always there, you have to assume it, and if it didn't get you the first run, it's waiting there on the second, the course by then having changed—more rutted, more icy, a lump of something there waiting to deflect your outer, more load-bearing, carving ski—by thirty other competitors carving up the course, carving up your perfect line, which is always and never really there.

You make the perfect line. Moment to moment. In nanotime. Each run of the course.

Guaranteed, though, by gate thirty your legs are sending messages to you.

Danger. Down here, at gate thirty, a top-of-the-course, hard line around a gate with some odd railing and deflection, and you're going to get sloppy.

Possibly even thrown off the course, or worse.

To which danger you respond by pulling in tighter, trying to ride a bit flatter between gates without standing up. Your legs are screaming here at turn forty-five for you to *just stand up*.

Your body now feels like a pipe, air-in/air-out, it makes no difference which, you are a big, hollow pipe.

And here is the next set of gates, red, two more after these, and you angle hard left, riding your right ski into the apex of this turn, the g forces so great that your eyes are heavy in their sockets, as if some distinct and separate part of your body, and your legs in the apex are hit now especially hard. You are taking every risk at the bottom. You can feel the shock waves in your skis, which make them skip in the arc, your heart in your throat, because you know your skis might skip out of their arc entirely and catch again, but at the bottom here, you wouldn't have the energy to absorb what would be, this umpteenth time, a 4 g hammering, six hundred pounds aimed from unexpected angles at your legs.

But that does not happen. Your skis hold.

And aimed at the last gate, you're centered over your skis again, sucking it all in, all of it. You are one big hollow, no amount of air here enough to make up for the oxygen deficit you've racked up, yet you are turning right again. Anyway.

Just—one—last—turn.

Your outer leg, your left, is mush, and you give in the slightest, decide on a marginally safer line here, a *rounder* turn, which will cost you, and veering right, you hang on for all you're worth—any sort of chatter here will be the end of you, having spent it all.

So getting around the gate is nothing short of some kind of grace.

And around it you squat, hands thrust in front of you, reaching for the finish line, poles along your sides, weight back, more pressure on the tails of your skis, but the skis, at forty, forty-five miles per hour here squirrelly as hell with your weight back like this, there being the possibility you'll go ass over teakettle at the bottom, in front of everyone, though, more important, you need to jet here, cut perhaps hundredths of seconds off your time, *just over the finish line.*

And *now* you can stand—God, but does that feel *good!*—skidding to a stop and craning your head around to see your time.

Which is—*almost*—never fast enough.

WHY WE LOVE RACERS

Anyone, and that really is *anyone*, can get down an Alpine racing course. That is, *if* you can so much as make a snowplow turn.

"I skied Exhibition" was once a common skier's refrain, which usually meant this boaster had fallen, slipped, skidded, and otherwise clattered to the bottom of Sun Valley's famous bump run. And that in view of everyone on the chairlift.

Grizzly, at Snowbasin Resort in Utah, the site of the 2002 Olympic downhill competition, for example, can be navigated by the near neophyte. All it takes is a great deal of wedge turning, traversing, and maybe, for the truly uninitiated, an ice ax to stop that long slide to the bottom after the inevitable fall.

Still, all skiers—even the most timid—will let their skis run at times. This might be for a truly phobic skier a dashing, heart-whomping swoosh down First Time at Park City at the intoxicating speed of twenty-five miles per hour. It could be a run straight down Seattle Ridge in Sun Valley at sixty.

No matter.

Each skier is, in his or her mind, a *star* in that moment, pressing the envelope of what is possible.

These days, if you're a girl, you're Julia Mancuso, picking up an Olympic gold; if you're a boy, you're bad-boy Bode Miller, winning the first American World Cup overall title in twentysome years.

From the time skiing becomes not some plunking around on the hill, but a hyperfocused activity, the ski gods loom large. Their names are molded on our goggles, embossed on our gloves, painted and laminated on our skis. Their names are talismans, some of them, in film-fame fashion, like Jack, Bob, or Diane, becoming single names: Stein, Killy, and Picabo.

None of this really means a whole lot, though, until you stop dreaming of being a star and take to the gates yourself. In one run, pitted against others more experienced than yourself, you are no longer the "Hermanator," or Susy "Chapstick" Chaffee, or Playboy Tomba. As Bode Miller put it in an interview with *Newsweek*, "Defining your criteria for success is easier when you suck. As you get better, it becomes harder. The steps are smaller."

Which is where the insanity enters, albeit a *cocky, joyful* insanity.

Very early on, you discover that if you're going to get anywhere in this sport of ski racing, you need to rise to the level of your competitors' daring. And you find out in no time at all that there are lots of folks out there ten times crazier than you are.

Guaranteed certifiable, some of them.

Like the rubber-limbed kid with the dimples in front of you now, who walks pigeon-toed and who's just cleaned your clock. Beat you by seconds on this crappy little course at Buck Hill, in Burnsville, Minnesota, because he's not afraid of breaking his legs in two.

And he doesn't, run after run, break his legs, so what's *your* problem? So what if you fly off the slalom course and do three somersaults on your head? What's a little pain? After all, your damn ski boots hurt so much, what would be a little more pain? But there is this self-regulating, ingrained spirit of self-protection in you. It's this little voice you have to both listen to *and* overcome if you want to truly ski fast.

After all, whisking down seemingly near vertical slopes at forty miles per hour between bamboo gates that could rip your legs off somehow doesn't exactly fit into that old Darwinian evolutionary picture. Imagine a Cro-Magnon, club slung over his shoulder, navigating a run at Chamonix. Is he smiling? Or is he terrified?

The would-be *racer* is smiling (albeit grimly). (Especially if there is a woolly mammoth coming down the slope after him.)

So, taking your shot at the Buck Hill gates again, you ski way out of your comfort zone, and still you lose. It's part of the early racing picture. Here, you either despair and quit, or you get really pissed off and focused. When you do the latter of the two, as Lindsey Kildow did endless times at Buck Hill, you learn a few things: first, when you simply try to put *more* energy and heart into it than that laid-back–looking pasty kid, you lose yet again, each time pushing you farther over your comfort limit, each time more humiliating.

So you focus. In your head, you're cold and calculating; in your body, you are a seething mass of thwarted will.

And what you focus on are the ski gods, taking from the current crop whatever you can steal.

It's a bit like Prometheus stealing fire from the gods. Only, whereas Prometheus was punished for it by having his liver torn out by raptors every evening, you have your legs, back, head, and feet pounded nearly numb time and time again. Or you suffer a boot-top fracture. A broken clavicle. Nearly frostbitten feet. It hurts, but there are those moments when what you've been stealing from the ski gods *works*. Early on, you learn to keep your hands out in front of you. You learn to feel the length of the bases of your feet, and how to move your weight from the ball of your foot (a turn initiation, attack position) to the heel of your foot (a jetting, end-of-a-turn position). You learn the power of keeping your shins pressed into the tongues of your boots. You learn that your skis, too front-weighted moving from hard snow into soft snow, will cross their tips and send you onto your head. You learn jetting on your tails is a risky business at best, and that skis so weighted turn unpredictably and can, worse yet, tear ligaments if you fall like this, "riding the backseat." And over and over again, when you get serious, racing, you look to those racers who built this whole business before you. Who dreamed of doing the impossible, and then did it.

That's why we love the ski gods. They show us, over and over, that the seemingly impossible *is* possible. Even if they are from a town too small to warrant a dot on a map (Picabo Street, from Triumph, Idaho, near Sun Valley), or raised without electricity or indoor plumbing (Bode Miller), or they crashed so ferociously we feared for their lives, not for their ability to stand up and win a gold medal days later (Hermann Maier).

Up before dawn, shoveling in breakfast, and out into—in some geographical locals—blistering cold, if you are a racer, your mind is on *speed*.

Getting *down* a course is nothing; doing it *faster* than anyone else, *anyone*, on a given day, is skiing into the realm of magic.

As Bode Miller said recently, he doesn't master the mountain, *he masters speed*.

And speed, in Alpine racing, takes a daring kind of grace. One competitors buy with their at times extraordinarily daring lives, a handful of these competitors so singular in their talent that their names have become synonymous with the sport itself, skiers such as . . .

STEIN ERIKSEN, THE NORSE SKI GOD

Stein Eriksen was the first major figure to influence skiing following World War II. Realize that although the first Winter Olympic Games were held in 1924, and races had officially been public events in northern Europe since the 1880s, Alpine racing as we now know it did not exist until the 1950s.

This coincided with new technologies gleaned from wartime engineering applied to ski equipment, which, of course, changed skiing itself.

Tension-release bindings, laminated ski composition, Cellulix bases (and later P-tex bases) gave rise to new performance possibilities, which no one exploited more than racers.

Stein Eriksen, a handsome Norwegian not well known in the then-very-tight circles of European racing, stunned the world by winning the 1952 Olympics slalom event. Stein using a never-before-seen style: coming at a gate, he, instead of turning his upper body *into* the gate, turned his shoulders square to it—*away* from it—while carving the opposite direction with his skis, his skis so perfectly parallel that spectators were awed.

Stein had contemplated hanging up the ski life and working in the family business, farming, but on this day, he won his race by some tenths of a second, and an entirely new life was born.

Stein, as are many racers, was recruited by a major resort to run its ski school, Squaw Valley in California. And the story of Stein might have ended there, but for that damnable style of his. For those fifties and early sixties skiers on long Head Standards, *skiing like Stein was the ultimate.*

In part because it was nearly impossible. First of all, skis do not carve well when the boots they are attached to are set side to side. They can't be sufficiently canted (edge angled to the slope). And when skiers added to that the Olympic-winning and oh-so-very-stylish reverse shoulder move, most skiers went over in a heap in the white stuff. Yet in film after film (and book after book), here was Stein, flying as gracefully as a bird down the steepest of slopes, oftentimes in showy, gorgeous powder, which only a handful of skiers in the world skied well at that time, much less with the appearance of effortlessness.

And again, this totally self-possessed grace.

And, Americans loved Stein's story. Small-town kid with a dream applies himself with all his heart and—presto, is rewarded by the gods themselves. Wins Olympic gold and becomes a media darling.

Stein was *pure* charisma.

Stein became *the* symbol of skiing's royalty in the United States. There were Stein Eriksen goggles, and Stein Eriksen poles, and Stein Eriksen skis and boots and jackets and pants. Stein, Stein, Stein. He had a thick mane of blond hair he brushed back from his archetypal Norse face, a style men came to adopt in legion.

Even his heavy Norwegian accent, which made him seem hesitant, almost unsure of himself when speaking English, endeared him to us.

Into his seventies now and after a quintuple bypass, Stein is still somehow preternaturally youthful, Stein running Deer Valley in Utah, *Skiing* magazine's reader's number one American resort, Stein appearing in Deer Valley's promos, seeming to float through snow as if weightless.

Stein, even though his style is now outmoded, still the image of the master skier, a legend which has stuck with us for well over *five decades.*

KILLY, THE SOPHISTICATED SCRAPPER

Jean-Claude Killy burst onto the scene in the 1968 Grenoble Winter Games, changing the way we skied forever.

Killy raced with an explosive, fists-out-front style, Killy seeming to as much punch through gates as carve around them. He was exciting to watch, this dark, intense Frenchman who skied on Dynamics (*Dee*-na-meeks), a then relatively unknown manufacturer. So successful was Killy, that his skis, VR-17s, would become the most sought after for some time following his second-only-in-the-history-of-Olympic-racing win of all three Alpine events: downhill, giant slalom, and slalom. And why do we not remember Toni Sailer, who was the first to win all three? Sailer had no memorable, radical style.

Such as Killy's legendary *avalement.*

Killy discovered that if he weighted the *tails* of his skis *after* clearing the apex of a gate, at the very moment the turning forces were exponentially decreasing, he could generate yet more energy from his barely carving skis, which move, done cumulatively on courses, would cut tenths of seconds from his time and win him races. His method went counter to all previous thought on skiing. Weighting your tails was death, and skiers, if they did anything, literally got shin splints from banging their lower legs into the tongues of their boots. In fact, this was core to the Austrian technique, the thinking behind it having no less credence in skiing circles than holy writ. Weight forward, even today, is gospel, but added to it, by Killy, is the end-of-turn, on-your-heels trick, so dubbed by the American press, the . . .

Jet Turn.

No doubt, *avalement* would have been relegated to the status of racing arcana but for the racy name. And the fact that *we could see it.* As we could see Stein's reverse-shoulder and boots-jammed-together trick.

And as with Stein's trick, every aspiring racer and wanna-look-like-a-racer got "into the backseat."

Killy's style, which was 90 percent smack-on old-school balanced carving work, was mistakenly dubbed by the press the "sit-back style." So pervasive, and so pernicious was the press's mistaken coverage of Killy's innovation, that the director of the spectacularly successful Burke Mountain Academy, Warren Witherell, penned an entire chapter addressing this new *sit-back style* in his highly influential text *How the Racers Ski.* His chapter begins, "The life of a ski coach is often devoted to fighting senseless habits and fads. One year racers are waving their arms wildly about; the next year they are bobbing their heads. The current rage is 'sitting back.' " Witherell went on to say, "Killy . . . made use of the whole ski, [employing] forward, neutral, and back leverage to carve precise turns. The skiing press has, unfortunately, printed pictures of Killy . . . in low-hip, sitting back, *off-balance* positions that are way out of proportion to the actual use of such a stance." And, Witherell concluded, even then "back leverage is used more often in soft snow than in hard." Yet almost all racing is done on hard snow: hardpack, boilerplate, and ice. No matter, *Ski* magazine wrote at the time, in an article titled, "Back Is Beautiful" (a pun on the then-popular saying "black is beautiful"). "The S [jet] turn is destined to become the advanced parallel form to which all good skiers will aspire in the 1970's." "Sitting back" and *avalement*, as used by Killy, were two different things, racers everywhere were cautioned.

But they were not to the public. They had seen the pictures of ski god Killy, and they were believers.

INGEMAR STENMARK, THE ULTIMATE CARVER AND FINESSE SKIING'S LAST HERO

If there had ever been any question about the winning power of the pure carved turn, Ingemar Stenmark answered it, and then some. The winner of a most-likely never-to-be-equaled-again eighty-six World Cup victories and two Olympic gold medals, Stenmark quietly holds the crown as the most successful Alpine racer of all time.

Stenmark means *skiing*.

But even more important, Stenmark was the first glimmer of yet another revolution in skiing—what was to become the *parabolic ski*, a new instrument that would turn the skiing world on its head some ten years later. Even to this day these new "pure carving" skis and Stenmark's techniques are profoundly impacting the way skiers get down mountains.

Stenmark, a successful though not world-shaking competitor in his own right, was racing with moderate success when he met embittered and motivated Ermano Nogler, who himself had been a former champion. Nogler, after many years coaching the Italian team, had been told he was no longer needed, and had gone in search of a star—in, of all places, Sweden.

He found Ingemar Stenmark, whom he coached in a new and scientific method, all of it aimed at the technique of the *pure carved turn*. Whereas competitors prior to Stenmark had hammered through courses, sat back through them, and now were banging through breakaway gates (as did Alberto Tomba, who would usher in a new kind of ski racer years later, the brawler), Stenmark, coached by Nogler, came to navigate courses with almost total efficiency, translating gravitational energies into turning energies *without* skidding, sliding, or "up-course" forces.

Stenmark, with the help of Nogler, went on a grueling regimen of experimentation, wherein, with the aid of much filming, he and Nogler refined the *timing* of edge sets, the *use of leverage*, and the *mechanics of the body* to produce the cleanest-run competitions ever.

Again, this competitor's revolutionary new style could be *seen* in his radical, gravity-defying, skis-distant-from-his-body arcs around gates.

Nothing short of total focus, however, could produce these results—at least not on equipment such as Stenmark was using at the time.

It was a costly program, and not one just any competitor could abide by or thrive on, and we were relieved, really, when the bruisers, such as Alberto Tomba, gave us a breath of fresh air with their flamboyant, knock-down-the-gates style, made possible by the advent of spring-loaded, breakaway gates.

But, you may ask, how did we come to have such skiers as Stein, Killy, and Stenmark?

OLYMPIC AND "WHITE CIRCUS" RACING—
A SHORT HISTORY

The international ski racing scene as we know it today began in Europe with the expansion of rail service in the 1880s. That's right. *Rail*. Rail access to mountain areas popularized the sport of downhill skiing, the rail companies aggressively advertising and glamorizing what had been, until that time, a pastime of the superwealthy or the superadventurous. (Is it any surprise, then, that America's "first destination resort," Sun Valley, was put on the map by Union Pacific Railroad advertising and dollars, as recommended by its European technician, Count Felix Schaffgotsch, hired by the Union Pacific's then chairman, W. Averell Harriman? Or that J. P. Morgan, of railroad fame, would be the first man to try the newly invented—from an endless-cable banana loader—chair lift, on Dollar Mountain at Sun Valley?)

New rail routes, which crossed the Alps from west to east, made access to resorts such as Saint-Anton and Kitzbühel possible even for those with modest means. And rail spurs to sanatoriums, which were poplar in Europe, gave rise to resorts such as Chamonix, Davos, and Saint-Moritz—a tandem pleasure of European skiing to this day, the common area spa and baths, an après-ski bonus.

This rail development continued over a forty-year period, a large number of British tourists, in particular, flocking to the Bernese Oberland after World War I, towns such as Wengen and Mürren becoming bastions of skiing. This interest in skiing was, really, a necessary outgrowth of a northern European fin de siècle obsession with mountaineering. As early as the eighteenth century, gentlemen of means and sophistication came to be compelled to scale Alpine peaks. And while many scaled Mont Blanc and the Matterhorn, other felt-hatted, less-adventurous souls, who desired to sniff at the danger rather than experience it directly, created an entire mountain resort industry, complete with charming chalets, but even more important, cable cars and cog railways to reach the summits without all the danger and fuss.

Still, skiing continued to evolve as a necessary *corollary* to the Alpine adventure, taking climbers across glaciers, and *down* them—so many, and with such great pleasure, that more than a few climbers decided that *skiing down* mountains was a greater pleasure than *climbing up* them.

Here modern skiing was born, in the Alps, the French, with that Gallic excitability and penchant for labyrinthine laws, going so far as to create the Fédération Internationale de Ski (International Ski Federation), which sanctioned "Alpine" events—races—for those daring climbers turned skiers. (A proud parallel development was taking place all the while in the United States. In the Sierras, Norwegian and Swedish gold miners were organizing downhill races with mass starts, the winners awarded from substantial betting pools.)

To this day the FIS remains, with the IOC, the International Olympic Committee, the most powerful governing body in Alpine events.

From the formation of the FIS to the inclusion of Alpine racing events in the Olympics in 1922 was a small step. Here was an already established international sports competition, with its own bylaws, infrastructure, history, and body of more than enthusiastic spectators. So the FIS simply petitioned for the inclusion of Alpine events in the Olympics, initially as a *demonstration* event.

The crowds went mad with excitement over these very daring Alpine racers, these human bullets on skis, and in 1924, the IOC, with the help of the FIS, put on the first Olympic Winter Games.

But not as we know them now. The original Olympic Winter Games event was "downhill," and downhill *only*.

One race, one course. Really, still more demonstration than full-on sport. (Could you imagine *one* track event in the Summer Olympics?)

Such was the case with the development of the sport that even when the second Winter Olympics were held in Saint-Moritz in 1928, local hostelers advertised a dozen winter events, among them skating, tobogganing, and bobsledding, but there was *not one* mention of skiing.

All this changed due to the efforts of Arnold Lunn, the progenitor of modern Alpine ski racing. Lunn, whose father owned the Lunn Travel Agency in London, was altogether familiar with the spectacular scenery around the Alps through his father's work and the visits it afforded him to such places. Born in 1888, Arnold was spending most of his time around Chamonix and Crans-Montana, in Valais, Adelboden, or Mürren in the Bernese Oberland, by the time he was in his teens.

Lunn, unlike his father who simply promoted the notion of romance in these mountainous areas, lived this romance, and managed to sell it to thousands, so impassioned was he. And, given his connection to tourism, he organized "gymkhanas" for those individuals wanting exercise and amusement.

Realize that Kitzbühel, just prior to this, had organized its first "downhill" event, which had been so successful that the following year special trains were offered to bring the spectators in from Innsbruck and Bavaria, tens of thousands of them.

So it was in this spirit that Lunn created the "slalom" in 1922, skiing's first official, codified event, a spin-off of his earlier gymkhanas. In the same fashion, he introduced and organized the first "combined" event, a downhill *and* slalom. Lunn then fought to have the International Ski Federation endorse his races, something it did not do until 1930.

Lunn was not to be put off. He teamed with then Alpine great Hannes Schneider of Saint-Anton to create the first of the classic competitions, the Arlberg-Kandahar, which became the true starting point of international Alpine ski racing. *Arlberg*, after the mountain range, Schneider turned into a skiing sensation (as well as the name he gave his graduated-steps skiing method, which was used into the seventies); and *Kandahar*, in honor of Lord Roberts of Kandahar, the hero of the British raj who showed himself particularly valiant during the battle of Kandahar in southern Afghanistan in 1879.

Established in Saint-Anton, the Arlberg-Kandahar was on odd years run in Mürren, where Lunn had one of his homes.

From the first, the Arlberg-Kandahar race was not without controversy.

In 1938, the race was to be held in Saint-Anton, but a few days before the event, Nazi Germany annexed Austria and the Gestapo arrested Hannes Schneider, whom they considered to be an enemy of Hitler's Germany. Lunn retaliated by canceling the race, which the Germans now figured large in. Lunn entered into negotiations with the Nazis over the next year's event long enough for Schneider to escape with his family to the United States, where he established a ski school based on his Arlberg techniques.

Lunn refused to let the race return to German-occupied Saint-Anton, instead moving it to Chamonix, France, where then downhill sensation James Couttet promoted and further developed the event.

The greatest difference here, though, was this: in the *earlier* Lunn-Schneider competitions, skiers had to qualify for the slalom competition held the second day by placing in the top forty in the *downhill*, held the first day. Couttet and his fellow organizers dispensed with this requirement and along with it the starting order it had generated (the fastest five in the downhill competing in a group of five in reverse order, then, likewise, the second set of five, etc.) and the true era of the *specialist* was born.

And with the specialist was also born the "French Method," based on the style of their world champion, Emile Allais, and sanctioned by the then secretary of the French Ski Federation, G. Blanchon.

At this time, as many as twenty thousand spectators would turn out for the Arlberg-Kandahar, which fostered spin-off races everywhere, such as the Engelberg world championships.

The outbreak of war in 1939 ended this period of racing, even though the Lauberhorn races were still run each winter in Wengen, Switzerland. Here, many racers who had fled to Switzerland, and as a result of their political status could not race under their own names, did so under names like "Donner" (Thunder) and "Blitz" (Lightning), though many brilliant careers were cut short.

Still, when racing resumed full force after the war, it was the Austrians who emerged as a world power, under the tutelage of Fred Roessner. So powerful was the Austrian "Wunderteam," that it dominated world racing events six winters in a row, introducing to the world its first internationally lauded Alpine racing stars, as we know them now: Toni Sailer, Karl Schranz, and Christian Pravda.

And here now, too, were for the first time the Americans, inheritors of spectacular resorts such as Aspen, Vail, and Steamboat, all set up by Tenth Mountain Division skiers who fell in love with the sport during World War II training, among them racers such as Buddy Werner (who, incidentally, died in an avalanche before he could truly compete with the Austrians).

But it wasn't until the 1956 Olympics, when Toni Sailer won all three gold Alpine event medals, downhill, giant slalom, and slalom, that television discovered it had a market in broadcasting Alpine events.

Which fueled, at that time, a sport badly in need of capital. Television coverage provided it.

And in turn, gave rise to more interest in Alpine stars. After a bit of digging, the media—not only television, but the newspaper industry, too—had a field day. These racers, it was discovered, not only went like lightning down the slopes, they also drove crazily, smashing up their cars, engaged fearlessly in affairs and mistaken couplings, brawled in public, and drank and smoked to excess.

They said crazy things, mixed up languages, cried in public, and crashed, while racing, spectacularly.

And leaped and danced when they won races.

They were colorful, our best and worst selves, and we loved them, these human generators of awe, surprise, and incredible verve. If they had the guts to do something as insane as steering skis down a mountainside at seventy miles per hour, why couldn't *we* do any number of things? Why not?

So great was our interest in these stars that by 1964, the Eurovision network was beaming broadcasts of these events to remote locations such as Algeria and Morocco, places where people had never so much as *seen* snow. And by 1966, television had so turned skiing into an international spectator sport that the sport was ripe for the creation of the World Cup Skiing Tournament, the companion event to the Olympics, which now generates enormous revenues for broadcasters and competitors alike. Makes millionaires of winners, many times over.

And all of this started through Lunn's travel agency, and his slalom for exercise-minded Europeans who wanted to spice up their vacations.

Well, Lunn certainly succeeded—for all of us, racer and weekend skier alike. Now we all dream dreams of glory, fueled by the exciting images fed to us by the Alpine-hungry media machine.

OLD SCHOOL: WHERE THESE PEOPLE COME FROM—

Worldwide, racers distinguish themselves at very early ages. Annemarie Moser-Proell, the greatest female racer in history, for example, was only fourteen in 1967 when she took part in her first World Cup race, on the very dangerous downhill at Badgastein, Austria. When she gave up racing in 1980, claiming she was "burned out," she was just twenty-eight.

So, how does a fourteen-year-old come to be competing in an international event like the World Cup?

Through school, the *old school*. In communities where there is a tradition of racing and ample snow, all the would-be racer needs to do is sign on the dotted line. Teams are always looking for talent—and the younger the better.

In America, states such as Colorado, Utah, Montana, and Idaho; California, Vermont, New Hampshire, and Rhode Island; and Minnesota, Michigan, and Wisconsin all host serious racing programs organized around the European tournament system. High school teams, for that reason, are breeder programs, all hosting, through the United States Ski Association, regional tournaments: East, Mid-West, Mountain, Inter-Mountain, and West. In Park City, for example, there are serious programs for any level of competitor, from those under ten, to those bucking for genuine, bona fide membership on the U.S. (or National) Ski Team. Here, world-class champion Picabo Street oversees race and ski schools. There are the YSL (Youth Ski League) starter programs: Love to Race, Farm Team, and Devo (Development) Team. If you show stellar promise (and it must be stellar in Park City, home of the National Ski Team since the mid-1980s), you will win a spot on the C Team, then B Team (by which time you will have a sponsor, be it Fischer, Rossignol, Atomic, K2, or other), and finally the A Team. The A Team competition is international class, A Team skiers competing in FIS races in Germany, Austria, France, and Switzerland, and it is a small step from the Park City A team to the National Ski Team. (Fewer than *one in one thousand* very gifted racers make it onto the National Team.)

The Park City/Salt Lake City area, site of the 2002 Olympic Winter Games, claimed having over seventy competitors in the 2006 Turin Games.

In fact, the only two members of the U.S. Ski Team to take home medals in the Turin Games, Ted Ligety (who took a gold medal in the combined) and Julia Mancuso (who took gold in giant slalom), both hailed from Park City. Mancuso, in colorful fashion, it is worth noting, endeared herself to the Italians at the Turin Games by claiming to have forebears who were liquor runners for Al Capone in Chicago, where her family had its roots. (In Tomba fashion, she wore a faux diamond tiara when racing in slower slalom events and competed in "Super Jules" underwear, which she designed herself, something the style-conscious Italians also loved.)

Lindsey Kildow, who, were it not for a terrible practice run accident, would have taken home some kind of medal, also claimed Park City as home.

But having noted that, many racers permanently relocate to the Wasatch Mountains area to race on the National Team. Most are from elsewhere. The 2006 Olympic Games medalists, Ted Ligety and Julia Mancuso, got their starts in local California racing, and Lindsey Kildow, one of the finest women racers in decades, got hers on Minnesota slopes—particularly that of Buck Hill, a molehill of a resort, boasting all of two hundred and some feet vertical and one of the most successful Alpine racing programs in the United States.

You mean, you ask, two *thousand* feet, don't you?

No. Two *hundred*.

And on any night you will find dead-serious racers carving runs around gates as if their lives depended on it. Thousands upon thousands of runs.

In a state such as Minnesota, where the skiing surface is more often than not boilerplate, and there is not that much vertical, you either simply fool around (and become a weekend skier) or get nearly intolerably serious. If you begin at an early age, winning the Junior Olympics competitions are something to shoot for, the equivalent of Park City's A Team. Or, as I did later in Sun Valley and Jackson Hole with former U.S. Ski Team members and Burke Mountain Academy graduates, you can *privateer* in ski races sponsored by car companies such as Toyota and Chevrolet, or by ski manufacturers such as Head or K2 on your own "dime and time," picking up trophies and the purses such privatized races offer, none of which is sufficient to float your life. For that reason, privateers, skiers without sponsorship dollars, have to get on podiums quick, thus winning sponsors, or get out. (Imagine the AFL having only *ten* top spots. *That's* the kind of competition there is in Alpine racing.)

But even then, privateers are hardly that: if they are at all successful, privateers all bear the stamp of high-caliber training, as racing at this level demands it. And you only get such training in the old-school programs.

To judge a program's seriousness—its caliber—you simply have to look at its success in producing nationally ranked competitors. If a particular skier has more talent than his or her local program, and has terrific ambition, a move to a better "school" is warranted. Some programs, such as the Burke Mountain Academy, are flat-out famous for producing winning racers. So finding a hot school, one boasting coaches who were nationally ranked competitors themselves, is critical.

No serious racer—not even a Bode Miller—escapes the need for focused, hands-on training with others more expert than him or herself.

It does not happen. Racers are *not* just born—talent *is* born, but it must be refined and focused.

If you ski dual events, as I did in my teens, downhill *and* Nordic jumping, and due to practice pressures only compete in one, which is not an Alpine event, NASTAR (National Standard Races) competitions, can show you how you'd stack up against the best of the best in slalom competition. NASTAR got its start in 1968, and has become the largest public recreational ski racing program in the world. Do note that it is *recreational*, for those not gunning for the A Team or Junior Olympics, or for those racers who need a reality check. In NASTAR racing, a World Cup superstar, such as Daron Rahlves, is chosen as a pacesetter and assigned a zero handicap and sets "par" on a run. Other pacesetters, who race on the same course against Rahlves, are then assigned a handicap from 1 to 999, based on their performance. These pacesetters move out across the country and race against others who also receive handicap scores, all based on how they would have done in competition against Rahlves's initial performance.

So, in theory, when you sign up to race a NASTAR course, you are skiing against Rahlves (or, for example, Bode Miller, Picabo Street, or Julia Mancuso).

These results can be anything from thrilling to downright depressing, the difference between skiing fast and skiing magic right there in numbers for you. Talent, you learn quickly, is much rarer, and bought at a much higher price than you imagined. Though, if taken as a lark (NASTAR awards medals and other bric-a-brac), NASTAR racing can simply be a great deal of serious—sometimes even *extreme*—fun.

The cost of this, even now, is about $5 a run. And some ski areas, such as Park City, have NASTAR races daily.

Which again bring out the contenders and the real thing: in Park City, Sun Valley, or Squaw Valley, ex-Olympians are everywhere, as we would expect. But they are everywhere, too, in Wisconsin, Michigan, and Minnesota—but more so in the last than elsewhere in the Midwest.

Which brings me back to school. And the racing programs approach.

THE TECHNICAL ART OF SKIING FAST: A BRIEF PRIMER ON STRATEGY

So, you think you're a hot shot, do you? Coach Tadsen, of the Flying Spartans, in Minneapolis, asks.

Yeah, I do, you tell him.

There's this *Fuck you, kid* something in his voice, and when he swings his hand out to the course, motioning to you that the hill is now yours, you have to rise to the occasion. You are just fifteen and bucking for a spot on the Flying Spartans. You are not going to just get down the hill and the course on it, you are going to tear it up, carve it up, destroy it.

There is no place for a gliding start. You skate out of the starting gate, which gets your heart going, those two hundred beats a minute by the third gate, you are so focused here that your mind is like some hypersensitive monitor, with things your teachers at Highland Hills, Buck Hill, and Welch Village have shouted at you coming to you now—HANDS IN FRONT!—ON THE BALLS OF YOUR FEET!—QUIET UPPER BODY!—RELEASE YOUR EDGES ONLY COMING OUT OF THE TURN!—DON'T SIT BACK!— ATTACK, ATTACK, ATTACK!

At the time, you cut the nonbreakaway gates so close you banged into them, bruising your shoulders.

But no matter—you don't feel it (not until later), because your concentration is focused on the feel of the skis under your feet, which your far-too-tight boots allow you to sense, not *like* extensions of your body but your *actual* body. You can tell, instantly, when you are on ice, in your skis' suddenly quiet but heavy rush. When they encounter softer snow, there is this resistance, granular in frigid temperatures, sticky near or above freezing, either of which, when moving from boilerplate to soft, can pitch you dangerously too far forward. But there are an infinite number of soft snows, and your skis perform differently on each of them: powder (dry, or heavy—such as Sierra cement), windblown (snow that has set, or been compressed, or has set, then weakened into sugar snow), snow that has surface hoar, snow that is glazed, snow that has strengthened and hardened to the consistency of Styrofoam. There is firnspiegel, rimmed snow, mashed potatoes.

You ski them all differently, and there may be as many as five or six surfaces on a downhill course.

There is sluff snow, also, which packs around gates, which has a braking effect, and if you are in too much of an attack position, on the balls of your feet, weighting the fronts of your skis, and you encounter sluff, you can be thrown so far forward that your tips will cross. (As did gold medal favorite Giorgio Rocca's in the 2006 Olympic slalom competition, sending him head over heels.)

Imagine standing on a hard, wooden ball three feet in diameter.

Put the ball on a thirty-five to fifty-degree slope. Allow that the ball is rolling, but you remain at the top of it, regardless of what the ball encounters in the way of resistance or irregularities.

This was, actually, an exercise for racers: standing on a ball of this diameter (on a flat surface), and so refining your balance that you could lean, roll, or stoop in any direction without losing your balance and falling. (Some skiers still use it.)

This is what it feels like, skiing gates at thirty to forty miles per hour.

Which you cannot do—unless your balance is exquisitely sensitive, exquisitely flexible and responsive.

Which it is, you having already been on skis what seems forever, in those childhood years, each year an eternity.

But you've been waiting for this. At school, you are an average-sized kid, not taller or shorter than the other kids in general. You might play football, baseball, soccer, but size has not been an advantage. Skiers, until recently, were *not* large people. Size was not an advantage until the advent of the breakaway gate, and size remains a questionable advantage at best.

So you focus on being faster *or* quicker (realize that you can be *quicker*—in time—around a gate, *cutting a shorter line*; or you can be *faster, staying on the outside and maintaining a marginally greater speed as a result*), or both, depending on the gate. A gate on a flatter section, say a twenty-five- to thirty-degree slope, and you want ultimate quickness—the straightest line around the gates with the least exhaustion of inertial energy. Gates on very steep slopes demand hard carved turns, more fully rounded, which in turn scrubs off quickness, but prevents the skis from "getting away from you." A skier may want to carve around such a gate while maintaining speed, though this may require a more radical turn at the following gate, which, if skidding or chattering resulted, would lose both time and speed.

So a strategy is required.

And there is the distance *between* the gates to consider. Technique for slalom is akin to a quick fistfight. You make the most of each of your punches, staying centered and putting everything into quickness and power over a very short duration.

Since slalom turns are so hard around the axis, the gates, a critical consideration is *not skidding the tails of your skis.*

If you edge too severely, apply too much attack energy, banging into the tongues of your boots and forcing your turns, your skis will skid at the tails—which will spend an enormous amount of your energy. So you must not only with lightning sharpness *enter* your turns at the exact place where the designed arc of the skis you are using will carve around the gate without skidding, you must exit effectively also. Here *leverage* is critical—to prevent the tails from skidding, your weight goes back, on your heels, though only for a fraction of a second, enough to counteract the hard carving decayed turn skid.

Then, as before, you are neutral on your feet, earning as much speed between this gate and the next, until, again, at that last and precise moment, you—*ATTACK.*

With a giant slalom course, the equation is far more complex, because the spacing of the gates is more variable, the pitch of the slope is more variable, and, as the course is longer, the snow conditions are more variable.

Which, for skiers who excel at the giant slalom, is a joy—in that the GS is a totally mind-consuming challenge.

Because if slalom is a punching match (and it has been since the rise of the brawlers, some even wearing shin and forearm strike plates), GS is an all-out, no-holds-barred, kickboxing, wrestling, running-and-striking affair.

Realize, since any ski has only one true, designed radius that it carves, forcing the GS ski to perform in a variety of carving arcs—short to the point of skidding; moderate g turns; and long, downhill-like sweeping arcs—requires extraordinary talent. And this also on a greater variety of snow surfaces and pitch—and over a much longer run. GS races then are "technical challenges," the speeds here reaching that of the low end of downhill, nearly fifty miles per hour or so, making GS crashes more violent.

Downhill, skied on the steepest pitches, and at speeds that can maim or kill you, is a white-hot pursuit of the cleanest line. While being a winning GS competitor requires the greatest degree of *technical skill*, downhill requires the most flat-out *daring*. Which is, of course, why we love it. In Alpine skiing, it is always the biggest draw, that due to the raw beauty of it, and the very high degree of risk.

Downhill skiing is the high-wire act of Alpine racing. You can't take your eyes off these men and women.

In downhill, finding and being able to hold—an almost impossible task due to the very high g forces—the straightest line down the mountain wins the race.

And most of us can only imagine what it feels like to ski such slopes at such speed. (To truly appreciate a downhill course, or a super G, GS, or slalom course, one must stand on an actual hill, and there watch racers. Film, as anyone who has ever taken a shot of a mountain slope knows, absolutely flattens perspective. And television even more so. Granted that if these courses appear steep on television, imagine how steep they *truly* are.)

But the course you are on here, as a team hopeful, is a slalom course.

And you punch through gate after gate, cutting as cleanly and brazenly as you possibly can.

When you reach the bottom, you play Jean-Claude Killy, sitting back on your skis and jetting.

Tadsen, to your surprise and delight, is leaping down the hill alongside the course. He has a watch in his hand, and there is still plenty of that *Fuck you, kid* look on his face, but there is also excitement.

Ten years you've been skiing, but there was no reason to say that up at the top.

You simply had to stay on your feet and run the course gate for gate with one of the best Alpine skiers in the Central Division. A harsh brawler of a kid who has the reflexes and reactions of someone permanently on bad basement speed (which he really did use). Muttonchop sideburns, eyes that burn, he glares at you, you breathing hard after your run. He hates your guts. Number one seed on the team, he's been up half the night playing poker with the other guys on the team.

They all have that raw, punchy meanness about them—but also this inside-joking, wised-up something.

"Suit up, kid," Tadsen tells you, and Tadsen's first-seed racer, Larry, impossibly older (though all of just eighteen), and looking as if he'll punch you in the face the second Tadsen's out of sight, gives you a lopsided grin.

"So, you did okay," he says, giving you a knock up alongside your head.

What you are not telling yourself is: *Congratulations!* You made the team . . . you think, though not without a certain irony.

In the schools, you lose more than you'd like, you now competing against older, more-experienced skiers. But you can't give up. Because when you lose, you lose small, by seconds. Say, three, against kids who are bucking for the God's Honest Real Live United States Ski Team.

If your school has clout.

Racing in Park City, Utah, for example, you come to rub shoulders with so many Olympic hopefuls that you not only don't think of them that way, products of media attention and hype, you think of them as "those people" you see three, four, or five times a week. Just like yours, their hair, under their hats and helmets, gets greasy. They slip on the icy cement bricks in the courtyard, walking to the lift. They crash at times, and they are not always good sports, or even interesting ones.

Picabo, on a bad day, can be petulant, even harsh. Ted Ligety sometimes puts his foot in his mouth. Bode, as we all know, is more than a loose cannon on deck, a magnet for controversy. (Just recently, I was at the Base Patrol hut in Park City, and there ran into none other than the Flying Tomato himself, Shaun White, winner of the Olympic Gold medal in the halfpipe. Waiting for a ride in his helicopter, he turned his back to all but his support staff, resorting to the protection of the nearly hour-long conversation his cell phone provided.)

But you're all in it together. Good, bad, and indifferent.

The whole machine of competition for the racer is so tied into specific resort protocol, such as dealing with irritable coaches and course preparation, and with everyone from resort brass to support staff, such as hosts keeping recreational skiers off courses to cat drivers who groom and build courses, that there is a blessed simplicity in getting on the damned course and *having at it*.

Finally.

So while the media creates major inflation by hyping expectations for specific racing hopefuls, as it did in the 2006 Olympics with Bode Miller and Hermann Maier, the truth of the matter is that each competitor, especially in ski racing, feels more so a part of some vast and hoary old beast—which makes the racing itself all that much sweeter.

Out on the mountain there is a certain purity in competing, but even then, really, you are not racing against any other competitors but yourself—this being something Bode Miller, one of the most colorful and successful Alpine racers of all time, tried, unsuccessfully, to point out.

Self-possession and mastery don't make the copy that a good, drag-down, beat-'em-up fistfight does.

When a competitor runs a course while aware of being seen during the run, though, he or she performs poorly. (Alpine racing, in this, is the near opposite of snowboarding competition, where the entire point *is* being seen—whether that's throwing 1080s and cab indies or grabbing stale fish.)

Which makes of Alpine racing, especially at elite levels, an even greater mind game. *Never* is talent alone sufficient.

There must be an absolute application of energy to that talent. And all racers, from the first, must gamble, and gamble large: there is always, with greater edge angles, as well as skiing straighter lines, and pushing the course speed limits, the possibility of not only "blowing out of the course"—what happens when a skier simply cannot control his or her skis given the irregularities of the course and the g forces—but of also suffering serious, and in downhill possibly fatal, injuries.

And in this is a necessary refinement of skills born out of experience of an almost infinitely variable terrain, these skills (including modes of thought) becoming so subtle that the racer, really, only "thinks" of edge angles, the position of his body, or the location of his hands when having to correct his or her line or recover from some course irregularity.

Racers, without exception, race "out of their minds."

Really, there are only three possibilities for improvement: improved physical training, improved equipment, and improved technique.

The first two are matters of calculation; it is the last we live, breathe, and sleep. Where the *art* occurs.

Realize that, for example, a turn initiation that is a *tenth of a second off* on a giant slalom course will produce a turn six to nine feet *short* (fatal, in that the skier possibly straddles the gate) or *long* (also fatal, as the cumulative effect of such errors means the skier must compensate on the following gate or gates, most likely skidding, or having to apply greater edge angles or body English, and thus losing more time).

Racers must also learn to overcome natural ways of seeing. One of the principal causes of aiming too straight at gates is that *your skis follow your eyes*; and most neophyte racers focus their eyes at the *bases of the gates*, when they should focus their eyes on the exact line their skis should follow *through the gates*.

Newton's laws—"For every action there is an equal and opposite reaction" and "a body in motion will continue in the same direction and at the same speed until acted on by an outside force"—are critical considerations here. If you so much as lift your arm, for example, you change the way in which your skis are carving—hence all the hysteria about your hands and upper body. A corollary to the second law here, force equals mass times acceleration, is also useful. The more speed the skier has, the more energy; hence the need for greater forces to change direction (and also the greater forces of deformation when the skier falls).

Pivot-pole plants, critical in slalom racing, are anathema in GS, super G, and downhill.

"Inclination," the angle you must lean to keep from falling to the outside of a turn, must be controlled by subtle movements of the knees—laterally, forward, and backward.

"Leverage" adds another axis to inclination, and in it, "twisting," using the upper body to direct the skis, if used at all, should only *assist* leverage and inclination to carve turns.

Friction, too, is a consideration: the friction of the skis on the snow, but as important, the friction of the skier *in the air*. One way to minimize this is to decrease the skier's overall drag coefficient by putting something slippery on her. Spandex and Lycra not only make you *look* faster, you *are* faster. Denser air produces more friction, so higher elevations (having less-dense air) *are* faster. Basically, air resistance increases at the square of speed, so slight increases in speed create marked increases in air resistance (in bicycle racing, at a speed of thirty miles per hour, more than 90 percent of the rider's effort is used to overcome air resistance). So, if you are racing giant slalom, super G, or downhill, *decreasing* your surface area results in far faster times; conversely, *increasing* your surface area (especially quickly) can be disastrous, such as coming out of a tuck to regain balance, a not unusual reason for a fall at high speed in the downhill. Still, as master skier Killy himself said, "It's how you make your turns that really determines your speed down the mountain."

And following the best line. Which is always the shortest distance between two points—the gate you are at, and the gate following.

Simple enough, it would seem, but for gates being set at different *angles* to the fall line: the nearer the gate is to the fall line, the fewer degrees you must turn to get around it. The farther from it, the larger the turn.

All this, to be negotiated in one seamless, maximum speed run in flat light, gray light, lightly falling snow, fog, or in brilliant sunshine—all of which greatly influence snow surfaces and visibility.

And, for Americans skiing in Europe, there is the different terrain. In Europe, most competition is done *above* the tree line. This may not seem significant, but, when I first turned skis down German, Austrian, and Swiss slopes, the lack of trees gave those mountain slopes the feel of something alien—even lunar. It can give you a bit of vertigo, initially, the lack of trees and ground cover, the feeling that you might simply fall off the side of the mountain. To mitigate that negative, there is, of course, the excitement of being in Garmisch or Chamonix, the charm of six-century-old pubs and restaurants, the thrill of European style. But on the mountain, it is all business as usual. Ski tuning, early mornings, cutting around gates all day, your life counting on your focus and passion.

In the 2006 games, Julia Mancuso, having grown up skiing Squaw Valley, was not much put off by the Italian fog and *flat light*.

Which talent might just have won her the gold.

Many racers—and skiers in general—become disoriented in flat light. In flat light you cannot see the surface under your skis, so you must rely almost entirely on "feel"—a not terrible condition for recreational skiing, but for skiing on the edge, racing, flat light makes things very difficult.

Given the complexity of courses (spacing and orientation of the gates to the fall line), snow surfaces (profoundly variable), light, and differing ergonomics of each racer (heavier skiers have an advantage now on slalom courses, so nearly superhuman speed and finesse in slalom are required from those who are not heavy) only thousands of on-the-edge runs can make any one racer consistently successful—which is why so many racers suffer serious injuries.

You cannot practice for winning by skiing losing times. Free skiing helps refine balance and keep you sharp and in shape, but those on-the-edge-runs must be the focus. This cannot humanly be done without exception, without periods of rest and temporary poor performance.

Coaches then, at times, become insufferable, because they—in general—very vocally discourage lukewarm performances. And quietly, but with a certain wariness, reward improvement. (Once-only breakthroughs are not of much value—skiers must be able to break through time and time again.)

Being on the edge of challenge is exciting, but it can also be exhausting.

So much so that skiing at FIS-sanctioned events requires both phenomenal talent *and* extraordinary heart. You have to be tough. What no spectator or anyone not familiar with the racing scene can ever know is the time and energy that goes into winning races.

You absolutely have to love it, the speed, the refinement, the challenge, the very extreme skiing life (early mornings, blizzards, travel, fierce competition, danger), or you will never succeed.

In Minnesota, when I skied in the Central Division, we practiced with the team three days a week minimum—for four to five hours each day. In Nordic jumping, this was not a problem as our meets were held at night, and we could get to any of the local "hills," the Bush Lake Olympic Training Center, Carver Park, or Theodore Wirth, by three on school days and still have hours until our meets. Training for Alpine events, though, required missing school on some days, and on weekends pushing even harder. Saturdays and Sundays, up at four, or five, you would eat a heavy breakfast, and you would pack a likewise filling lunch, all protein and sugar (candy bars, or fruit bars to get your blood sugar up later), as you would, oftentimes in Minnesota, be skiing in subzero temperatures. You would get on a Duofold union suit, ski socks, a turtleneck, a sweater over that, ski pants, ski jacket, then check your remaining gear: gloves (dried over a heating vent), goggles (with nonfogging stick), ski poles (light and not bent), and skis.

Your skis you would have, before you slept, lovingly (if they are still your babies, your allies in sport) tuned.

Your house stinks of wax, a perpetual, all-winter smell that emanates from the basement where you have your equipment.

Tuning your skis is a labor of love—and just a plain old chore. So there is something in the ritual of it that compels you to ski hard. It's a bit like some mad scientist refining the aerodynamics on a rocket through much effort and experimentation: he'll want to see if it is going to work well (a thought that might give one pause when considering all those missiles out there in silos). Even *prior* to your day of racing, then, you are thinking about speed.

Preparing one ski at a time, you first fill any and all gouges in your bases with P-tex, making sure not to get any carbon into the new material. Carbon creates friction. You have to keep the flame on your P-tex stick "clean" by dripping the dirty P-tex on an extra metal scraper. When the P-tex has cooled, you scrape the melted P-tex flat with a metal scraper.

You then set your straight edge on the ski, to see how flat the base is (a concave or "railed" ski will "hook," carve erratically and sharply). The ski base should be flat. If it isn't, even slightly, you flatten it with a block and #100 sandpaper. When the base is flat, you brush it with a brass brush, which will remove fibers left from the sandpaper. A rule of thumb here is, the more you brush with the Fibertex, the faster the ski will be. Which makes it hard to simply give your skis a "once-over."

If you are cutting tenths of seconds from your time, how much brushing with Fibertex is enough?

To make the ski carve more easily and to eliminate any "grabby" feel that it might have, you bevel the ski's base and side edges. To do this, you take a roll of half-inch masking tape and wrap layers around the handle end of your file, and with the ski flat to you, run the teeth of your file at an angle across the width of the ski, beveling the opposite base edge. Each layer of tape on the file's noncutting surface will further cant the cutting surface. If you want the now standard one-degree base bevel, you use two layers of tape. You repeat the process for the second base edge, then you set your ski side-up in your vise. Using a side filer, such as a Base Beast, you now sharpen the side edge at one to four degrees, then do likewise with the second. Using a polishing stone, you remove any burrs on the base and side edges.

Years ago, when side and base edges were cut at ninety degrees, detuning was in order for particular uses. Now, though, the skier can anticipate conditions and tune for them: for example, if the surface to be skied on will be boilerplate or ice, a half degree of base bevel might be used to give maximum edge hold (cutting). If the ski is to be used on a porous surface, a two-degree base angle might be used to prevent the ski from railing unpredictably.

And with snow conditions in mind, you wax (in this, a necessary consideration, too, is air temperature—often, snow temperature and air temperature will vary greatly). In years past, there was a color coding for waxes specific to conditions, though now most waxes are clear.

Using an iron (formerly your mom's, ruined for clothing the first time you prepped skis with it, so now yours), you melt the proper wax to the base so that it puddles at the tail. You must make sure that the wax does not smoke—again, indicating "burning" and the formation of carbon, which creates friction. (If money is no object, Fluoro, a fluorine compound that actually binds chemically with the P-tex base, will be your choice—Fluoro, *just* a few hundred dollars a salt-shaker-sized container.)

You then run your scraper the length of the base of your ski, which turns up paper-thick curls of wax.

This done, you buff with a horsehair brush until the base gleams—like the medal you are going to win—and reach for the other ski of the pair.

This tuning of your skis is *just for starters: a drop in the ocean of what it takes to consistently win races.*

Done with the second ski, you wrap each in plastic film, so the newly "tuned" ski bases do not directly contact each other, and bind them using the skis' brakes.

(Some racers—even barely teenage ones—will have as many as *five* pairs of skis, and will "prep" as many as three in a prerace evening.)

You turn off your radio, make sure the iron is off, sweep the steel filings, wax curls, and P-tex bits into the wastebasket. You reach for your skis, switch off the light, then trudge up the stairs, where you set your skis by the front door.

You'll know where they are the following morning—in the dark, when you leave for your race.

Only *when*, and *if*, you rise to the level of national competition will you be spared this prerace ritual, will you have your own personal ski tuner.

You skip it a few times, and when you do, you curse yourself (your skis skid when dull, carve unpredictably—even drag).

Sliding into your bed, what your coach has shouted at you until you've found yourself mouthing it with him comes to you—

Don't make excuses. Win.

You consider your tuning. Your skis, which you've chosen out of hundreds, are now as close to magic as you can make them. You consider that tendency you have, on your left side, to release your edge too early.

And when you stand at the top of today's course, having suffered the jostling of your teammates, the dumb, sullen jokes, the long ride, and the constant film running in your head of previous races, you are more than ready.

It's five degrees out, the slalom course in front of you steep, the light bright, everything lit with new snow, brilliant and blue white.

You've made every effort, and you are more than ready. You are ferocious. You want to eat this course up.

Rip it up.

It's right here in front of you. A whole world of possibility, and it all comes together right here, right now.

Out of the gate.

BAD BILLY—A WARNING

Just prior to the 1984 Olympics in Sarajevo, business in the skiing world was going on as usual. With the exception of Americans Phil and Steve Mahre, Europeans were dominating the sport, and nowhere more so than in the ultimate speed event, downhill. Top Austrian downhillers Peter Muller and Anton Steiner were, *almost* without exception, beating all contenders in World Cup events, and the coming Olympic gold medal seemed assured for either one of them.

In the middle of all this, and amid a fury of rumors about eligibility, and rumors of adolescent criminal behavior, one young racer, Bill Johnson, made the U.S. Ski Team. The rumors turned out to be true. Among other questionable acting out, Bill had stolen a car when he was seventeen, destroying the car through joyriding. Bill was the antithesis of European calm and calculation. He was loud, boastful, and rough. (Among the Austrians he was known as "that American nose-picker.") Yet the season before the Olympics, in wind-tunnel testing, he had 5 percent more speed in his tuck than any other skier who'd been tested. And, going into the Olympics, at a World Cup event at the notoriously difficult Lauberhorn in Wengen, Switzerland, Johnson had won big—something the Europeans wrote off as a fluke, an accident. Which brought him to the Sarajevo games with major attitude, of a kind that nearly killed him later.

But at Sarajevo, Johnson was a star. He mocked his rivals. "They should hand the gold medal to me. Everyone else can fight for second," he told the press, prior to his downhill performance.

Bill's run at Bjelasnica was genius. Full of straight, flat sections, the course ideally suited his ultra-tucked style. The Swiss and Austrian racers later claimed Bill had only won the race because the course was so *easy*. So why didn't they win then, given how "easy" it was? Bill raced sixth, finishing the course in one minute, forty-five and fifty-nine hundredths seconds, watching fifty-five other racers attempt to beat his time—which they did not. Bill took gold, a first and not yet repeated American win in the downhill. And even while we were cheering for Bill, he was already souring our victory with bad sportsmanship. Bill spoke freely with the European press about how good it was to "stick it to the Austrians," while crassly claiming his gold medal would earn him millions in endorsements.

(Of course, it *could have*, but winners don't say these things, not at Olympic events.)

Even then-president Ronald Reagan threw a reception for him at the White House, telling him, "You gave your country something beyond description. And believe me, all Americans—Republicans, Democrats, Independents, from whatever race, religion, or creed—we're all on the same team, cheering you."

It turned out Johnson's fame was short-lived. His cocky, brash—even abrasive—personality did *not* win him endorsements.

His was not a face we wanted to see in shoe and soap ads.

His marriage fell apart, and he was living alone. Then, in 2001, Bill Johnson made a comeback attempt at the U.S. Alpine Championships. No longer the swaggering, reckless youth of twenty-three, but still a very fast skier of forty, he approached the downhill gates, some press members said later, with a certain trepidation not characteristic of him. No doubt, Bill was still a world-class skier, was the possessor of a very unusual talent—but trying to stage a comeback in skiing at *forty?* In Whitefish, Montana?

Bill, on his qualifying downhill run, lost control in the middle of the course, crashing through two safety nets *headfirst*. While rescue crews stabilized his airway, he nearly chocked on his severed tongue and broken teeth. He suffered terrible brain damage and lay in a hospital in a coma for three weeks. Upon waking, he spent four months in therapy, learning to walk again.

Said Bill, later, "I didn't know who I was for three months and didn't think that I needed to be alive."

Doctors, not long after he'd regained consciousness, had wondered the same, so great were the uncertainties surrounding his brain injuries.

Bill joked, "I don't remember anything in the 2000s or a lot from the 1990s. But I have two sons, one who is seven and one who is nine, so I must have been around."

Even a year later, though, Bad Bill, despite permanent weakness on the right side of his body and his slurred speech, was back on skis—albeit, now, just as someone taking in the fresh air and sunshine.

And when he was interviewed, after helping carry the torch into the Olympic Stadium in Salt Lake City in 2002, we couldn't help being both horrified at his all-too-apparent permanent injury, and very sad.

For here was one whose reach truly *had* exceeded his grasp.

Brash and abrasive as he was, we wanted to see him, at forty, put on that mantle of supreme downhiller. To win again. Why not, if he could have pulled it off? But it had been so, so long over. Could we blame him for what happened? For having the wherewithal, the guts, the flat-out *balls* to try, all over again—*at forty!*—to reenter what truly is a sport of young and supremely talented competitors? And even while he struggled to mount the steps with the torch, this now crippled, humbled Bill Johnson, part of us *wanted that crazy kid back*. The one who said, just before his Sarajevo run, "Nothing can stop me."

Nothing but time, and fate, and circumstance.

A sobering reminder that even the champion, the king, must at some time hand down his scepter, even his life.

BRILLIANT RACERS FOR OUR TIME—
AND FOR ANY

All-time great racers not only impress us with their prowess on the mountain, but with the very force of their personalities.

Hermann Maier was one such racer, a teammate of his, Hans Knauss, commented on him, "He is for sure *not* one of us." Said another teammate, "He's from another planet." Though known in skiing circles long before the 1998 Olympic Games—he dominated the World Cup circuit in the year prior to it—we came to know him best through those games at Nagano.

Tight-lipped, preternaturally focused, and by occupation a mason, which made him extraordinarily strong, he rarely gave interviews.

Going into the 1998 competitions, he was favored to win the downhill, super G, and giant slalom events. Even then two-time Olympic champion Alberto Tomba said, "It will be difficult to beat Maier in Nagano. He is so full of confidence he can take all the risks he wants."

And take risks he did, right out of the gate.

We all knew he was good. But the World Cup somehow always figures, in the United States, anyway, as poor cousin to the Olympic Games. So we wondered how he would perform in Nagano.

That he was known for being relentless piqued our interest. But in a sport where extraordinary performances are ordinary, we watched with divided attention. Until the *Sturz*.

The big accident. (One only rivaled it—in sports coverage anyway—Yugoslavian ski jumper Vinko Bogataj's "Agony of Defeat" fall on *Wide World of Sports*.)

Very nearly flying on the downhill, Maier lost an edge. The results were catastrophic. Maier was turned sideways in the air, caught by wind, at a speed we could only guess at. Maier stayed in the air what seemed forever, then finally hit the hill with such explosive force that we were reminded of the possibility of total catastrophe that lies under the surface of every seemingly controlled run, Maier tearing through two orange rows of safety nets to come to rest in a heap.

In an instant we were again made aware of why this sport is so thrilling. But then, too, we felt for this competitor. No doubt, we thought, a wheelchair, or worse, would be waiting for him—*if* he so much as survived.

Maier did. And more. Lying on the hill as if paralyzed for just moments, he—to our astonishment—got to his feet, shaking himself as if from some moment of absentmindedness, then snapped into his skis and continued down the hill.

Disqualified, of course, and those of us watching, astounded, were thinking, Well, great! But there's the end of the '98 games for Maier.

Not so. He skied into Olympic racing history, and our collective memories, when he not only took gold in his first event following the crash, the super G, but that by an almost unheard of margin. And if *that* weren't enough, three days later, he went out and placed the fastest times in each run of the giant slalom, again taking gold.

*Un*believable. And also unbelievable was that he did not leap into the air, wave to the spectators, or kiss his skis; or blubber incoherent and ecstatic nothings to the first reporter to get to him.

He said, "Yesterday was not so good. But today I am happy."

Not so good? Happy?

Not long after, fellow Austrian Arnold Schwarzenegger gave him the moniker "the Hermanator" (the name a play on Schwarzenegger's world-famous role as the cyborg/robot that, in its perceived duty as savior, would not be stopped—not by bullets, bombs, or even an industrial-strength metal crusher).

The name stuck, though Maier's Austrian teammates came to call him "the Monster."

Then, as if this weren't enough, Maier suffered another terrible *Sturz*, this time, though, when riding his motorcycle. A car struck him at an intersection, sending him flying through the air yet again—though this time into a ditch. He sustained compound fractures in his lower right leg and nerve damage in his left. In addition to this, there was life-threatening internal bleeding and swelling.

During a seven-hour operation, doctors debated whether they should remove the more damaged of his legs. So profound were Maier's injuries, he went 675 days before returning to racing, a move most—given how painful his recovery was reported to be—would never have so much as considered. Maier, initially, had great trouble just walking, to say nothing of skiing. And forget racing in world-class circles.

But, still astounding—just *two weeks* after his return to competition, he was on top of the winners' podium again, in Sölden, at a World Cup event.

Two . . . *weeks*.

It was *here* that the almost superhumanly reserved "Hermanator" tossed his skis in the air, then hurled himself screaming to the ground. For Maier, not just another historic win, Maier also superseding all but Ingemar Stenmark's total number of World Cup victories.

But what did he say to the journalists?

"I was happy to compete again today after some small problems last month."

Small problems? No doubt, Maier would have to be dead three times over for him to recognize a *real* problem (as *we* see them).

Maier's recovery proved so successful, he went on to compete in the 2006 Olympic Games in Turin, Italy. And while he did not take home a medal from the games, he placed in the top ten, skiing for all the world like the absolutely extraordinary athlete he is.

One for all time.

●

For fans worldwide, Bode Miller exemplifies the iconoclastic, can-do American spirit.

Born and raised in a house without electricity or indoor plumbing, in the woods near Franconia, New Hampshire, Miller learned to be self-reliant. Truly *not* like other athletes, his approach to his sport, born out of what he learned growing up, was one that demanded self-invention, oftentimes to the frustration of his coaches.

His very philosophy, as embodied in the title of a book he co-authored with Jack McEnany, *Bode: Go Fast, Be Good, Have Fun*, ran against the grain of most European programs, which still embrace obsession with technique and refinement through time-tested methods, all amounting to a kind of pedigree.

Miller's approach, given that, was a breath of fresh air (for Europeans, too, who loved his style: as many as seventy thousand of them showing up to watch races in Germany, Austria, France, and Switzerland, and the fans chanting, with profound enthusiasm, his name, "Bo-DEE, Bo-DEE, Bo-DEE!").

Says Miller in his book: "Get a plan, stick to it, and trust your instincts."

It is this last bit that caused those around him so much anxiety and trouble, but also made of Miller something new.

Miller's *instincts*.

Miller, for example, was the first racer of his caliber to switch over to the new "parabolic" skis. For doing this, he was thought crazy, though when he won on them, his detractors jumped on the new skis themselves.

And even under pressure, Miller's demeanor was warm. He had a boyish smile, but, at his best, was blisteringly fast—*if* he could stay on his skis. Because more so than for any other racer in recent history, he was also known for being *inconsistent*—or, it could be said that he was *consistent* in one way: *he either crashed big or won big*.

In the 2002 Salt Lake City Olympics, Miller caught an edge, as did Hermann Maier in the 1998 Olympics downhill combined, but instead of falling, he pulled off one of his many, often-photographed, unbelievable midrun saves—getting back over his skis and finishing the run to win a silver medal. Shortly after, in a similarly irregular performance, he made a flat-out end run in the giant slalom, reminding crowds of Tomba and Phil Mahre.

The Phil Mahre comparison turned out to be prescient, as in January 2005, Miller became the first American in twenty-two years to win the World Cup overall, Mahre having been that earlier American winner. And Miller competed in all five events, this being unheard of. Concerns were that perhaps competing in all events would tire him, which raised questions, too, about his training, and about his unconventional views on performance drugs—some of which he claimed would help eliminate exhaustion and prevent serious accidents.

The kind that his brother, Chelan (a world-class big-mountain snowboarder), had while motorcycling just prior to the opening of the World Circuit competitions. A terrible accident, Chelan suffering such brain trauma that surgeons had to open his skull to treat the injury. Miller, who'd traveled from New York to be at his brother's bedside, was forced to leave for Europe just after the surgery.

While en route to the World Cup competitions, and distracted, as anyone would be, Miller changed his mind about how and what he would ski at the event.

He had been persuaded *not* to race all events, but after his brother's accident, he was going to go full tilt into it, as he had in the past.

"It's a source of pride for me," he told a reporter. "I don't feel like there's any reason to back off and half-ass it. It's good for me in terms of style, too. When you're skiing in every race, there's less downtime and that's less time to stay out partying."

Partying? While in competition?

And here was the advent of a true media circus, one that had been *brewing* for some time (pun intended).

So big did this story become that a year later, and just weeks before the Olympics started, the cover of *Time*'s January 23, 2006, issue read: *American Rebel: He speaks his mind—and apologizes later. He loves to party—and doesn't care about winning. Yet Bode Miller is poised to strike Olympic gold. On the slopes with skiing's bad boy. Newsweek*'s issue that same week was much the same; *Miller Time* (a pun on Bode's partying, employing Miller beer's advertising slogan): *The Truth about Bad-Boy Skier Bode Miller*. These titles were the direct result of a CBS *60 Minutes* interview, in which Bode made the comment that he'd skied "wasted," and the final straw for a Bode Miller disgusted by the media's digging into his life.

But this is all getting ahead of Miller's story.

Miller had been the target of such speculation and media interest for some time because, as already noted, he *was* truly different, on the slopes *and* off. On the slopes he was radically daring, but so too off. He was outspoken, as was Bad Boy Bill Johnson, but in an entirely different way. Miller was the kind of "Bad Boy" we love. He had a charming sense of self-irony, could be funny, profane, and insightful, but most unusual was his honesty. He simply did things his own way, even where his exercise regimen was concerned, which again made for good copy.

For example: All snow sports athletes train for power and strength, aiming for the maximum power-to-weight ratio (which means maximizing the components of power that rely on quality of movement: rate, range, coordination, balance, and muscle fiber recruitment). Miller, concerned with this as are all world-class athletes, though, created his own training. For endurance, he pushed a wheelbarrow with fifty pounds (twenty-two kilos) in it, or sometimes friends, up a steep hillside. For refining his balance, he practiced "slacklining," tying a one-inch-thick rope three or more feet high between two trees, and not only walking on the rope, but performing one-legged squats and other drills there for hours. For agility and quick reflexes (and mental anticipation) he ran in dry streambeds, "rockhopping." A superior exercise for developing lightning-fast edge changes, rock hopping is also an easy way to injure yourself. And, to add to this, Miller was equally unorthodox in tuning his equipment. Especially his famously punched-out boots. At one point Bode discovered that if he slid PowerBars (a brand of high-carb candy bar) between the backs of his boots and his calves going up the lift to a race, by the time he got to the top, the backs of his boots would have "firmed up again, nice and high in the back. Worked like high-test gas," he said. *PowerBars?*

Was he joking? (Sometimes he was.) Yet, when he truly *did* discover something new, that a composite-metal foot bed gave him superior feel (recall, when racing, you don't just *ski on snow,* you have to sense what *kind of snow you're skiing on*), he horrified his coaches by sharing what he'd discovered with his competitors—because, he said, he didn't want an unfair advantage.

All this coming from some backwoods recreational skier would simply be the stuff of genuine eccentricity.

But Miller *won* races—world-class races, and lots of them, and in a style that thrilled spectators. He had legs that worked magic, and one of the straightest lines in the history of ski racing. Miller wowed us in Salt Lake, and again at the 2005 World Circuit competitions, where he took the World Cup, thereby joining such legends as Jean-Claude Killy, Ingemar Stenmark, and Hermann Maier, who'd won his fourth title the season before.

Setting Miller up for a sweep at the 2006 Games, as it had Maier.

And there began the fierce media hype, pitting Miller against the Hermanator, seemingly back from the dead. This hype so vexing to Miller that at one point he claimed about the upcoming Olympics that "If it wasn't such a cluster-fuck for me to pull out now, I'd consider it."

(Since the age of three, he had been racing, going fast, and had won so many trophies he felt he didn't need more. His leaded-glass World Cup trophy, the highest honor in the skiing world, shattered in his luggage while returning to the United States. Which said something about Miller's feelings about it: any other racer would have padded his trophy in three layers of bubble wrap and carried it in his lap on the airplane all the way home.)

The two weeks of the Torino Olympics, Miller skied in world-class fashion, but nowhere near his best. He made a—in retrospect—*peculiar* decision to use an untried pair of Atomic skis, which proved to be slow, in the downhill minutes before his race, and was about to win, it seemed, the combined, when he straddled a gate. On the slalom, he blew out of the course (nine of the twenty-nine competitors did not finish the first run because they crashed or straddled a gate).

When story-hungry reporters headed for Miller, he jumped a fence, retreating to his recreational vehicle.

No matter. The following week, or the next month, in typical erratic, but predictable, Miller fashion, *he just might have won all five events*.

That we all believed it, knew it to be true, in the way we know rain is wet, or sunshine warms, just goes to show how great a skier he was.

A one-of-a-kind champion.

A FINAL CONSIDERATION: GOOD GUYS *DO* FINISH FIRST, LEO

Of all the recent world-class Alpine competitors, Picabo Street looms large, not only because of her reputation—being perhaps the greatest *downhill* skier, male or female, of all time—but as much for her winning spirit. While many pundits commented that Hermann Maier made winning look painful, Street made winning races look like pure joy.

There was something charmingly youthful about her, girlish, pixieish. Even effervescent. When she smiled, it wasn't just something for the cameras, but something that came from her love of what she was doing: *skiing*.

Make no mistake, though: Picabo Street was a fierce competitor.

"You put a roadblock in front of me," she told one reporter, "and I'm going to find a way to either get around it, under it, or plow right through it if I have to."

Street, the only American skier to ever win a World Cup downhill, was named not after an infant's game, but after a nearby town. Picabo, pronounced "peek-a-boo," means "shining waters" in the language of the Sho-Ban, a Native American tribe who once inhabited the region. Street, though, for the first three years of her life in tiny Triumph (population: 50), Idaho, was called just "Baby Girl." Born of counterculture parents, her new name was given to her when her father, Stubby, a stonemason, took a job in Central America, and a new, proper name was needed.

Back in Triumph, later, the Streets grew their own food and chopped wood for heating their home.

There were only eight children in the town of Triumph, seven of them boys, among those boys Picabo's brother, Roland, just a year older. As a result, Picabo grew up as the quintessential tomboy, competing with the boys racing bicycles, playing tackle football, and boxing, the last taking out a few of her teeth in her early years.

Street began skiing at the age of six, but was unusual in that she was obsessed with speed, was a born risk taker. By the time she was ten she was beating girls years older, and by the time she was seventeen, in 1989, she won a spot on the U.S. Ski Team (recall, less than one in one thousand *gifted* racers make the team). Picabo, though, was such a wild child that she lasted on the team barely a year. She was told by one coach that she would never win because she couldn't "follow the rules."

(Of course, all this time later, we are reminded of Bode Miller's style, and his early racing problems.)

Picabo took her dismissal from the U.S. Ski Team as a wake-up call. She finished her high school education, trained as if her life depended on it, and in six months was back on the team. In 1993, she won a silver medal in downhill at the World Championships.

Spectators discovered her, though, a year later, at the 1994 Olympic Winter Games in Lillehammer, Norway, where she won a silver medal in the downhill. Picabo amused fans with her humor: at one point when asked about her love of speed, she cheerfully, and with an infectious grin, responded that she thought the police should give tickets to people for driving too *slow* in the left lane, *her* lane.

The two years following proved Street's claim to that left lane, but more so her genius on skis.

In 1995, she won the World Cup title in downhill, then repeated this feat in 1996.

Overall, in this period, she won six straight World Cup downhills and nine total World Cup competitions.

And then, in December 1996, came her first bad fall, which tore the anterior cruciate ligament on her left leg. (This despite the good luck charm she always carried on her, a cross and pin.)

The 1998 Olympic Games in Nagano were fast approaching, and there was some question as to the possibility of her recuperating in time. Street spent eleven thousand hours on stationary bikes, Stairmasters, and treadmills. She swam laps, walked countless miles, surprising her trainers by hitting the slopes one year after her accident.

She got back to training, hitting it hard, finally entering pre-Olympic competition in Are, Sweden, in January 1998.

At the end of a race, traveling at seventy-five miles per hour, she crashed into a fence.

And, like Hermann Maier, she—miraculously—got up on her own power and walked away from the crash.

For most competitors, crashes such as Picabo's in Sweden are anathema. That selfsame *other* who skis faster than is consciously possible, and makes adjustments to terrain that are truly superhuman, now works in service of self-preservation. That *other*, in effect, *puts on the brakes.*

That is why it is so difficult for skiers after a hard fall to pick up the pace, ski that line just this side of survival.

Picabo was having none of it. "That crash was a blessing in disguise," she told reporters. "I wondered what would happen when I went down, and I proved to myself I was 100 percent healthy. I took confidence out of that incident." She then added, in characteristic Picabo fashion, "Adversity makes heroes."

Realize, she didn't say *she* was a hero, as would have Bad Boy Bill Johnson. She said she would rise to the challenge she'd been given. Admirable stuff, given the severity of her fall.

Then, weeks later at the Nagano Olympic Games, still suffering from her earlier fall, Street took gold in the super G, a feat all the more spectacular in that she'd never won a race in super G in World Cup competition—it wasn't even her event.

Street placed a disappointing downhill time, putting her in sixth place, but racing fans were thrilled. On the winners' podium, Street again radiated that infectious joy so characteristic of her.

Which made her fall, later that season, all the more dramatic.

Misreading a bump at a World Cup downhill race in Switzerland, she crashed, again, into a fence, at seventy miles per hour. This time, though, she did not get up and walk away. Broken in nine places, her left femur protruded through the quadriceps of her thigh. And her right anterior cruciate ligament had been torn.

For most competitors with Street's record, this would have been a time to call an end to her racing career.

Street, amazing the racing world, got up yet again. (After, she commented: "It hurt my heart more than other crashes have and I think about it. I cringe when I see it and remember it.")

This time, her rehab took two years, Street battling feelings of depression for the first time, mornings when she "just didn't want to get out of bed." Though even that didn't defeat her, as, she claimed, "I'm carrying that light inside of me. It's making me hold my head up." And when she did return to her sport, went on to race in Switzerland, then Alberta, Canada, with her performances showing steady improvement until she won a Super Series down-hill event at Snowbasin, Utah, on the course where the 2002 Olympic downhill would be held, on Grizzly.

Though Street eventually placed, as sports pundits put it, "a disappointing sixteenth" in that Olympic competition's downhill, her fans were not disappointed.

In fact, during the first downhill training session before the Salt Lake Games, Street posted the fastest run of any competitor.

Street, after the games, gracefully announced her retirement.

Thirty, and having overcome countless obstacles, having gone under, over, and around all difficulties, she still radiated that win-some joy, though just then, in it was a bit of melancholy. Hers, too, was a story we loved. All of it, the unusual upbringing, the stellar performances and falls, the spectacular comebacks. But, in the end, it was the way she lived it that most touched us.

Whether winning races, or training, or recovering from upsets, Picabo Street lit up the racing scene with a truly rare talent—*the ability to find joy in life itself, in the application of oneself to that which can be seem impossible.*

And if anyone showed us that the impossible could be done, and with a song in our hearts, Picabo Street did. And for that, we're forever grateful. Which is why, whether we are skiers or not, we love racing.

But even more so, *racers*, who show us what we *could* be; or, in some cases, *can* be . . .

Makers of magic.

THE CURIOUS AND ARCANE WORLD OF NORDIC SKI JUMPING

UP, UP, AND *AWAY!*

Picture yourself standing on top of a tower, one that is 240 feet tall, or twenty-six stories high.

A tower named, it seems ironically appropriate to you just now, "Suicide Hill."

You are going to jump from this tower in a few moments, but let's not go into that yet. Let's just take a look around. Let's enjoy the view.

If you face the rear of the tower and look down, you'll discover, to your surprise, that you aren't 240-some feet above the carpet of trees below, but more than 600 feet—because the tower has been built on the crest of Copper Peak (so named because of the copper ore in it), which rises roughly 400 feet out of the surrounding plain.

Look long and hard from this height, you can see into three states: Michigan, Wisconsin, and Minnesota. It's one hell of a view, below a patchwork of trees, deciduous and conifer, Lake Superior looming off to the north so close you'd think you could fall into it.

You might wonder if the height is making you a little dizzy, a bit unsteady on your feet, like some cartoon character who has been hit over the head with an iron frying pan. But, you find now, there really *is* something vertiginous about this tower you're standing on. The tower, which isn't much more than a post with a ramp running down its front side, is very subtly swaying in the wind, which is constant, but you tell yourself that's fine. After all, the engineers who built this tower built it to withstand winds up to a hundred miles per hour.

Today, though, the tower is only weathering a wind of twenty miles per hour and sways just enough to be felt.

But enough of the view. You're here to jump, take a ride down that just-mentioned front-side ramp. Reason tells you that you could always climb down the ramp, there are steps off to one side of it. But you don't do that.

No. You are one of a handful of jumpers who have qualified to compete here at Copper Peak today, in Ironwood, Michigan.

No one who makes it up to the top of Suicide Hill walks down the inrun steps. And you are not going to be the first. Not today. You'd rather die than do that. Which you just might—really—do.

Only a month ago the brother of one of your teammates was killed competing on a jump half the size of this one, Harris Hill, in Brattleboro, Vermont. So your general anxieties here at Suicide are real ones. And having watched your teammate's brother's fatal crash on TV doesn't help quell those fears. Having landed well enough, Jeff lost his balance in the transition, his head striking the hardpack there, Jeff dying hours later at a local hospital from a brain hemorrhage. Jeff Wright had been a member of the U.S. Jumping Team, and a very skilled competitor. Though just unlucky, you tell yourself.

Your luck, you assure yourself, will hold. As mine did, until that unlucky day that proved otherwise.

So, up top waiting your turn, you try to shake it off. You dance a little. You joke with your buddies, who are acting tough, as you are. You and your teammates are all first timers at Copper Peak. The Austrians, the Germans, and the Swiss Kid in front of you in the jumping order are all Olympians, they've been here tens of times. As a result, you're at the end of the tournament roster: a rookie. And, now, you're just trying to fit in. Move up a notch.

It's a cold day, the temperature hovering around zero. You are wearing a one-piece suit, a helmet, goggles, and square-toed boots. (Because air that is trapped inside a jumper's suit adds in lift and distance, your suit cannot be thicker than five millimeters, to prevent you from having an advantage.)

Waiting for the tournament to start you absentmindedly toss and catch your skis, a tic of sorts.

Out from the competitors' platform, seventeen hundred feet and more in front of you, and six hundred feet down, are scores of spectators in green, red, yellow, and black snowsuits, on what are called the flats—the area beyond the outrun, where you'll skid to a stop after you jump.

Also on the flats, huddled around vans, are sports journalists with their cameras and satellite equipment, coaches, parents, sweethearts and wives, and friends.

The spectators will tell you they're here to watch you fly (but you know they are also here to see you crash—like that guy on *Wide World of Sports*—at least some of them).

Everywhere down on the flats is motion now, which is typical of a tournament. There are vendors hawking hot dogs and hot cocoa and pins and memorabilia from stands with red and green striped awnings. A couple kids are playing hacky sack. Now and then strains of music rise up to you, tinny and small. There's a sharp, nervous energy in the air—as if scientists were about to launch some fighter plane they'd been tinkering with. (Only here it is coaches launching their prized jumpers.)

But more than anything there is *excitement*. An absolute *thrill*. Even a kind of peculiar *joy*. Again.

That's what you're feeling just now.

Because this son of a bitch, Copper Peak, or Suicide Hill, is *the* challenge in North America, the biggest jump on the continent, but also the *world's* largest freestanding jump, and the better part of you, all those years of club competition, regional tournaments, and practice at Central Division sites (Bush Lake, Theodore Wirth, and Carver Park in Minneapolis; Chester in Duluth; Cloquet in Minnesota, and the list goes on, thirty or so jumps, each set off in trees, on some lonely hill), all of that tells you: *You're ready.* You wouldn't pass up jumping here for anything. You've *earned* this.

And now, down below you, just off the end of the jump, a man crosses waving two green flags.

All clear.

The front-runner, a jumper from Austria, slides out onto the bar over the inrun.

Distant, from the PA system, comes the jumper's name and his tournament standing.

The Austrian glances in your direction and grins. He's not going to just go off this thing, he means to beat you at it. There's a moment of intense quiet in which you can hear him breathing. Then, as simply as standing from a dining-room chair, he lifts from the bar, jets down the slope and, at the lip of the jump, hurls himself out and over his skis and . . .

Flying, clears the knoll of the landing hill and is gone.

Seconds later, you get his distance over the PA: 140 meters, or 459 feet.

Here, at Suicide, a P-point jump: It's good, very good. But it's not great. And his style points, 55.4, could be better.

Standing at the top of Suicide on the competitors' platform, getting ready to take your turn, *stoked* is not the word for what you feel.

This could be your day. You could—*if* your timing is perfect, *if* the snow isn't slow, *if* the wax you burned onto your skis is a better fit for the conditions than the Austrian's, *if* your style is *here*, admittedly, more fluid, more graceful than you know it is . . .

You could *win*.

So you are feeling . . . a *wild possibility*. You're looking for *magic*. Standing in your gear, waiting your turn, the whole world yawns open.

You squat now, leap into the wall of the waiting area. Good. Very good. (Doing all those leg exercises, the squat leaps, hundreds a week in season, has very nearly made you a human frog. Girls tease you about your weird-looking legs—frog legs. Pants never fit right.)

Your name is called over the PA. Coach pulls you close, whispers in your ear, *Keep it low in the inrun, watch your timing. Knock this son of a bitch dead.*

You kick your square-toed boots into your skis.

Elans. You love the name: *Elan*. For grace, for style, for . . . well, world-class jumpers have been winning tournaments on Elans for years. Your Elans are roughly 260 centimeters, or eight and a half feet long (because longer skis also generate more lift and distance, the maximum length of any competitor's skis is determined by multiplying that jumper's height in centimeters by 1.46), nearly five inches wide, and have six tracks down their P-tex bases, which you have painstakingly waxed. The skis are a navy blue, a sober, tool-like color. The bindings hold your toes in place, but the heels are free, connected to the skis by spring-loaded cables. You can adjust the angle that the skis will articulate from the ball of your foot, and you test your skis on the platform now, make sure the heels come up the exact distance you want them to, on this equipment a few inches, until the cables provide resistance.

Nice. Just right.

And now it is your turn. You step down to the bar and, sliding yourself to the middle, place your skis in the grooved center track. The track drops those earlier mentioned 240 vertical feet (and nearly 400 horizontal feet) to the takeoff point, which is from your perspective, the width of a gloved thumb.

You sit, hands on the bar.

At moments like this, that jumper from the *Wide World of Sports* who crashed off the inrun at Obersdorf, Germany, is—again—in your thoughts. Though, if you go off at the top here, you'll fall five times the distance he did.

Your name, team, and tournament ranking is announced, which you only hear the first few words of, so intensely are you in a bubble of concentration.

Chest down in the inrun. Timing at the takeoff. Still body in the air.

You take three breaths. One, two, and on the third you lift off the bar onto your skis, which you tuck over, in your inrun position, on the steepest portion of the inrun, nearly falling vertically.

The track, you realize, is not fast, and that is why the Austrian didn't go over the P-point.

Accelerating down the track, thirty, forty, fifty, sixty miles per hour, you are minutely, intensely aware of the plantar portion of your feet, where your weight is precisely balanced. Too far forward and, when you come off the jump, you'll angle into the knoll. Too far back, you'll come up vertical and catch wind. Either will cut your distance drastically.

The takeoff of Suicide approaching, you are now traveling over seventy-five miles per hour, or 110 feet per second.

The takeoff pine boughs, eight pair on either side of the ramp, flash by you in near otherworldly slow motion.

8-7-6-5-4-3-2-

Your job is to explode up and over your skis and into nothing, at seventy-five miles per hour, at the exact one-thousandth of a second when your ski tips reach the last pair of pine boughs.

A nearly impossible task, but you have been anticipating this move now since you passed the first set of boughs—

Or, eight-thousandths of a second.

If you jump early, if you jump *before* your ski tips reach that last set of pine boughs, the force of your leap will be directed downward and into the inrun structure itself, which will result in pitching your body too far over your skis, forcing your skis into an "attitude" in no way optimal for generating lift ("attitude" being a term used in aviation for the angle at which an aircraft penetrates the air it is moving through).

And if you are late?

If you jump *after* your skis have passed the last set of pine boughs? You will have no purchase on the inrun and will spend most (if not all) of your jumping force on air, will have no height, and will be carried by momentum alone down the landing hill. (The ends, or takeoff portions, of Nordic ski jumps, *un*like ramps for freestyle jumping, are usually *negative* five degrees from level. Hence, a Nordic jump does not "throw" the skier "up" into the air. The more "power" a jumper has, the more height he can generate off the ramp—thus buying himself significant distance on the landing hill.)

Both early and late jumps spell failure.

But when your tips reach that impossible point, that hoped-for, aimed-for, practiced-for perfect moment, you burst off the jump, *up* and *out over* your skis, your timing perfect and, the knoll of the hill dropping out from under you—

JOY! You are *FLYING!*

Over the knoll, if you were to drop a plumb line from your hip to the ground, it would measure nearly thirty feet, but you are flying down, down, down *hundreds* of feet now, flying on a thick cushion of air, which you navigate with your skis, wings now, your hands behind you at your hips, and there is the blue stripe on the slope, the P-point, where you *could* land, but you still have energy, you still have altitude, even though you are jockeying your hands and body now over the skis to keep control of them, the air buffeting them severely.

You do have enough altitude to get to the K-point, out beyond the blue P. But the question rises, how much danger are you willing to take on?

How much risk of injury?

If you push the jump, try to land around the K-point, which is nearer the transition from the nearly vertical landing hill to the horizontal outrun, the forces that can crush you in the transition are greater. Which makes a K-point and beyond landing much riskier. A truly extraordinary jumper, such as Happy Harada, can "outjump" the hill, or at least the recording equipment, and survive intact. Which sounds good, but taking risks like that can as easily maim you as make you in jumping.

And, if you come down in the transition, *out* of your telemark landing (legs *not* scissored in a near crouch to prevent falling forward or backward) you could be thrown backward and strike the rear, most vulnerable part of your head, as did your teammate's brother who died at Harris Hill in Vermont.

But this is your day. You'll push it. You're high as a kite on THRILL. So you hold it, and hold it, and just short of the K-point you pull back off your skis, standing in air, and the wind strikes you the way it does if you put your head out the window of a car on the highway. That wind brings you right down.

"Pock!" Your skis strike the hill.

You land in that telemark, which you hold through the transition, the transition—in a nanosecond of near panic almost sending you over backward—and you jet out onto the flats, braking, a roar of voices and clapping there, and you skid to a stop and turn to see the two things you want to know.

On the scoreboard, your distance: 478 feet. Your all-time best. Which makes you ecstatic, nearly crazy with joy, until your style points come up: 46.3.

The point totals for distance and style, combined, yield a total score of 110. In world competition, lousy.

All right, so you're not Matti Nykänen, the greatest jumper of all time, who you wouldn't want to be anyway; or Jens Weissflog, second only to Nykänen; or even crazy one-eyed Jerry Martin, who set the North American Ski Flying distance record on this hill just last year.

But you're thrilled anyway. What a *ride!* Not only did you take a run on Suicide, you placed a respectable distance, and that on your first time out.

A friend scrambles to you from the crowd. "Wow!" he says. "That was great! I mean, you gotta work on your hands and stuff, but—four hundred *seventy feet!*"

Four hundred seventy-*eight* feet, you correct.

You shoulder your skis and head for the landing hill, which you will climb, but before you do, you turn to your friend and say, "Wish me luck!"

You're so wired, climbing the landing hill feels good. Your legs are elastic, strong.

What was it that made the skis shift from side to side like that in the air, you're thinking. (How did Yukio Kasaya do it? Look so good?)

How can I be more *still* in the air? you're thinking.

And suddenly, you're on the bar again, Coach's single admonition ringing in your head. *Work on the style.* Coming from him, it's the closest thing to a pat on the back you've ever gotten, and you swell with it, but remind yourself to stay focused.

Six hundred feet up, over the whole, messy world, you take those three deep breaths. *This* time, you think, and you lift off the bar.

Icarus, again.

HOW DO THEY *DO* THAT?

No one, obviously, throws a pair of skis over his shoulder, climbs a 140-meter ski-flying "hill," and takes a run. In fact, less than a hundred expert jumpers worldwide are qualified to compete on ski-flying hills—jumps 140 meters or larger. Jumpers don't start on big hills. Jumpers, as I did, start very young and on small training hills.

Granted, though jumping on these smaller hills might not be as exciting for spectators to watch, for young kids, these hills are *as* thrilling, if not more so, than the world-class hills they'll compete on later.

Why?

I'll get back to that. But first, consider this: I am at a friend's house watching the Winter Olympics on TV. My friend is a social worker for whom riding a bicycle is a dangerous activity. Mowing the lawn is dangerous. Navigating icy steps to the car in winter is dangerous. Eating a potato skin is dangerous. We are opposites, and I suppose this is part of what makes our friendship work.

Of course, when the jumpers come on I mention my having

been a jumping competitor (which can be akin, in some circles, to saying you brush your teeth with a Black & Decker weed whacker. What, are you *insane?*)

At which point, my friend, Ed, says, "It doesn't look very hard. They just come off the end like that, right?"

I can only laugh. (I'd like to see *him* come off the end like that. He'd do Eddie the Eagle proud.)

"They all sort of look the same, don't they?" he adds.

"Yeah," I say, "they do 'sort of all look the same.'"

And I have to explain. That "same" look, that "style," takes a minimum of eight to ten years to perfect—and that only *if* you have the talent. Which is *very* rare. The jumpers you see in the Olympics are some of the most highly trained athletes in the world. Any one jumper at the Olympics has made thousands of jumps, has had thousands of hours of training and instruction, of coaches shouting at him, cajoling him, sometimes praising him— though, in skiing, the shouting is more common.

And there are things about jumping now that competitors deal with that I never dealt with.

There is a saying now, proven by testing: *Fat don't fly.*

Jumpers with appreciable body fat are not competitive at national, much less international, levels. Your average jumper may have to keep his body fat down to 5 percent. Some do this by resorting to purging, which has caused concerns about bulimia among jumpers—and these are *male* jumpers. Jumpers, over time, also suffer impact-related spinal deterioration. Knee problems. Hip problems.

Accident-related injuries are common. Once, at Cloquet, Minnesota, after a heavy snowfall, I was given the honor of "setting the track" on the Big Jump. I was thrilled to be so honored, but quietly terrified.

In "setting the track," the first skier to jump a hill after a snowfall stands on the platform over the nearly vertical ramp, or inrun, which has been sidestepped and now has no ruts, or ski tracks, on it. The jumper places his skis the exact width they *should be* on that inrun ramp. The jumper then kicks off the platform—trusting gravity, and his form, to take him down the center.

On a fresh, trackless ramp like this, though, all that would be required to send you crashing over the side would be, say, an inch or two of that old track under the fresh snow to catch one of your skis (a "snow snake"), going over the side like that called in the sport "pulling a Vinko," after Vinko Bogataj, famous for his *Wide World of Sports* "Agony of Defeat" run.

But that wasn't what got me that day. I didn't pull a Vinko. Something else was waiting. I made it down the inrun, rode the takeoff instead of "jumping" from it, as track setters do, and landed just over the rise of the knoll. All exactly as it should be done.

However, when I threw down my telemark landing, the fresh snow on the knoll peeled away in an avalanche, leaving me skiing on milk-jug-thick glare ice.

At sixty miles per hour.

Whereas it had snowed ten inches elsewhere in Minnesota, in Cloquet, it had rained first, the temperature had dropped radically, and *then* it had snowed—a good foot or two, covering the ice. Around the jump, and on the road in, the snow had adhered to the ice, but on the landing hill, which was facing north and was much colder, the ice had formed without an intermediate (warmer) layer of snow over it, so the snow only adhered enough to balance there.

Surprise! (I'll get you yet, my little pretty—and I'll get your dog, too!)

When I shot down the landing hill, the ice was so glossy it was like being a watermelon seed squeezed between a thumb and an index finger. Down I went, performing every known ballet posture to keep myself over those skis, to finally cartwheel like the Road Runner onto the flats, where I lay in a relieved heap.

In the chalet we all had a good laugh and the tournament was called off.

So, each jump has its dangers. When you leaped from Chester, in Duluth, the wind off Lake Superior could throw you nearly sideways. Theodore Wirth, in Minneapolis, could have a kicker, a slight positive elevation, which could play havoc with your in-flight balance and landing. Carver, which was a steel jump just outside Minneapolis, felt smooth but had trees too close to the landing hill. And there were other foibles.

The last meet of my club career, I stood at the top of the Theodore Wirth jump, took the all-clear wave, and kicked onto the inrun. I'd been wearing the same jumping suit for three years (albeit washed regularly), and at that moment, the seam running up my backside decided to quit on me. This left me flying down the inrun, as I experienced it, with my bum (as the Brits would say)—red Duofold clad—hanging out for the whole world to see.

In my usual fashion, I burst off the ramp, held what advantage I had for as long as I could, and put down my telemark, skidding to a stop on the flats. I must have placed all right, because I have no recollection of my score and I did well enough to go on to the Central Division competition. But it was an embarrassing moment, completely unanticipated, and not really earned by me. (Or so we like to think.)

Walking around like some advertisement for anal-retentive posture (shoulders back, head erect) to hide my ruined suit, I got my gear on the car and drove home. Later, at Bridgeman's, where we congregated after meets, I tried to, without giving up what really happened, find out if anyone had noticed my errant jump-suit.

No one had, but after a bit of Chivas I related the incident to my teammates, who, of course, never let me forget it.

At the state high school meet the end of that month, I was given the honor of being the first man off the jump—again. (I should have figured it out by this time, shouldn't I? They may as well have been asking if there's a kamikaze in the group, could he please step forward?)

We had practiced all afternoon and taken our usual break. It was, however, March now, and the jump was angled so that, in the late afternoon, the sidewall of the inrun, about shoulder high, shaded the inrun track, while the landing hill was still in full sun-light.

With the usual fanfare, we competitors marched out of the chalet, prepared to do battle.

We had, that early evening, a few hundred spectators.

At the top of the jump, in my newly repaired, triple-stitched jumpsuit, I waited for the all clear.

Fortunately for me, my first run was a performance test for the tournament, or so I thought, to make certain there was no "kicker" at the takeoff point or irregularities on the inrun, land-ing hill, or transition that would pose threats to the tournament competitors. In other words, I was a guinea pig, but so honored because I could do the job the director of hill safety wanted done.

I got the all clear, kicked off the ramp, this time completely calm, completely centered, the inrun track glare ice and very fast, and, so encouraged, when I hit the takeoff point, I double-pressed up and out over my skis (I had, even then, been working on a technique like the V Style, where I got so far down on my skis that they would nearly strike me in the head), pressed it for all I was worth, flying far, far down the hill, and at that last, critical moment, I threw down my telemark.

Onto glue-sticky, resistant mush.

In far less time than I could so much as *think* to get my weight back, I found myself riding the right side of my face on that rough snow, through the transition, knocked dopey.

Rudy, my coach, ran to me and got me on my feet.

"Remember the drill," he said.

Which was, *You don't have a concussion until you have a concussion.* (The standard expression from injured jumpers was "Tomorrow I might need surgery, but I'll make it today.")

While the meet went on around me, I had a doctor shine a pencil-thin beam of light into my eyes and ask me what year it was (1975), who the president was (Ford), and to repeat unrelated strings of words like *Sunday, walrus, Ticonderoga* and *helicopter, tooth-brush, tits* (doctors back then said those sorts of things, at least to boys such as myself). When I grinned at that last, he gave me a big whomp on the shoulder and sent me back onto the hill, saved by the doc's love of pulchritude.

We went on to win that meet, and in doing so, took home a trophy the size of a commercial coffee urn, gold-plated with wings on it. We couldn't have been prouder, especially me, face swollen all out of proportion, and smiling for photos, looking like that demented doll in *Revenge of Chucky II*.

So, you might ask, why do it, if it can be so dangerous?

Really. After all the near sanctimonious talk of Icarus and flying, and this short-lived rush, what's the big deal?

Why? As with other extreme skiing, *it's some of the best fun on earth.*

CLUB JUMPING

All jumpers get their start here in the United States in *clubs*. Some of these clubs go back to the 1880s. Norwegians, in particular, were crazy about the sport and brought it with them to the Northeast and the Midwest from Oslo and other parts of Norway. The Nansen Ski Club in Berlin, New Hampshire, is credited with being the first in the United States. Established in 1882, the club was named after Norwegian Fridtjof Nansen, who crossed Greenland, solo, on skis.

In the Midwest, Cloquet, Minnesota, has the oldest jumping club, followed by the Minneapolis Ski Club, the St. Paul Ski Club, and smaller school clubs, such as the Flying Spartans, which I jumped in during high school.

Realize that the sport of skiing did not come to the United States in the form that we're most familiar with now, downhill skiing; it came to us as *jumping*. Jumping was a thriving national sport in the United States over fifty years before the first recognized downhill resort, Sun Valley, in Idaho, was built.

Clubs, unlike Alpine racing *schools*, were organized around specific jumps—for example, the Ford Hill Jumping Club on the East Coast built and maintained Ford Hill, but traveled to tournaments elsewhere in the Northeast Division, in Maine, Rhode Island, and Vermont. Some jumping clubs had particularly colorful names. The Suicide Hill Club, in Michigan, is one such club. And each had its own history, hill, memorable characters, and inside jokes.

Clubs, unlike Alpine ski schools, had this amateurish feel to them. *On the surface* they were mom-and-pop organizations with hand-painted signs, bake sales, and—sometimes—crappy gear. But under all that silliness, that plain old fun, was a core of seriousness—the best skiers jumping to win, even go on to the Olympics, which they did.

So, jumping clubs, nationwide, attracted a range of competitors, anything from guys with nicknames like Crash Cassady, who did just like that, to gifted kids who rose out of club competition before they were even in their teens. Years ago there were even family dynasties of Olympic jumpers in certain clubs, such as, in Minnesota, the Denneys, a fierce bunch of Norwegians, or, in Michigan, the Flying Bietila Brothers.

If you were a kid, say, at a meet in Duluth, at Chester, and you saw on the tournament roster a Denney, you knew you were looking at some very serious competition.

Clubs, for younger kids like me, were a riot.

One afternoon at Theodore Wirth, practicing for a meet, I made an especially uninspired run, skidding to a stop on the flats beside an old guy in a blue down jacket and wool hat fashioned to look like the Swedish flag. It was probably, without exaggerating, ten below zero.

I was disgusted with my jump, and sighed audibly.

"You gotta *pump* the fuckin' hill!" the old man said, squinting at me.

Never one to be rude, I said, "Okay, what was wrong with it?"

And this former Swedish national champion, a onetime world-record holder, gave me a lesson right there.

(I was levering over my skis at the waist, "jackknifing," he told me, a common error and one that's hard to overcome once you start doing it.)

Clubs *not* connected to high school athletics (and high school skiing in Minnesota is as serious a sport as football or basketball) tended to bring out a wider range of jumpers: the weekend thrill seeker who could be mean-spirited or a good time Charlie; the

aspiring youngster; the Olympic wannabe; the near mentally re-
tarded; and the just-plain demented. In the clubs, there was as
much irritated shoulder bumping, cursing, spitting, and backbiting
as there was awe, admiration, unbelievable courage, generosity,
and . . . yes, *élan*.

Style.

And here I return to my social worker friend's comment, *Olympic jumpers all look the same.*

Yes, at the world level, and *no*, at the amateur. (And, to the
trained eye, *no*, for both.)

Club jumping and high school jumping are so exciting because
club jumpers are *not* that good. In fact, some club jumpers are
awful. The truth is that there are infinitely more Eddie the Eagles
jumping than Simon Ammanns.

But this makes for absolutely riveting competition. In my
teens, I never knew when going to a meet if Jim Denney, Greg
Winsberger, or Kip Sungaard, all of whom made the U.S. Olympic
jumping team, would be there, or if I'd have a field of Bucky
Boehmers to knock down. (Greg, his real name, was a sweetheart
of a guy, but he'd suffered some kind of neurological trauma as a
child, and moved, in general, as if he had mild CP. Jumped like
that, too. Funny thing was, I discovered, he could run like the
devil *off* his skis, which he did once, beating me in a fifty-yard
dash. A very educational experience.)

Club jumping, in essence, was this: *Seat-of-the-pants flying. As-
big-as-your-balls-are jumping.*

My first season out with the Spartans, we had one kid jumping
with us who was a hockey player. Brent later made it onto a National Hockey League team that won a Stanley Cup. Brent was one
of the roughest competitors I ever ran into. He jumped like he was
taking out rivals using body slams into the boards. And he intro-

duced us to codeine, in the form of prescription cough syrup, which he took tugs of before meets.

"Here, fuckface, drink this," he'd say.

He meant no meanness by it, it was just Brent's gentle way. Codeine you had to be careful with, it could remedy that propensity to jump early, if you got just the right amount—but if you got even a *drop* more than you wanted, you flew like lead and became a danger to yourself.

And, if that happened, a little speed fixed that, Brent's "whites," but then if you were *too* speedy, well, then, a bit more of the old codeine, etc., etc.

Sometimes, on meet nights, Brent's eyes darted in his eye sockets like pinballs.

Then he'd climb whatever scary "hill" we were jumping and hurl himself off, making the greatest distance, beating all and anyone on distance points alone, until we graduated to jumps so large that Brent's punchy style ruined him.

He jumped like a fifteen-round fistfight—and on jumps over seventy meters that just doesn't work.

And there was Bob Best, another nut. Even in the early seventies, Big Bad Bob had a Dan Quayle haircut, looked like some demented politician. (God knows, even now, he's probably selling ice to Eskimos.) Bob wore hard contact lenses, something I discovered when I threw a snowball in his face and one of them popped out. He gave me this strange look, then chased me through the oaks around the Carver fifty-meter, threatening to kill me with a hatchet he'd been using to cut brush from the landing hill. I worried he might really do it.

BB (short for Bad Bob), like so many jumpers, was affable, funny, a really nice kid. But there was that extra *some*thing in him that every jumper I ever knew had: some need to scare the living bejesus out of himself (or other people), to test himself.

BB was the craziest. Scary crazy. Here we were, barely in our teens, on a club outing to Carver Park. We were supposed to be jumping the twenty-meter (good for a sixty-foot ride), to work on our style: inrun position, takeoff timing, in-the-air form, telemark landing, all of which we did at best perfunctorily. (No, actually, we all were nothing short of god-awful just then, the closest thing to spastic.)

We were just kids. Just into the double digits.

That weekend, the St. Paul Ski Club brought in some ex-Olympic jumpers to coach us. For three hours, we—the Flying Spartans—jumped on the twenty-meter, some Austrian guy named Wolfgang screaming his lungs out at us.

"*Scheisse! Scheisse! Scheisse!*" he'd scream as we came off the end of that ratty, creosote-smelling old ramp. Shit! Shit! Shit!

"Get your head down. Chest down. You're too far forward. You're jackknifing. You're on your heels, that's why you're late."

In jumping, you improve your style by increments, overcoming by degrees the unnaturalness of it, and the just plain old fear. It can be an immensely frustrating sport. After all, why *can't* you look like those Olympic guys? you ask yourself.

Well, Wolfgang told us why.

We were little scaredy boys, letting fear get the better of us. What was to be afraid of? *Ja?* What was a little broken arm or a stick through the side of our heads? (Well, all right, he didn't say that about the *stick.*) All morning we worked on that twenty-meter, easily making a dozen runs each.

For lunch, the St. Paul Ski Club brought in a guy who had built a jump on some lakeside slope, one to be used in the summer. You stood on a little box with wheels on it, went hurtling down through the trees (any of which could poke out your eye or break you into a zillion pieces) and, at the end of that sheet-metal ramp—you jumped, you and that little box, into a lake.

We saw jumping footage (also on eight-millimeter film) of then international superstar Yukio Kasaya, who would take the gold at Sapporo. We got more dry-dock coaching. Now schematics on blackboards, ones detailing the physics of Nordic jumping. We had a few Olympic hopefuls there who were training on the Carver fifty-meter, a stone's throw from our twenty, give demonstrations. Some of these skiers were so skilled, it was almost painful to watch them.

When the hoopla and coaching were over, we ate, we Spartans taking our food outside for some fresh air (and a nip of codeine).

Jake Kaufman sat beside me and we compared lunches. I had a headcheese sandwich, an apple, and some *krumkaka*. Jake had cold matzo balls, a jellied fish thing, and some kind of apple dumpling.

"Trade?" he said.

Which we did. At least it was different. We sat munching that stuff, and here came BB, though now wearing a pair of those black-framed rocket scientist glasses, a red strap holding them on his head. He swept up his skis from alongside the chalet.

"Where you going?" I said.

"The fifty," he replied. "No one's callin' me scared, piece-of-shit Nazi bastard. I'll show him."

"Yeah, right," Jake droned.

But we got off the bench, all seven of us Spartans following BB to the fifty.

Realize that even a fifty-meter jump, if the inrun is built above ground, puts you high over any trees. You are *up* there. If you look over the side of the jump, your testicles pull up into your body. Your stomach clenches.

So, here is BB, looking like some demented—but pumped up—barely teenage Dan Quayle wearing jumping gear and those weird glasses. At the top he fluttered around a bit then set himself in the track.

"All right, real funny!" Jake shouted up to him.

BB gave us the finger, then kicked off the platform. Seconds later, eyes wide with terror, he schussed off the end of the jump, arms all over the place, his skis going every which way, and disappeared over the knoll. We heard that familiar *puck!* sound—Bob landing—then saw him spit out onto the flats, his fists raised over his head in triumph. Yeah, he'd looked worse than awful, but he'd done it. All of us—Bucky, Brent, Jake, myself, and the others—stood in that bright sunlight blinking. Well, who was going to be the first coward? That was the question.

"Goddamn it all," Jake cursed as we headed back from the chalet with our skis. "That *idiot!*"

Rudy, our coach, marched alongside us, thrilled. He hadn't thought he'd get us on the fifty for a month at least, or even that year, and here, thanks to BB, we were at it the first afternoon of the clinic. Just then, Rudy must have thought he had some real go-getters on his team. (Which, it turned out, he *did*. Years later, our team won state, no small thing, considering the competition.)

Rudy, now, was another interesting fixture in my jumping life. He was an Austrian, someone I'd met long before I was a jumper. Rudy, on his weekends, taught ski lessons at a local resort, Highland Hills—a rope tow, backwoods kind of place in south Minneapolis. Just nine, I'd gotten lessons at Highland Hills for Christmas along with my sisters, two older and one younger, had stood that first morning of lessons in my gear, when an efficient-looking man in a rumpled red jacket marched out of the ski school office with a clipboard.

He read off the names of my older sisters, and paused, coming to mine.

Which he read, slowly, thinking, taking in the next name as well, my younger sister's.

"Are you brothers and sisters?" he asked.

I said, *"Duhhhh!"* which truly endeared that old Austrian to me right then and there. My mistake, I know that now.

Two weeks later, and a better skier, I was happy to leave that class, and move on to others, and never made the mistake I had with Rudy again—in any situation. So imagine my surprise when, joining the Nordic jumping team in high school, I met my new coach. He marched into the room with that—most likely—same clipboard, read off our names, and, coming to mine, hesitated. I was tempted to say, No, I'm not related to anyone here, but I didn't. Rudy said it for me.

"Paul there beside you isn't your brother, is he?"

"Nooooo," I told him, Paul giving me a sidelong glance, confused. His last name was Sorensen, not Johnson, so?

Rudy just didn't love you, an acquaintance in New York told me, when I mentioned the rigorous training I'd gone through, Rudy's manners being a significant part of that training.

This woman had competed in tennis tournaments, a genteel sport by comparison. Rudy, I told her, didn't love *anybody*. But what I meant was—he showed you you were his guy by pushing you, by poking you right where it hurt worst, by getting every last bit of performance he could out of you, making you your best.

Which, with teenagers (especially jumpers), had to be hell.

And if he called you shit in the process and was disgusted with you half the time, oh well. *Das ist aber schade, ja?*

We knew what Rudy meant. Even when, in comical paroxisms of rage, he shouted at us in German.

(*That stinks! Scheisse! Are you brain dead? What did I just tell you? What do you mean, you aren't ready? I know when you're ready, and you're ready. And do it right this time. What's wrong with you, are you a little heavy back there after lunch, or are you just trying to look like you're trying to relieve yourself in the air? Are you going to do it this time, or are you going to just fuck up and quit because you stank last time? Huh? Don't make any excuses, I hate excuses. Yes or no?! Well, get to it then!*)

At one time, Austrians held the bulk of coaching and teaching positions in this country and over in Europe.

My tennis acquaintance told me that a coach like that in New York would be fired his first day.

Would he?

Oh, those Austrians! They were explosive, perfectionistic, angry, powerful, and supremely talented on skis (and they usually had a way with the ladies). Back in the dark-old days, resorts like Sun Valley, Stowe, and Alta boasted of having full quivers of Austrians in their ski schools, all former national champions whose pedigrees could be quoted by the employing ski school—or, in our case, jumping club.

TOURNAMENTS

As unlikely as it may seem, high school meets were held on weekday evenings *after dark*.

On those days, skiers all over Minnesota, Michigan, and

Wisconsin (and, in the Eastern division, Vermont, Maine, and New Hampshire) would be released from class early so they could spend a few hours warming up for meets. This meant three hours of daylight in which to practice.

Those afternoons you had to pay attention to your gear and the tuning of it. If it was warm during practice, especially above freezing, you had to rewax your equipment before the meet when the temperature dropped below freezing again.

You wanted to get enough runs in, say six to ten, but not *too* many, which could tire or discourage you.

Jumping, like so much of sport, is a mind game. But in jumping, it is also flat-out a courage game. How much heart do you have? is the question. Do you dare to outjump the hill, if you can? Or do you put more into your style to earn points?

Style, in jumping, will take you a long way, but it is not enough. You have to have that fierce, explosive *something* . . .

So, in jumping there was always a cocky, *fuck this shit* combativeness in the air. Sometimes competitors, especially high strung ones, would go off on a coach—have a Jimmy Connors moment.

If they were good enough, they would survive it; if not, they disappeared from competition, expelled.

Some kids who jumped in Minneapolis Ski Club events came from Fordtown, a down-at-its-heels corner of Richfield, where Ford Plant assembly-line workers lived. Those kids were fighters. Midway into an argument over something as small as not giving someone enough room on the steps up the landing hill at Wirth, say, you'd find yourself fending off punches—expert ones—which you had no option but to return.

Mind you, all that fighting stopped when competitors went on, placed in the bigger tournaments. (Which were held on weekends, at the Bush Lake Olympic Training Center seventy-meter, good for as much as a 240-foot ride). Then you modeled yourself after those Austrians who'd been your coaches.

At those meets, you'd damn near die before showing something had hurt you. Comported yourself like a champion, as you were told to.

So you practiced afternoons, saving that extra something for later, for the tournament.

Around five, the "hill," as it was called, would close, teams would retire to the chalet where the competitors—anxious, and springing here and there, having teammates help them "shake it out"—would eat next to nothing, and talk and, as boys will do, play pranks on each other.

Usually such pranks were directed at rival teams.

Our rival team was the Hornets, from Edina, a well-to-do (and some thought snotty) suburb of Minneapolis. The Hornets dressed in green jumping suits and skied on the finest and most expensive gear, drove to their meets in new Mercedes, while we Flying Spartans got to our meets in a Ford Econoline van, owned by our parent organization, Richfield High School. Such inequities were a part of the ski scene back then—in competitors' resources, equipment, coaching, and ease of getting places—as they are now. For example, Alpine racer Marc Girardelli, in a 1980s competition, had the use of his father's corporate helicopter so he could land on mountaintops before rival competitors, thus making a show of his position and also avoiding the wear and tear of lifts and trams.

So those inequities brought yet another edge to those high school and club meets. And all jumpers, as I said, begin in the *clubs*. It is only when a jumper truly distinguishes himself, through pure performance in tournaments, that the division—for example, the Central, the Eastern, or the Rocky Mountain—reaches in and plucks him out for grooming. Even then, sponsored, the Olympic hopeful must come up with tens of thousands of dollars to compete worldwide (particularly in Europe).

This the competitor raises through soliciting sponsorship wherever he can get it: from the local bank, Fireside Pizza, his disgruntled father, Big O Tires, Eunice, whose lawn you mowed—in short, anyone who will consent to help.

It's a humbling experience. You've just had the best season of your life, knocked the competition flat, and you're sent begging.

(You mean, like that guy on TV? What's his name, the "Agony of Defeat" guy? And you want *what?* Money?! For *that?!*)

Maybe it's healthy—it makes you grit your teeth, and, dammit, when you get the sniffles, or feel a bit off, *so what?* I paid for this ride, you think, and by God, I'm going to make it count. No beer, no cigarettes, no nothing. You haven't got an ounce of nonsense in you at that point.

But in the clubs there was plenty and then some—night meets were magic. Were a rough *joy.*

When you come out of the chalet, punched and pummeled and a bit sick from those awful Twinkies you ate, and the five cups of coffee you drank to get you jazzed—you smell woodsmoke.

The hill lights are on, mercury oxide, cutting a blinding strip of blue white in all that dark.

From the knoll at Wirth, where you congregate with your team, you can see out over Minneapolis, a bed of jewel-like lights winking in the sharp, cold breeze coming *up* the hill. *Excellent.* It could buy you some distance on the landing hill. And because it was warm this afternoon, you sweep up your skis and head for Rudy. Rudy, old Austrian that he is, the wonder worker of wax.

The four of you, the team's best jumpers, huddle by a section of jump superstructure, over your gear.

"Okay," Rudy says, a lilt in his voice.

You start the propane torch Rudy hands you with a striker, in the quiet the flame popping alight, then hissing, and you, like some medieval acolyte, melt the soap-sized block of wax in your left hand over the base of your left ski. When the wax hardens, after seconds—it is around zero out now—you set the ski upright against a rail of the jump, then take a block of cork and buff the P-tex base.

Just now, you have a pair of skis that were, two years ago, the closest thing to wings: Gafallers. They're French, red, with ornate gold decals, very Old World. If you *place* tonight, though, given your performance this winter, the club will give you a pair of Elans, the very best, so you polish now with a certain excitement, and even—yes, strange as it may seem—melancholy affection. These skis, your beloved Gafallers, have taken you down some big hills. They're your pals. (Skiers always love good gear. But we are irrationally attached to great gear—which is, always, that magic wand we're looking for. That object in the world with which we can cast spells.)

You lift the left ski now, sight down its length, using the bluish glare of the mercury oxide hill lights.

You make out spots not perfectly glossy, or thickish—if a thousandth of an inch can be called "thickish."

And you buff and buff, using the edge of the cork to eliminate irregularities, then the face of the cork to get overall flatness. You check again.

Music floats up from the landing hill, as always. Even at a small club meet like this, down on the flats a vendor selling hot drinks, candy bars, and pastries, coming from there also a hum of talk, parents, friends, brothers and sisters having arrived, and—tonight, since this is a crucial tournament—two or three television vans from local stations.

Waxing, you picture those people on the flats, clasping cups of coffee, cocoa, and cider, and chatting, those reporters with microphones navigating lengths of cable.

Left ski done, now the right. Same ritual. Rudy, behind you, rubs his mitted hands together, Kaufman tells some joke about Norwegians trying to put in a lightbulb, which they haven't realized is a rock.

Your teammate, Paul Sorensen, who is a Norwegian, glares. "You trying to tell me something?" he says.

"It's a squarehead joke," Kaufman says.

"Blockhead," you correct him.

In the ongoing war of insults between Norwegians and Swedes, Norwegians call Swedes "squareheads," Swedes call Norwegians "block-" or "rockheads." It's amusing, since the two groups are really one in the same, just divided by a national border—a fact any squarehead or blockhead would refute until you were so sickened of the explanation you'd have to do bodily harm to escape the catalog of differences, most of them having to do with different vowel sounds and fine points over, maybe, kinds of headcheese, or the lengths of certain male body parts. Or, if you are from outside the culture, you might comment that there really are only two kinds of Norwegians or Swedes, those who commit suicide, and those who cause others to commit suicide, thus ending the argument on a high note, while starting another about work, or duty, or . . . say, Martin Luther.

A Fordtown Flyer goes by, bumping you with his shoulder.

"Hey!" you shout into his back.

Skis slung over his right shoulder, he throws up his left hand, middle finger raised.

"Yeah, you too," you call out, Rudy swinging you around by the elbow and pointing to your skis.

Skis prepped, Paul, Jake, Larry, and you stand shoulder to shoulder, Rudy five or so feet out in front of you.

"Okay," Rudy says, then, down on one knee, he calls, "Hit it!" and Paul leaps from his crouch, Rudy catching him at the waist, Paul pressing himself over Rudy, then rolling off.

Then the others, and now, you. (Imagine clowns popping out of one of those tiny cars at the circus—one after another. It goes something like that.)

You squat, imagining hurtling down the inrun, balancing expertly on your feet, until that call from Rudy—*"Hit it!"*—and you leap out, and Rudy catches you at the waist, straight-armed, over his head, and you practice your in-air style, until Rudy, with a huff, rolls you off.

You do two or three rotations, after the first your teammates catching you. Rudy, all the while coaching, pulling your hands back along your hips, or forcing your head down—"like that, *down*, you're not looking *over* the landing hill, you're looking *down*. Got it? And keep that back straight! *Don't* jackknife!" he tells you.

There is a call to start the tournament, and you, your team mates, and Rudy march to the stairs at the end of the jump, the takeoff point, which is about six feet off the ground, right at head level.

"Okay," Rudy says, eyeballing each of you.

But you he punches in the shoulder. No love tap this (although that is exactly what it is), for you who can move up tonight.

"Make it count," he says, to all of you.

Then he's gone, and you are in line, on the stairs. You turn to watch as the tournament begins.

On a small hill like this, execution and style are critical.

Across the hill from you, and halfway down the landing

hill, is the judges' box, a wooden affair the size of a small mobile home on stilts. Four large windows face the landing hill, in each a man wearing a tomato soup–red United States Ski Association jacket, with his eyes intently on the hill, three of them judges, clipboards in hand, the fourth man the hill safety supervisor.

An official crosses the end of the jump now, waving green flags, and the tournament begins.

At the top, way up over the trees, in the blue-white light, a jumper stands, waiting. Green jumpsuit—a Hornet. But, when he gets the go-ahead flag from the judges' box, you call along with the others anyway, in an off-key chorus, "Make it good! Make it count! Show 'er the stuff!" some old Scandinavian shouting through that chorus the one thing that really sticks, "*Yump* the fuckin' hill!"

There is a hush, and then the jumper kicks off the backboard (here, at Wirth, there is a box around the platform). The wooden jump thrums under your feet, and with a "Hufff!" Edina's best is off the ramp, then flying over the knoll and out of sight, there coming seconds later that distinctive *puck*, this jumper's telemark landing, the jumper squirting out onto the flats where he skids to a stop. There is a round of applause, but you are watching the judges' box.

Edina's finest has run up a slightly less than P-point jump, here, on this club forty-meter, just 115 feet, for a score of 45.9 distance points, but 51.9 points for style.

All of this you understand in a flash, the point system very simple, really.

At the top, a jumper starts with a perfect score, or 40 points per jump. 20 points for distance, 20 points for style.

A 20-point jump for distance is one *into* but *not beyond* the

P-point (or "norm point"), which is the average competent but not inspired distance on the hill. If the jumper goes *beyond the P-point*, as jumpers often do, into *the K-point* (the "critical point"), as truly Herculean jumpers like Happy Harada do, special compensation points are yet again added. So a jumper can have well over a "hill-designed" distance score: he can have an *inspired* score.

A 20-point jump for *style* would be the sort you'd see with world-class jumpers—body parallel to the skis, the skis in perfect V formation, the body entirely still, no jockeying of the skis, no sawing back and forth in heavy air or wind. A 20-style-point jump is *art*—even the world's best, as in gymnastics, are almost never given 20 points for style. There is always something *less than perfect*, which makes this aspect of the sport so trying, and exciting.

In competition, you have to look like you were *born* to be flying, not just be flying. You have to make it look *effortless*.

And if you land roughly, nearly fall, or make the landing appear awkward or difficult, more points are deducted.

If you lose your balance while landing and touch your hands to the snow to prevent yourself from going over backward in the transition, or from falling in any direction, you receive zero points for style.

At higher levels of competition, one mistake like that can ruin an entire season. "Touching down," it is called.

The remainder of the math is simple. Two jumps in each tournament. Three judges. A hill-designed perfect score then would be 240 points: 40 for each jump, times 3 judges, times 2 jumps, equals 240 points.

However, to be competitive, at even the regional level, you have to jump beyond those hill-designed "normative" scores.

Jumpers like Finn Matti Nykänen, or East German Jens Weissflog, put down one daring, far-over K-point jump after another, to amass point totals of 260 and more per tournament.

Nykänen and Weissflog proved nearly unbeatable.

●

But you are here tonight at Wirth, hoping to earn your new wings, the coveted club Elans. And now the front-runner, the Hornet, has earned respectable style, but poor distance, points.

So it will be a battle of *heart* tonight—to see who can take it farthest down the hill.

It'll be fast and furious, forty-five or fifty competitors jumping in rapid succession.

A club jumping event is a bit like a stock car race. Colorful characters, fights, spectacular crashes, and a good deal of humor.

It's a bunch of amateurs giving a dangerous sport a go. The word *amateur* has as its root *amare*, to love, which is exactly why these competitors are here. For the love of it. There isn't any money, not at this level. And there aren't crowds of people as there are at other sports conducted during winter, such as basketball and hockey. (Granted, when you're younger, your parents will try to come, or your—if you're lucky—girlfriend, who will bite her fingernails to the quick watching.) There aren't those cheerleaders tossing pompoms over their heads. (We Spartans joked about that, how we were going to get cheerleaders, *the Iciclettes*—our cheerleaders, as elsewhere, scantily clad but ours waving pompoms of corn snow.)

Club jumpers do it for the thrill. For that *oh, so memorable* right jump out of all those awful jumps.

A good jump is like nailing a ninety-mile-per-hour pitch with the sweet spot on the bat, the ball, as if magically sailing high and over that outfield barrier, almost as if the ball never touched the bat.

At club level, you're lucky to get one of those runs out of thirty.

There's a very, very *elusive* something to the sport that is almost indefinable, such that you *can't* train most kids to do it right.

While the sport is explosive and violent, it is also, in its own way, as subtle as, say, a near-perfect game of golf—one where you could drown in the water traps.

At a tournament, or in practice, you'll schuss down the inrun, making every calculation possible, your last jump, for some reasons you know and some you *don't*, a disaster. So you focus on correcting your balance and timing on this round—let's say you were a couple thousandths of a second *early* on that last jump, so approaching the pine boughs you hold on a nanosecond longer, and *then* give it your all. Somehow, you find yourself *so* high over the knoll that it startles you, those men down below, measuring distance with cane poles, noticeably smaller. Right then, you realize, this is one of those magic runs, and, inspired, you'll hold on over the landing hill, down, down, down, and throw in a perfect telemark landing.

Your distance? Equal to the hill record. Your style points? From the three judges, 18.5 each, for a total of 55.5. For you, extraordinary.

You're thrilled, and meeting with Coach up at the top, you'll tell him, This is it, this is the night. He'll give you a slap on the back, look hopeful. *Same on the next run: head down, balance, timing,* he'll tell you.

So, on the next run, all the way down the ramp, you're trying to *think* yourself into all that made the last jump . . . magic.

You have this son of a bitch now, you tell yourself, and this time you'll give it even *more* muscle.

Bang! You're off the ramp, and—maybe you're high over the hill again, but—sonofabitch! You've pushed *too* far out this time now, and are wheeling your hands to get your body back on top of your skis. (Or you could have jackknifed, or your skis were uneven, one catching the air in such a way it nearly levers up into your head. Or any other of an infinite number of disasters.) But what you've done here is go too aggressively out, and pulling back, you land on the tails of your skis, which in turn necessitates bracing your hands against the hardpack in the transition so you don't go over backward and truly injure yourself.

On the flats you collect yourself, toss your skis over your shoulder, and passing the brightly lit scoring box, you don't even look.

Your hands touched the snow in the transition: You received zero points for style. You're out.

And you'll have learned, again, that old lesson about jumping: you *cannot* muscle your way through it.

And that's the addictive thing about jumping. You get one of those Olympic-caliber runs, and there's *nothing* like it.

It's the real thing: *Flying. Everything just so.*

And you want it again, and again, and again, and again. You can't get enough of it, but, dammit all if you don't get beaten up trying.

And in club jumping, rookies get just enough of those runs to keep them coming back.

But tonight, here, *now* . . .

You are standing at the foot of the stairs to the platform, trying *not* to watch too much of the hand wheeling, jackknifing, skidding, and crashing. Your body remembers all that.

All that you've honed out of yourself—though it's still there—could, if you are careless, express itself again.

On the top, standing on the platform, you take in the view again. Beautiful, the city lit up, and the trees dark, the inrun a ribbon of white through it. You move to your left, another jumper schussing down the inrun and gone. Then another. And then this, just before you step into the track on top . . .

A serious crash, the last skier before you now crumpled out past the transition. There is a flurry of activity, the hill safety director, judges, and hill doctor with his bag, running out onto the flats, the boy's coach and teammates standing over him already. While they are huddled over the injured skier, an ambulance rolls out onto the snow, EMTs scrambling from it, pulling a collapsible stretcher through the rear doors.

You watch all this with a detached dread. Probably just a concussion, but it might be this kid's last run as a jumper.

Somehow, one of the younger kids, in Junior Division, maybe just fourteen or fifteen, has gotten onto the PA system in the judges' box.

"GET THE BODY OFF THE HILL!" he says into the microphone there. "GET THE BODY OFF THE HILL!"

And, since the hill doctor gives a wave—the skier is conscious now, and probably just fine, though they're taking him to a hospital for observation—there is an outbreak of clapping, and relieved laughter. You feel your spirits lift, you breathe easy.

The ambulance pulls out of the tournament area, but no lights on—a reassuring sign—and all take their places again.

You shake yourself—head, neck, shoulders.

There is something so beautiful up here it is almost indescribable—not just the height and the view, but the feel of it, this adventure, the smell of damp wool, woodsmoke, hot wax, tobacco, and the carnival-like tournament sounds, the distant putter of a generator, and this sharp chill fixing it in your mind for all time, like some old photograph on glass, a daguerreotype.

You kick off the platform onto the steep inrun. You are in that bubble of expanded time again.

Picking up speed, the rails of the inrun flash by; you center yourself over your skis.

Your body is lit up, fluid, focused.

The pine boughs come at you, and at exactly *that* nanosecond your tips reach them, you burst out into space. Press out over your skis, riding the air, having hit that sweet spot.

Flying, yet again.

CLUB EXTRACURRICULAR CONFIDENTIAL

After the meets, trophies in hand, the victors (and losers) retire. A little talk with Mom and Dad, milk and cookies, and they slide between those flannel sheets for some good, well-earned rest.

Not.

For club jumpers, as in downhill skiing, there is always the *après-ski* scene. For each club in Minneapolis, whether the Hornets, or the Fordtown Flyers, or the Flying Spartans, there was a specific hangout, and I'm sure there still is. For the Spartans it was Bridgeman's on Sixty-sixth Street. Imagine the Mel's Diner of *American Graffiti*, but in winter, snow covering everything but the street. In the lot are jacked-up junk cars with ski racks on their roofs, but these skis so long they extend a good length of the car. In the cars, the kids are taking toots off bottles of whiskey and going over their jumps and the jumps of the other competitors.

And, remember, you *won* tonight—so you have that big, bulky trophy in the car with you, which, tomorrow, will go into the Spartans' trophy case. Though, tonight it's *yours*. As are the Elans, the club's best skis, which you will pick up at the end of the week—*magic* skis. You're already thinking of driving to Michigan, where you could give them a go at Pine Mountain, take a 450-foot ride.

It is all you can do to sit (for the most part) in the car—so you and your friends don't.

Jumpers, you won't be surprised to discover, are risk takers off the hill, too. They ride motorcycles, fly hang gliders, scuba dive.

And, back then, we hookybobbed after a meet, just to loosen up again, you'd get so badly wired.

And it was fun. In hookybobbing, you needed a substantial new snowfall. This would slow cars going in and out of the Bridgeman's lot.

Our hookybobbing was fueled with Chivas. My father, who didn't drink, got every Christmas from one of his patients a bottle of Crown Royal. These he never touched but to make "highballs" for guests, storing the bottles within easy reach in a cupboard. I took it upon myself to fill flasks with that Chivas, topping the bottles up with water and coloring the lot of it with red dye number four, to give what was there that authentic amber hue—something that got difficult as the bottles came to have different hues of gold, and me, out of necessity, becoming a sort of hobby colorist.

Some twenty years later, my wife and I were amused, considering my father making drinks with that watered-down Chivas. His friends must have thought him either tight with his booze, or just ignorant about what made a good drink.

Damn, but Doc Johnson makes a lousy drink, they must have said. This old-fashioned is all *water!*

In hookybobbing, you'd target, say, an older couple having the shrimp baskets and coffee inside, and when they, ever so slowly, crackled out of the Bridgeman's lot on that fresh, still falling five or more inches of snow, you snuck up to the rear of that Chrysler Imperial, or Cadillac Fleetwood, and took hold of the bumper, making sure the driver didn't see you in his mirror.

Hanging on like that, you bumped shoulders with your teammates, the car accelerating, fifteen, twenty, twenty-five miles per hour, taking you up Sixty-sixth Street, snow blinding you, your feet skittering crazily under you. Usually, you could barely cling to that bumper for laughing, and dropped off a few blocks away, walked back to Bridgeman's, where, sometimes, teams from other parts of the city slowly drove by, oftentimes shouting epithets at their rivals.

Which inspired retaliation. Such as the night our crazy Italian teammate, visiting from St. Paul, had his nonna's black Crown Victoria—a real old ladies' car if there ever was one. Eddie, wearing his grandfather's hat, one of those fuzzy pointed jobs with the little dapper feather in the band, eased the car through the Bridgeman's lot, this on a night after the Spartans had taken a sound beating from the Hornets.

And here they were now, two of them ducking from a big Mercedes and scooting to the rear of that Crown Victoria. Eddie, hotheaded, and never one for moderation, steered the car not just up Sixty-sixth Street, but onto the Crosstown Highway. Before they knew what was happening, those Hornets on the rear were hanging on for their lives, snow billowing around them, the two crying for us to stop.

Inside that big car, at first we were weeping with laughter. New snow, and it was slow out on the highway, the cars barely doing thirty. But then Eddie hit the gas. Forty. Fifty. Sixty miles per hour. It was all we could do to get him to back off, since one of the Hornets on the rear had personally insulted him. (Somehow, being called a "fucking piece-of-shit greasy wop bastard" didn't sit well with him.)

Every year, kids were killed hookybobbing, and we dropped those two Hornets off on Penn Avenue, some six blocks up the highway, more than a little relieved—even apologetic.

That what we'd done brought on more fights at tournaments that winter didn't surprise us.

Jumping inspired a punchy, let's-get-to-it sort of spirit—in competitors *and* noncompetitors alike—noncompetitors sometimes making creative use of jumps.

●

One New Year's Eve, it was all I could do to talk a friend I'd bought a hang glider with from taking it off the Bush Lake seventy-meter in the dark. He hadn't so much as strapped himself into that thing, yet thought he could put on my jumping skis, head down the ramp with the glider on his back, and fly.

But fly *where?* I asked him. Into the *trees?*

●

A friend of my father's, an attorney, and a very even-tempered and quiet-spoken man, brightened at the mention of my competing at Wirth. Had he been a jumper? I asked. No. But he had accepted a dare when he was just ten, to ride his new bicycle off the Wirth Parkway jump. This would have been about 1936. Well, did he? I asked. Orrin laughed.

It was written up in the *Star Tribune*, he told me. And he hadn't come out too badly, either—only broke his collarbone and his arm.

Late at night, and after meets, you could ride the landing hills of jumps on your back, curled up like turtles in your then popular "wet-look" jacket. The landing hill of Suicide, in Michigan, was good for a fifty-mile-per-hour ride, only that millimeter of wet-look cloth between you and the hardpack. The FIS banned that clothing the year after it became popular, because when skiers fell on mountain slopes they couldn't be stopped, that wet-look material so slick that downed skiers picked up tremendous speed until they met with that inevitable immovable object. Or fell from a precipice not made to be skied or fallen over.

You used that gear to your advantage. You had races, hurtling down those landing slopes, spinning circles and laughing hysterically.

●

Almost daily, getting around the Twin Cities on Highway 494, you passed by the Bush Lake seventy-meter.

I compete on that, you'd say.

Really? most people replied, shifting away from you in the car, as if you smelled funny, or had tendrils of smoke snaking up out of your ears.

By then, you knew those "hills" as friends, enemies, challenges, as places where you'd had some of the best times of your life. *That* was club jumping. Where you started, where you cut your teeth on "little hills," twenty-, forty-, fifty-meters where you got your first real "rides," where you learned to "do it."

And when you went on, which only the most gifted did, all that silliness and kid stuff ended. You focused. Cut out the horsing around. And you hit the road to find sponsors to buy yourself those flights to Germany, Austria, Switzerland, Norway, and Sweden, and to Poland and Slovenia.

But the *club* was where you got your start.

OLYMPIC AND WORLD CUP COMPETITION

At the Olympic and World Cup level of Nordic jumping competition, hairsplitting, Herculean efforts, raw *talent*—that indefinable *some*thing in a competitor that makes his efforts consistently superior—*and* technology win events.

Here we return to those jumpers who "all sort of look the same."

They should, because each progressive group of jumpers since the first competitions in Norway, at Trysil, in 1862, discovers and adopts some new variation on form that will maximize the distance competitors are capable of jumping, and the style with which they do it.

Style, when the father of jumping, Sondre Norheim, set the first world distance record at thirty meters (ninety-nine feet) in 1860, was to stand up at the end of the jump and sail down the hill upright. If you were ballsy enough, you waved at the spectators. So enthralled were the Norwegians with their flying athletes that, by 1882, when the second Nordic Athletic Contest was held, more than twenty thousand spectators attended.

That upright style, and Norheim's record, lasted some thirty-three years, until Norwegians Thulin Thams and Sigmund Ruud pioneered what came to be known as the Kongsberger Technique (named after their hometown), in which the upper body is bent at the hips, the skier has an extreme forward lean, and his arms are extended *in front of him*—which made jumpers look as though they were diving out over their skis. This so radically improved jumping distances that the "Magic Line"—or the hypothetical distance jumpers were thought capable of—was set at a hundred meters, a distance that wasn't exceeded for decades.

During the period of the Kongsberger Technique, jumping exhibitions became so popular that Barnum and Bailey made them part of their circus. In 1907, Carl Howelsen, a Norwegian immigrant, nightly thrilled circusgoers by leaping over either *the Mountain of Death*, or a row of six elephants. Crowds *loved* it, Barnum and Bailey billing Howelsen's jumping as *"the Greatest Show on Earth,"* here the origin of that later famous expression for the P. T. Barnum and Bailey Circus in its entirety. Following suit, hucksters built temporary ramps at places such as Soldier Field, in Chicago, to improve ticket sales at baseball and football games: between innings or at halftime world-class jumpers leaping on snow that had been brought in by truck. One promoter, in New York City, even went so far as to build a jump on the roof of Macy's, the jumpers schussing down that ramp on a mixture of rice hulls, borax, and salt. In February 1934, the Auburn Ski Club of Truckee, California, put forty-three thousand cubic feet of snow on six Southern Pacific boxcars and shipped it to steep Hearst Avenue, just north of the UC-Berkeley campus. About forty-five thousand people, including thousands on "Tightwad Hill," gathered to watch the Auburn Ski Club jumping exhibition. The event ended in a riot— the jumpers landing in a mass of UC-Berkeley students engaged in a snowball fight.

Of course, too, during this Kongsberger Technique period, there were refinements which further improved jumpers' distances. Anders Haugen brought to the sport the skis-exactly-parallel-in-flight improvement (which put an end to the *flying scissors* technique, where one loose ski would smack you in the head).

Distances again changed so radically that hills had to change with them.

At Steamboat Springs, Colorado, in 1917, the world distance record was set at a thrilling 203 feet, more than double Norheim's distance.

This improvement in performance positioned jumping for inclusion in the first Winter Olympics in 1924. At that time, jumpers competed on what was called the "Normal Hill" (90 meters); the "Large Hill" (120 meters) wasn't added until 1964.

When I began jumping at the end of the 1960s, the Kongsberger Technique was still de rigueur, though a further-modified form of it. Developed by Andreas Daescher in the 1950s, the *Daescher style* placed the arms backward and alongside the body. This proved to have definite aerodynamic advantages over Thams and Ruud's first variation, and yielded distances, on ski-flying hills, in the near-five-hundred-foot range.

In 1985, Swedish jumper Jan Boklov changed all that with what came to be called the "V Style," which all jumpers use now, the skis parted in a radical V open in the direction of motion, and the jumper's body and head right down between the skis.

The V was experimented with as early as 1969 by Polish jumper Miroslaw Graf, who got a distance advantage with it, but lost that advantage to low style points in competition as his form was thought to be ungainly, Graf's teammates teasing that he was trying to hit himself in the head with his skis.

The V Style radically improves lift in the air (wind tunnel tests measure by 28 percent), and decreases landing speeds (instead of landing at nearly sixty miles per hour, a competitor now lands at around forty).

This new V Style changed the sport radically, particularly in the 1990s. Now skiers were routinely jumping well over distances of five hundred feet on "ski-flying" hills such as Suicide in Michigan. Older jumps, as a result, were torn down and rebuilt so that competitors using the new ski-flying technique would not injure themselves by "outjumping" (jumping beyond the transition into the outrun) older-style hills.

These *new* hills have been contoured in such a way that now jumpers are not more than twenty feet off the ground in flight—though they are covering distances that were unthinkable thirty years ago.

I have jumped on both kinds of hills. The older hills, where the landing slope dropped precipitously from the knoll, would put you as much as forty feet off the ground, which made jumping those hills very dangerous. (Yet, I will also add, there was no thrill on earth like crossing that knoll, when the hill dropped out from under you, and you were, in a nanosecond, truly flying.)

Once, at a meet at Pine Mountain, in Michigan, I saw a skier carried by wind over the heads of those marking distances on the landing hill just out from the trees, the skier desperately steering back over the center of the landing hill to slap down a perfect telemark, for a jump of 430-some feet. Not a hill record, but a very memorable effort.

Had this jumper not been able to steer himself back onto the hill, out from the trees, the outcome would almost certainly have been his death.

The jumper's height, at that hill, made him vulnerable to a cross draft, only his command of style saving him.

So style is *what works*, what *wins tournaments*, and year after year new styles emerge, and competitors adopt them with a vengeance, seeking to refine those styles for further advantage. And, for that reason, jumpers come to look alike in their technique. (The last jumping competitor to successfully use both the Kongsberger

Technique and the V Style was Jens Weissflog of East Germany, who took Olympic gold in 1984; since then, competitors who have been unable to master the new technique have dropped out of world-class events.)

But, you might ask, is all this focus on style and equipment really making that much of a difference?

Consider this: the current world ski-flying distance record (as this book is being written) is 784 feet (239 meters), set by Norway's Bjorn Einar Romoren, at Planica, in Slovenia.

Seven hundred eighty-four feet. That's nearly *three football fields* set end to end, or, *two long city blocks.*

In Europe, where there is a mania for the sport, the Magic Line is now thought to be 300 meters, or 984 feet.

Let's just call that a thousand feet. Fair enough? About a fifth of a mile.

Outrageous? No, just a matter of time. And the place. The men and the women who will do it are already here.

I know, because I've met them.

WOMEN JUMPERS

Women's inclusion in Olympic Nordic jumping competition is only a matter of time. Currently, the FIS is considering an international petition by women's jumping teams to add women's competition to the World Championships. This is important, as the "Eddie the Eagle rule" (see page 165) bars from Olympic competition jumpers who have not competed in the top fifty at World events. At the latest, a women's competition at the World Cup will take place in 2009, paving the way for the women's Nordic jumping competition in the 2010 Olympics.

In the last two years, both Lindsey Van and Jessica Jerome, American Inter-Mountain Division jumpers, have been in the top five in world competitions, Van placing second only to Anette Sagen of Norway.

In single event jumping (not Nordic combined), *no American has medaled since the inception of the Winter Olympics in 1924.*

Why? American jumpers don't receive the necessary training or resources. The famous Denneys, for example, *built* themselves a wind tunnel—when they couldn't get access to one in the United States—*out of an old bus.* The Denneys cut the nose off a bus, attached an enormous sheet-metal wind catcher, something like a huge, snowplow-sized scoop, to the front, and, to generate wind, drove the bus down an old, rarely used length of highway at . . . exactly a jumper's speed in the air, fifty to sixty miles per hour. Imagine encountering the Wind Tunnel Bus on that section of highway, at the wheel an old (drunk on aquavit) bearded Norwegian shouting to the kids practicing their in-the-air performance behind him, *"Yump! Yump the fuckin' hill!"* Funny? Sure, especially at the Olympics, where those wind-tunnel-earned extra thirty to fifty feet distances, and more refined style, would buy the U.S. Nordic Jumping Team not only some medals, but some respect.

Given her current performance, and a fair piece of luck, Lindsey Van could be the first U.S. Olympic medal winner in Nordic jumping. And if not Lindsey Van, another woman.

In 2010, the women will be there—though even now they are competing, and very successfully, in World Continental Cup events.

At present, the longest flight recorded by a woman, Austria's Daniela Irascho, is . . . 656 feet (200) meters.

Over *six times* Norheim's original record.

UPSETS AND IDIOTS

In Nordic jumping venues, as in all sports competitions, there are historical upsets, amusing events, and disasters of memorable proportion. Most recently, at the 2002 Olympic games in Salt Lake City, a competitor from a country that did not so much as have a Large Hill defeated one of the finest veteran jumpers in the world, Sven Hannawald, in the 120-meter competition.

I am referring to, of course, the then-twenty-year-old Harry Potter look-alike, Simon Ammann.

Bespectacled, mop-haired, and smiling a smile that seemed not to have so much as a hint of world-weariness in it, Simon Ammann jumped right through our television screens and into our hearts.

At the onset of the Nordic competition, Ammann was one of the event's entrants that was least expected to medal. Ammann had little experience when compared to jumpers the likes of Adam Malysz, Sven Hannawald, and Kazuyoshi Funaki. And, just months prior to the Olympics, Ammann had sustained such serious injuries at a World Cup tournament that it was thought he might be unable to compete in the Olympics, much less take home a medal, even a bronze.

When, on the Normal Hill, the ninety-meter, Ammann beat top-ranked rival Sven Hannawald, taking gold, his performance that afternoon was touted by sports journalists as a fluke, those journalists predicting Ammann's certain defeat on the Large Hill.

Four days later, on the Large Hill, the "Swiss kid," Ammann, hit two magic balls right out of the park, not only defeating dour superstar Hannawald, but soaring over the closest competition by *11 points*—an almost unheard-of margin. But what spectators loved best about Ammann was this.

So genuinely ecstatic was he after his second, winning jump on the Large Hill, that, when he was mobbed by reporters, he couldn't so much as speak a coherent sentence.

Big-eyed, and loopy with shock over his good fortune, he kept glancing in the direction of the scoreboard as if he couldn't believe his eyes.

That day, Ammann went down in the records with Finnish jumper Matti Nykänen as the only other competitor in the history of the sport to take gold in both the Normal and Large Hill competitions.

●

At the 1994 Olympics games in Lillehammer, the Japanese suffered defeat in one of the most memorable upsets in the sport's history. But in this case, their defeat wasn't due to the stellar performance of a rival jumper, such as Simon Ammann, but something else. Japan went into the second round of the team event (especially prized by the Japanese) with an overwhelming lead. The Japanese team widened that lead with stellar second-round performances, leaving Harada, Japan's strongest jumper, the last man in the competition at the top of the Large Hill.

Even a poor jump by Harada would win the Japanese team the coveted gold. Harada had, on his first round, placed stellar style points and a world-class distance of four hundred feet.

Harada raced down the inrun, leaped from the takeoff point.

From the moment Harada was airborne, it was obvious to everyone watching that something had gone *very* wrong. Harada knew it, too. He threw down his landing far short of the P-point, and with a smile cemented on his face, skidded to a stop on the flats. Harada's second jump was just *319 feet*—the *lowest* score of the competition—which gave the gold to Germany.

Harada said, afterward, "In the past, a well-raised Japanese would have to commit *hari-kari* after such a mistake."

Japanese fans were horrified.

In Japan, where ski jumping is a national passion (some seventy thousand spectators turn out for locally held World events), jumpers are celebrities with the cachet of Joe Montana and Terry Bradshaw.

Still, it was Harada's winning smile and affable manner, even at that moment of terrible defeat, that won him the nickname "Happy Harada," and made him an all-time favorite. The Japanese simply *loved* Harada.

And so, beloved by his fans, he was put back on his skis and sent out to do battle again four years later at Nagano.

There, on the Normal Hill, Harada established himself as the front-runner, but on his second jump, he—*again*—choked in world-class fashion, placing fifth and out of medal contention. A Tokyo paper printed as its front-page headline the following morning: HARADA HUMILIATES JAPAN. Harada responded by taking home a bronze in the Big Hill competition—though his performance there was still nowhere near his best. Which left the team event on the Big Hill in question. It was here that the Japanese *most* wanted to succeed, especially given what had happened at Lillehammer, thanks to Harada.

In his first round of the team event, Harada faced genuine bad luck—a freak headwind—which gave him a woeful distance of 260 feet: not just a *bad* jump, but a *disaster*.

Japanese fans cried out, "Not Again!"

So, poised for his second-round performance in the team event, Harada's very life seemed at stake (or some life that he might actually *want* to live). He sped down the ramp, leaped for all he was worth and, sailing down the landing hill, he went on, and on, and on, until he'd gone so far down the landing hill that he *outjumped the recording equipment*—in one effort, *tying the world record on the hill*, and *possibly* earning the Japanese team the points they needed to take the gold. But would Harada's points be enough? (Harada had jumped *so* far the Olympic judges had to hand measure the additional distance, temporarily postponing the competition to decide how many distance points to award him.)

Harada was awarded a stellar score.

But this time it remained for Harada's teammate, Kazuyoshi Funaki, to jump last, which he did. (Funaki said, later, the pressure he experienced prior to his run was a near-crushing, physical weight in his chest.)

At the bottom, on the flats with the spectators, all four team members turned their faces to the scoreboard, waiting for Funaki's score.

When the scores came up, the Japanese team had won the gold. Harada threw out his hands in victory (or was it relief?), then collapsed onto his back. His teammates—in very *un*-Japanese fashion—pounced on him, crying with joy and tossing each other into the air, the whole world at that moment, it seemed, happy for Harada.

●

Occasionally, a particularly poorly turned-out competitor—so much so that he becomes comical—catches our attention. Such a competitor was Eddie "the Eagle" Edwards, the "World's Favorite Ski Jumper." Eddie, or "Mr. Magoo on skis," as journalists called him, was a plasterer from Cheltenham, and looked like one—five feet eight and 180 pounds, in a sport where most competitors are lanky and under 160 pounds. He wore bottle-bottom glasses and had an oversized, owlish head. Eddie got into the Olympics because no other Brit applied in Nordic jumping that year, Eddie only eligible because he'd recorded a 252-foot (77-meter) jump on a hill in, of all places, *Australia*. Since there was no snow in Britain, or suitable hills, Eddie trained, at least initially, by jumping over double-decker buses—and at that for only two years.

At the 1988 Olympic Nordic jumping competitions in Calgary, Canada, record crowds gathered daily, Eddie being one of the chief reasons. It was said that the thrill would be in seeing if this "idiot" would crash and kill himself as he leaped from the Olympic jumps. Even George Herbert Walker Bush, president-elect then, stopped a conference to watch Eddie jump.

Eddie was awful, ungainly, no eagle in the air, but he did *not* kill himself. Out of a field of fifty-seven jumpers, he placed fifty-sixth, and that after the fifty-seventh was disqualified. Prior to his second jump on the Large Hill, he said, grinning into the cameras, "Hello, mum! It's *me!*"

Other competitors, and the IOC, were so outraged by Eddie and the "circus" he was making of the sport, that a rule was put in place following the 1988 Olympics called the "Eddie the Eagle rule," which states that competitors must place in the top 30 percent in international jumping events before being eligible to compete in the Olympics. Still, Eddie had cut through the sometimes sanctimonious feeling that can permeate skiing events, skiing being so fiercely competitive that hundredths of seconds, or inches, or a tenth of a point, can make the difference between a star and a has-been. At the World level, skiing demands a degree of focus not conducive to breezy nattering and antics. Eddie, though, if nothing else, showed us the power of will and courage, of which he had an abundance.

Eddie was not just a jumper, but a bona fide fan of extreme sport. At one time he ranked number 9 in Amateur Speed Skiing

(106.8 mph), and held a record in stunt jumping (ten cars/six buses). Currently, a major Hollywood production company is making a film on Eddie's life. Failing to qualify for successive Olympic jumping teams, Eddie is studying law, to be a "legal eagle."

Eddie's happy legacy? His date of birth—December 5—is a *public holiday* for casualty (insurance) departments all over Great Britain.

I SET AN UNOFFICIAL DISTANCE RECORD, AND END MY JUMPING CAREER

Following club jumping with the Spartans, I went on to compete in the Central Division and elsewhere, but now I was at the University of Minnesota, and I didn't get out to practice as much as I should have. I was out a day or two a week at the most and still competing on big hills. This I did until 1977, when, one sunny January day, a young jumper called and wanted me to give him some pointers at the Bush Lake Olympic Training Center seventy-meter.

I was tired of studying, the light was pouring in through the windows, the temperature was around ten degrees, just perfect, and I said yes.

Out at Bush, the day was everything I had hoped it would be, the track on the seventy-meter set and the outrun sidestepped, fifteen or so skiers out and doing well enough, but my student was clumsy, not good at taking directions, and I was frustrated. One run after another he would jump late and jackknife, which also made him land on the tails of his skis, which in turn caused him to ride his hands on the snow through the transition. Poor distance, zero style points.

So David needed nothing short of a total readjustment. I tried to get him to simply *ride* the jump and by increments jump *out* and *into* the landing hill. (As I've already said, this is a very *unnatural* thing to do.)

David wasn't getting it. An hour or so of that went by, and I told him I wished I had my equipment. If I'd brought it, I'd just show him, I said.

What size shoe did I wear? he asked.

It turned out we wore the same size, though his skis were ones I would never have used—Fischers. (German, and, for me, too heavy.)

"Just use my gear," he told me, and, frustrated as I was, and feeling irritated with myself that I hadn't come prepared (but why, then, should I have, since I hadn't intended to jump?), I tried on his boots and they seemed a good-enough fit, if a bit too wide. (I mean, they weren't Koko the clown shoes after all.)

I'd worn my jumping suit, since it was ideal for the cold, and practiced a few stationary jumps on the flats, warming my legs up.

Suddenly it all came back. I was getting, as we put it back then, *jazzed*. I wanted to get up there, and *now*.

I wanted to *fly*.

Down on the flats, wearing David's boots, I kicked into his Fischers and checked the heel cables and blocks. Not great, but not awful. They would do. I fussed with those Fischers a bit more, readjusted the heel cables, then climbed the seventy-meter, falling back into my old routine, in me a mix of terror and excitement.

What I was doing was a bit stupid, not stretching or just taking a few practice rides to shake out the flutters.

David, as I'd instructed him to, took his place down from the takeoff point on the landing hill so he could see my run top to bottom. Up on top, south Minneapolis was lit in early afternoon sun, just beautiful. It had snowed and everywhere in the treetops were patches of blue-white, in the air that exciting, ashy, new-snow smell.

On the jumper's platform I was at the top of the world again and it felt better than good.

I slipped on David's goggles, David using a new kind with yellow lenses, which seemed to cut the glare but flatten perspective. I thought it might be the peculiar angle the lenses were set in the neoprene frame, canted forward, and tried to adjust them over my face, but wasn't having any luck.

In the end, I tightened the strap and simply made sure the goggles were secure. What the hell. Eddie the Eagle'd worn those bottle-bottomed jobs, so these would work well enough.

I waited my turn among a group of rookies who recognized me, the three boys jabbing each other.

"Hey, Mortensen," I said. "That you?"

I'd competed with his older brother, who'd gotten two concussions, and had had to stop jumping, doctor's orders.

When my turn came, I was alone on the platform, those boys all waiting below with David.

I stepped into the track, rolled my head on my neck, then loosened my shoulders. I squatted, practicing my telemark landing, and stood again, the boys, far below me, waving.

"Let's see it!" the smallest, in a yellow jumping suit, called up.

I waited until David gave the knoll and landing hill a hard look and waved the all clear.

I patted the lucky penny I kept in the pocket of my jumpsuit, took a deep breath, and kicked down into the track.

The ride down the inrun was sweet, the snow just right. When the pine boughs at the takeoff point came rushing at me I held back, in that bubble of no time, until the tips of those Fischers came exactly even with them, and there, with an almost indescribable pleasure, I kicked off, then pressed very hard into the skis, especially so, since David was watching, and the Fischers came up as I rode high over the knoll, nearly into my face, and— *dammit, but was my timing on!*

Sometimes, your intuitive jumps were the best, and *this* was one of them.

I had bought this ride big time, and like that, thinking I was Matti Nykänen himself, I sailed down the landing hill, held it, and held it, and held it, right on top of those Fischers, flying, those yellow lenses making it a little hard to see, I thought, and just like that, when I was thinking to throw in my telemark, in a heartbeat, one that sent a fistful of blood directly into my head, I saw, *not* the steep landing hill come up in front of me where I could set down, but the *transition*, and I got my right leg bent, which probably saved me, because when I struck the far end of the transition, almost on the flats, that bent knee turned some of my downward energy into forward motion, but still, I hit as if I'd jumped from a twenty-story building onto a sidewalk below.

I was thrown thirty, forty feet from the transition.

Jumbled in David's equipment, I lay there, my head ringing, not even sure where I was. I saw twittering birds, heard stars, I was that confused.

David, like some loose-jointed stick figure, came bounding down the landing hill, shouting, "You *OUTJUMPED THE HILL! YOU OUTJUMPED THE HILL!*" Those three kids who had been up on top were right behind him, palsied with glee.

I sat up, already aware that I'd done something to my right

leg, which I was more than afraid to try to bend. Moments later, David stood over me, thrilled.

"I think you set a record!" he told me.

A youngish jumping tech I recognized (who simply was called *Coach*) stood where I'd come down. He gave me a big grin and strode over with the kids to whom he'd been giving some pointers.

I got to my feet and pasted on my face what was, for me, an expression of surprised joy. I *was* thrilled, even *stunned* at what I'd done, though by then my right knee was aching so badly I feared I'd be sick. (Horking on someone's shoes was something I wanted to avoid at that triumphant moment.)

Coach slapped me on the back. He'd driven a stick off to the side of the outrun where I'd come down and pointed to it now.

"Is *that* something or what?!" he said.

I told him I thought it was, yes, and hoping to slink off before I lost my lunch, I wished him the same luck sometime.

There was more chatter and excitement and talk of trying to do something about making my jump an official record, since they'd all been there and seen it and Coach had marked the spot. I smiled through it all, then let David take his skis and boots, and we walked to his car. We got his equipment on the rack, and still thrilled to death with me, he said again what an awesome jump I'd made.

"It's a hill *record*," he said. "I mean, you *outjumped the hill!*"

He drove away, and I limped to my old Duster. ("With a top that looks like it came off a gold alligator!" rang in my head, the sales jingle Plymouth had used to sell Dusters on TV.) My knee was swelling something awful, and I wondered what to do. I was living off campus on busy Lake Street with my girlfriend, Alyson, and worried she might force me to go to some clinic, which I nearly felt I'd rather die than do. Realize that back then arthroscopic surgery was only a last resort; those undergoing it, as often as not, were *worse* after it, not better. *Gimpy* was the word used, which didn't inspire athletes to go under the knife for joint injuries.

I tested my right foot—after all, I had to push the gas pedal with it, didn't I?—then glanced over at that stick Coach had used to mark my jump, an arm's length of oak branch to the side of the outrun. It had begun to snow, the snow adhering to the side of the stick, so already it was difficult to make out from the parking lot. Another hour and you wouldn't know it was there, I thought.

Over on the flats, the younger kids were running circles around each other, making snowballs and pummeling each other with them, just as I had done years earlier. I felt choked up, somehow, watching them. I gave them a wave, and one whooped, doing a cartwheel in the snow.

I got to the apartment, and Alyson wasn't home. I took off my suit and looked at my knee. It had swollen half the size of a basketball. (And, by then, I realized I'd done something to my right hip as well.) I got ice from the freezer and went back to the bedroom. Alyson came in late and I told her I'd come down with the flu, and, after fussing over me, pills, pillows, and a peck on my forehead, she set herself in front of the tube, on the couch, where she slept that night.

I left early the following morning, came home late. The swelling in my knee went down, but it was hard walking, though, after a month, I could walk on it without limping.

I missed every tournament that winter, and didn't ski gates on the weekends as I had in the past. The year after that I left for Bozeman, Montana, where I continued my work in microbiology at Montana State University. After a year away from the sport, though, I thought to drop out of school and take up flying once again, at the national headquarters in Steamboat Springs, Colorado.

So late one afternoon I packed my gear in my car and, with the engine idling at the curb in front of my house (*Our House*, we called it, after the Crosby, Stills, and Nash tune), I studied a map, deciding on the best route.

Would it be best to take 90 east, then 25 south? Or 89 south around Yellowstone, to hook up with 80 at Rock Springs, and go east there?

In the end, I took neither route.

I never got there, to Steamboat Springs, but that is another story.

●

My right hip, all these years later, still clicks oddly sometimes when I walk uphill.

When I watch the Olympics, I'm insane for the jumping. I'm reminded of the indescribable beauty of flight, am buoyed up, thrilled. To say I loved the sport is not an overstatement. There was nothing like coming over the knoll, held aloft on your magic planks, the whole world there opening up under you.

"I did that," I'll say.

And whoever I'm watching with will always ask the same questions: How high do they go? and Why do they all sort of look the same? But most important, they'll ask, How do they *do* that? and Who *are* those guys? and, last of all, *Why* would anyone do that, jump off something like that?

But I don't have to tell you any of that now, do I?

You know.

WHO LIVES IN EAST BUMBLERUT, IDAHO, AND OTHER WEST OF THE HUDSON MYSTERIES

THE EXTREME SKIING HEAD COUNT

FIRST FATHERS

He stands well over six feet, has one of those handsome, rough-hewn faces you associate with John Ford westerns, wild gray hair down to his shoulders. He wears his shirt, faded denim, over a gray tee, the shirt unbuttoned to his belt, a thick leather affair tough enough to use as a tow rope. Everything about the man radiates some singular dynamism. In another life, this man might have been the president of a Fortune 500 start-up, the CEO of some wildcat Louisiana oil company, or a tough-talking senator from Idaho or Colorado.

But Dag Aabye is none of these things. He is, to those who are intimately connected to the skiing life, the father of extreme skiing.

Even sitting, there is something in motion about him. His eyes glitter. Women love this man. Dag loves women. He loves to ski, and he loves a good beer. The kinds of rewards that would have made him CEO of that offshore oil company mean nothing to him. Dag's life is about *adventure*. His dream home is a converted school bus, back in some pines away from the wealthy skiers who vacation here at Silver Star, in British Columbia.

To fuel his adventures, Dag washes dishes a few hours a week at a deli.

"Beer money," says Dag. "And you meet people that way," he adds, winking.

Dag, the father of extreme skiing. Just over sixty. Dag, who was in Warren Miller—like movies before anyone knew who Warren Miller was. Who, in his stunt man days, was a poker partner of Sean Connery, a pal of beautiful Ursula Andress, and who was, making one film, killed fourteen times in a single scene. Dag appeared in about forty films, including *Goldfinger* and *Die! Die! My Darling!* with Donald Sutherland.

Jim McConkey, the acknowledged father of extreme skiing here in the United States, recalled meeting Dag at Whistler, in British Columbia: "He was walking on his hands with skis on his feet at the top of the T-bar. Then he flipped over and skied off."

Others remembered first seeing Dag walking down the roof of Silver Star lodge on his hands, then flipping off and landing in the parking lot.

"My parents let me run back in Norway," he tells me. "I'd build a kicker on the steepest run I could find, and jump the whole day there."

Dag spent a portion of his childhood in Argentina, too. Land there in 1946 was a dollar for ten acres, but the family missed Norway and the snow and skiing, and Dag moved back with his parents, joining the Special Forces of Norway's army, where he further honed his acrobatics and skiing skills. Those skills took him to Scotland, where he was a ski instructor. He was seen by a talent scout, throwing 720 helicopters (a move that has since then been adopted by skiers and snowboarders alike) and was recruited to be a body double for Cliff Richardson.

Such was Dag's dynamism, his energy, that actors such as Michael Caine and Sean Connery, whom he met on shoots, were drawn to him.

As are people now—as I am, skiing in British Columbia.

The Dag types at resorts are legion, for where else can men and women who can't be bothered with blue-chip investments or working steadily or buying a condo for $1.5 mil, just three blocks from where Dag has his converted school bus, find a place for themselves in the world?

Meeting guys like Dag makes you ask yourself, if you're any kind of working stiff, is the *way* I'm living *worth it?*

When I was studying microbiology, as a premed, I sometimes wondered about the whole program: endless labs, and, at the beginning, a stretch of time staring you in face, roughly eight to twelve years of medical adventure, if you could see it that way.

At one time, I took to asking my classmates when they'd decided to do what they were doing.

"Oh," one student told me, "I've always known I was going to do this."

"But since *when?*"

"When I was seven or so. My dad's a doctor."

"Did you ever think of doing something else?"

"No."

I suppose it was the narrowness of it all that made me tune out. The suffocated feeling I got hearing all that, the step-by-step plan of assault on the safe, and revered, Good Life, one student's girlfriend telling me she was supporting her student husband, Bill, through medical school because she'd always wanted a Mercedes 450 SEL. (Had she said she wanted a lovely old Jag XKE, or a vintage Ferrari, say, a 250 Berlinetta, I might have had some respect for her, but that old Kleenex-box bodied Teutonic turd of a car? Where was the romance, the adventure in that?)

The year after I left Montana for graduate school, I put up an advertisement on a ride board at the University of Iowa before

Thanksgiving Day weekend. I got one rider, a chemical engineering student who was graduating that spring. Driving to Minneapolis from Iowa City, a six-hour jaunt, I asked him, "So, what now?"

"When I finish, I head right down to Texas, to Mosstek."

"Mosstek?"

He nodded. "They make keyboards for computers, that sort of thing. They need more plastics research."

This, of course, brought to mind that famous line in *The Graduate*. Benjamin Braddock, at his graduation party, bored and looking for an exit, is buttonholed by one of his father's friends, the friend telling Benjamin the hot ticket to the future and the good life could be summed up in one word, "Plastics."

At which point the audience, back then, anyway, always burst out laughing.

"What would you do if you could do anything you wanted to do?" I asked him, and found myself grinning.

"I'd take a year off and be a ski bum, somewhere in Colorado. Breckenridge, or Vail. I've skied there."

Bingo, I thought. I'd hoped there was some spark of adventure in this guy.

I told him I'd been a ski bum myself, at "America's first and finest resort" (as the advertisements read for years), Sun Valley. Even taught ski lessons there. I told him that being a ski bum was as easy as pointing your car in the direction of the resort of your choice and knocking on the door of the company's employment office. Just as I had.

I was lucky enough to have met Barbara Pigeon in Sun Valley, who, like an auntie, took me under her wing (God knows why), and made life easier for me, even giving me a single room in the best dorm they had, Washington, for a whopping $90 a month, a trout-filled stream running by right outside my window. (It was a single-floor dormitory, unlike the others, and if I reached out my window, I could nearly touch that stream.)

When I met Barbara, I'd been down in Hailey, just south of Ketchum, had been waiting for my U.S. Forest Service pay to reach me, and had been living the last few weeks on a fifty-pound sack of spuds (next to free in Idaho), slathering them with Gert's Golden Spread. It was something that looked like margarine but would barely melt on a baked potato. (I still have mixed feelings about potatoes.)

A woman I talked to at a bank almost daily, about my Forest Service money coming, took pity on me and lent me $10 for some meat—which, later, I very happily paid her back (such gestures are never forgotten).

But on the edge or not, here I was in Famous Sun Valley.

Home, for a time, to the U.S. Ski Team. Home to Ernest Hemingway, and now to his granddaughter, Mariel, who I'd see around town, and who, one day at The Hobbit, had lunch in the booth behind me ("I don't know who she thinks she is. I think her legs are fat," she said of some actress). And there was Slim Pickens, David Soul, and sometimes Paul Michael Glaser around, making a ski movie, *Swan Song*.

There was my friend Lisa, then top model for Maybelline. I met Clint Eastwood when I was teaching one afternoon, served as host to him, Clint giving me a $100 bill when I got him a coffee at Elevation 9,000 (he wouldn't take it courtesy of the resort, and making change was awkward).

Across the valley from Baldy, the Duponts were building a place, the foundation alone, in today's dollars, running around 4 million.

The season that year was slow to start, and I worked alongside the new owner, Earl Holding, of Little America gas stations and hotels, building Elevation 9,000, the new lodge at the top of Baldy, sometimes sixteen hours a day, making regular trips to the old mountain lodge, Roundhouse, which should have been put on the Historical Register, but was being used as a supply hut. There was so much old life in that lodge, on the lacquer-glazed knotty-pine walls, dream skis of generations past, Northlands, and Kastles, and Kneissls, on every wall, too, signed photos of the stars who had made Sun Valley famous, Clark Gable and Ingrid Bergman; Glenn Miller and Milton Berle and Sonja Henie, from *Sun Valley Serenade*, which had been filmed, at least in part, right in Roundhouse. There were signed eight-by-tens of Gary Cooper and Frank Sinatra and Ava Gardner. It had been that way from the first.

At the grand opening of Sun Valley, December 21, 1936, at the behest of visionary and creator, W. Averell Harriman, in attendance were Mr. Pullman, of passenger train fame; Mr. Otis, of elevators; and Mr. Fleischmann, of yeast and gin. Titans. Also in attendance were David O. Selznick and other well-known stars, among them Errol Flynn, who had a fistfight with a Chicago banker over who would have the honor of dancing first with Claudette Colbert. For six days those in attendance sang and drank and danced themselves ragged until the snow fell, and, en masse, the famous headed out onto Dollar Mountain to make U.S. history, *Life* magazine covering the whole event for a nation—here, for all to see (and ogle), the birth of America's *first* destination resort.

Skiers, stars, the wealthy, thrill seekers, adventurers—all were drawn to Sun Valley from that moment on, whole generations of them. (And nothing has changed in this, but for the addition of the snowboarder.)

So there were ghosts in that place, Roundhouse. You could feel them, all those high-octane lives, in that space nearly fifty years of mountain cheer. The place was a temple, the very cabinets and furniture curvaceously art nouveau, the light fixtures brass from the late thirties, keepsakes. And, there we were storing gasoline in five-gallon cans, flares, and canned chili, and condiments for hamburgers. Styrofoam cups in boxes of two hundred.

I was always struck dumb in Roundhouse when I was sent there for supplies. Most of us were. We went in, were awed by the feel of it, and got out as quickly as we could. It almost seemed some . . . sacrilege, to treat that space as we were treating it.

I'd been to small chapels in Italy, where in the vestibule, on an enormous board for such a thing, were testimonials of healing, and petitions for it, there also crutches, and medallions, and love letters, charms, a rose, a shoe, a lock of hair, a pair of glasses, all testifying to the range of people's hopes, and dreams, and aspirations.

That was what you felt in Roundhouse, but all of it filtered through the skiing life. Not just skiing, but the *skiing life*.

And here Roundhouse had been pushed off to the side, let go.

It was a time when Sun Valley was most down at the heels.

Houses could be had, when Earl Holding was taking the reins from Bill Janss, for less than a king's ransom, though we ski bums didn't even have the scratch for that. We ski bums bunked together in old miners' and ranchers' cabins. Places that were fantastically irregular, hammered together with tin, and chinked with cement, and painted pink, or blue, or just varnished natural. Or lived in the company dorms.

Now, the mean value of a single-family house in the Wood River Valley is $685,117.

Winters, I was on such terms with my boss in the company, that I could show up for work and say, "Gee, we have two feet of fresh snow out there. Business seems a little slow."

Dick Fox, a gem of a guy, would give me a nod, and I'd be free for the day—fiftysome days my first winter there.

Free to ski the bowls, to swoop down Seattle Ridge, to drink beer after skiing at Warm Springs, listening to some band belt out the blues, which none of us was feeling much of. (At least, not at first.)

I was as close to stone broke as I would ever be, and I was richer than my wildest dreams.

Said Jay Brunetto, an acquaintance on the mountain who'd been a professor of engineering at a prestigious East Coast school, "I used to dream all year of the three weeks I'd have in this place. I worked like hell to make sure it would happen. And then I thought, why not just live here, no matter what it took?"

Jay was instrumental in the manufacture of PRE (short for Precision) skis, and, later, snowboards of his own design.

Some wannabes bought life in the Valley with decades of focused labor, and some, the ski bums, and racers, and transients, simply bought it by making do, by living highly creative and eccentric lives. In Hailey, I'd lived in an apartment above the Mint Bar, which I frequented to use the old, weathered phone booth in the back, having no phone of my own. At closing, drunk miners and ranchers would stumble out onto the street, one calling loudly at 2:00 a.m., "Velma, I think I love you!" I slept on a box spring from a mattress set, suffered the snoring and incessant pot smoking of my roommate, who my racer friends jokingly referred to as Stone Blue Two. But up in Sun Valley, my life was something else.

Teaching ski lessons, and skiing, and racing. Anyone could race in tournaments sponsored by organizations like Chapstick, Toyota, or Head Ski, but in Sun Valley those competitions were *fierce*, world-class racers and local stars duking it out for substantial prizes.

In the Valley, millionaires mixed with racers, who mixed with movie stars (now Arnold Schwarzenegger, Demi Moore, and Bruce Willis, among others), who mixed with models and jet-setters, who mixed with hipsters and cranks and vagrants and drifters and ranchers and sheepherders and engineers and searchers. The Valley ethic being, whatever you were looking for, it was *here*, right in the Valley, somewhere. Up on Baldy, on skis. Or in town, socializing. Or just north, beyond Galena Summit and into the Salmon River area, breaking trail, in that stellar Alpine wilderness, where, after cutting down our Christmas tree in the dark, on a forty-degree slope, my roommate, Stone Blue Two, and I rode our tree down waist-deep powder, old Stone Blue Two whooping like the lunatic he was, and that hatchet in my jacket pocket the whole while.

In the car we got high, laughing about riding the tree down the mountain like real live Grinches, played Bizz, Buzz, Bang, a game in which competitors identify multiples of five, seven, and nine while trying to count to one hundred, which, when altered as we were, was an especial source of hilarity, given that both of us (my roommate, a mechanical engineer, and I, had had our heads crammed with calculus and higher math prior to our breaking away to bum in Sun Valley), and couldn't do it.

How high did we have to be? How could I have been much higher?

I was driving a Plymouth Duster, what must be one of the ugliest cars ever built. Others must have thought so, too, because, wherever I parked it, skiers passing would give it a kick. This made for some curious dents, which added to the car's already singular character.

One night I had mistakenly driven it like a dirt bike up what I thought was the back road to our dormitory parking and got the car aimed at the Sun Valley laundry loading ramp instead. My buddy Chris and I hit that ramp doing about forty, and it launched us right over the creek, *Dukes of Hazzard* style, the Motocross Cruster, as we were calling it, smacking into the parking lot we'd been looking for bumper first, so the hood whanged up around the windshield, blinding us as we slid to a stop. We got out, jumped on the hood in our shit kickers—cowboy boots—until the hood would lock again, and parked the car. "That bastard of a car's gonna kill you 'fore you kill it," Chris said, a warning I took to heart.

But that night of riding the tree down the mountainside I was ecstatic. Just that week, Stone Blue Two and I had been introduced to the U.S. Ski Team hopefuls and extreme skiers at a place, appropriately named, the White House, command central for the independent racers and extreme skiers in Sun Valley. At the White House, for Thanksgiving, we had duck, and goose, and venison, and elk, all bagged by those with us, and pies of ten types, wild rice, yams, potatoes, and we'd talked racing, and mountains, and powder snow, and climbing, and when it was dark, we all jumped in our cars, my roommate and I hitching a ride in a converted Eddy's Bread truck, and at Clarendon Hot Springs, in the subzero weather, and with a skiff of snow under our feet, we threw off our clothes, all thirty or so of us, and swam naked in the hot springs, Suzy Chase, who sang with a local blues band, belting out a tune from the diving board in her birthday suit, sleek and lovely, her friend and sidekick Wendy Poppin, another Burke Mountain Academy grad, splashing her. About then, my stomach, which had only had Idaho spuds and Gert's Golden Spread in it for weeks, began to revolt. It revolted like some Saturn V rocket about to launch, and I quickly wandered off into the dark, barefooted and naked, and, as had been said in those earlier days of NASA glory, we had lift off, Houston! When I rose from the launchpad, placing my hand on what I'd thought was snow, I realized, with a certain horror at first, I'd set my hand on fabric, in fact, many sorts of fabrics, which turned out to be some of my new friends' ski jackets, piled right there in the dark.

I slunk back to the hot pool, had a wonderful time, not saying a word to a soul that night, though, I related what had happened to Stone Blue Two the following day. We were hysterical with laughter.

What made it all that much funnier was that we'd just spent our last dollar at the Bald Mountain Hot Springs Resort, had gotten paper-hat jobs at a place frying doughnuts to cover our rent until the ski season started, and had been chased by a bear that afternoon in an abandoned mine shaft in the Sawtooths.

We'd run from the shaft, laughing so hard we were barely able to get down the mountainside.

"Was that a grizzly?" Stone Blue Two asked me at the Cruster.

"Well, I didn't exactly stop to ask him what he was, if that's what you mean," I said. And we burst out laughing.

Stone Blue Two was, in the end, a good roommate. He was absolutely unflappable. When I broke my skis just days before the part-time instructors' clinic, really a competition for a limited number of company spots, tore my bindings right out of my skis, and was beside myself, he gave me his Olins.

Boots, too.

Got the whole winter to ski, he said. And plenty of snow. Which we did. Got 160 inches that winter, most of it in February and March.

We skied, worked very hard, I won races and lost them, fell in love and out of love, we hot-potted, threw parties up at Elevation

9,000—simply hid in the snowdrifts on the roof until our manager took the lift to the bottom, then climbed down and turned on the wine taps, and voilà!

I remember skiing those three thousand plus feet vertical one night, by moonlight, on my rock skis, Day-Glo orange Siderals, skis that had, in their day, been magic skis. Skiing in that moonlight, they seemed to be on fire.

On heavy powder days, during whiteouts, when I was working one of the registers at Elevation 9,000 and not teaching, I'd get together with the cooks or lodge staff on break. We'd take the aluminum trays our bakery sent cookies up on, two and a half feet wide by three feet, and we'd sneak out the back, bend one end of the tray up, making a toboggan of it, and with another instructor or lodge employee doing the same beside us, we'd plummet down those three thousand feet, steering those trays by balancing to one side or the other, riding those trays like magic carpets on that soft snow, flying, sometimes at insane speeds (one nut back then was doing this sort of thing on a shovel, and was reaching speeds of seventy miles per hour). At the bottom of Warm Springs we'd leap to our feet, taking the trays with us, carefully placing the trays alongside the Warm Springs Lodge, where they would be picked up by the kitchen crew.

This we did until two girls out "traying" broke bones doing it, one her leg, the other her hip, and the resort management cracked down on it.

Days I was teaching, I'd climb the lee-side cornice of Elevation 9,000 onto the sunny roof, and the cooking staff would pass me up burgers and foaming cups of beer.

A very talented, and very short, racer friend of mine, Allen, was given the job of teaching racing school. He was a wonder at it, got the best from his kids, they just loved all five foot two of him, no one ever suspecting that on some occasions he liked his sunny days of instructing young racers made more sunny with Sunshine (LSD).

"You get all wound up, thinking too much," he taught me, "whistle. Just some dumb-ass tune to stop you thinking about your body."

To this day, it is something I do when I get too conscious skiing. It works wonders.

(Luckily for me, no one recognizes the inane and bawdy tunes that come to me from my Boy Scout years. And who could be serious whistling something titled "She Looked So Fair in the Midnight Air"?)

Saturday nights, we cheered for the Sun Valley amateur hockey team, always a prelude to some complicated dinner in Elkhorn Village, which we entered through a Pepto-Bismol pink archway, probably only three hundred units then in that entire development.

Weekdays, after skiing, we soaked in the hot-springs-fed pool in front of the lodge, Baldy rising up out of the steam like a mirage, or skated on the rink behind it with the well-heeled and famous. The lodge had been built by Harriman in '34 and '35 to create more passengers for the then declining numbers on the Union Pacific Railroad. We flew small planes out of the airport in Hailey, and sometimes helicopters to remote, untouched slopes of pristine snow.

Skiing brought us to Sun Valley, but it was never just the skiing that kept us there. It was an entire world, this *ski life*, call it what you will.

But more than anything, it was about the people. People who dared to do, to climb, hike, ski, fly.

Ernest Hemingway said of Sun Valley, and the Wood River

area, "You'd have to think like a machine not to engrave all this in your head so you'd never lose it."

He was right. All that came back to me, talking to my soon-to-be Mosstek chemical engineer rider, my years in the Valley, spelunking in old mines, hiking in the Sawtooths, fishing for trout on the Salmon River and in Silver Creek, backpacking the Sawtooths, the ski clinic I went through, two days, and on the last, the temperature dipping down to fourteen below zero. Skiing down the last run, my hands were so bitterly cold I put my thumbs in my mouth to stop their aching, only to find, when I'd gotten to my strange little apartment over the Mint Bar in Hailey, that I'd frozen a portion of my chin. I worried I'd have to have part of my face amputated, this because the zipper on my ski jacket had funneled that frigid air right into the cleft in my chin. But it thawed. I thawed. To race, to ski the powder, to fly.

"So, what do you think?" I asked the engineer-to-be in my car, this Steve.

"I could never do that," he told me. "Take time off like that."

"Why not?"

"What would an employer think if he saw a year gap in my résumé?"

"What would he *think*?" I said, this guy's whole life clear to me in that exchange. Here was one who went by the book.

But don't we all at times want to throw that book out the window? If even for a few hours, or a day?

Which is why we love characters like Dag, the father of extreme skiing. I always search them out, the Dag types, they loosen up my Lake Wobegon, Minnesota, tightness. I laugh around them, breathe more deeply.

But talking to Dag that afternoon . . .

"Can I say something to you?" Dag says. It's like a tick, Dag prefacing almost everything he says with it. I can tell, by his ease, he's done this before, related his story to the curious.

Can he? I tell him, *Of course. Please do.*

And Dag proceeds to tell me about how he made the first descent of the Lions near Vancouver, peaks that stand five thousand feet above Grouse Mountain. "Real steep," he tells me, "some say as much as seventy degrees." This I take in. I've skied fifty-degree slopes, and your boot buckles will catch on the uphill slopes when you turn. So, *seventy?* Dag tells me some hotshot helicopter pilot dropped him on a ridge where the snow was three hundred feet deep. He was skiing down well enough when he triggered an avalanche, after which he bounded between trees, hanging on to those trees for dear life. Legend had it his employer at the Seymour Ski School quipped after, "Broke his ribs and one ski, and he was out skiing later that afternoon, his pants ripped."

In Dag's time, this kind of skiing was called *hotdog* skiing.

Such skiers were hotdoggers.

By the 1980s, when I was living in Bozeman, and teaching part-time at Bridger Bowl, hotdog skiing was called *radical* skiing.

Around 1990, the expression became *extreme* skiing (each generation pushing the envelope of what is possible, including the present generation of snowboarders, who call what they do *Ripping Sick*). But, regardless of what it is called, all sorts of people are attracted to this edgy *life*. There's a thrill in the air around resort towns, excitement over new snowfall, the promise of adventure. Up at Bridger, you'd run into Peter Fonda, or Jane and Ted Turner. Tom McGuane lived nearby, north of Livingston, a whole host of writers and crazy types in Griz Country, too, around Missoula, Jim Crumley, Bill Kittredge, Jim Harrison, A. B. Guthrie, and James Welch, drinking themselves blind and hunting in the mountains, causing a general ruckus year-round.

As in Sun Valley, it was this edginess, this sometimes-too-rough environment that made your pulse quicken.

And skiers, back then, were out on the farthest reaches. Radical skiers would take on the "cold smoke," use mountain-climbing gear to scale the Spanish Peaks over Bridger, and ski down the chutes, even in fairly high avalanche danger, the skier's only talisman against being buried his or her Pieps or Skadie (avalanche beeper) and his trust that his friends would do justice for him if he triggered a slide and got caught in it.

These chutes at Bridger, and at Chet Huntley's Big Sky, just an hour south of Bozeman, were so steep, and the snow so deep, that skiing in it was sometimes called snorkel skiing, where the skier, so as not to be suffocated by the powder, or cold smoke, would wear a snorkel, one that exited well over his or her head. While this might seem like fanciful exaggeration, such is not the case.

In skiing cold smoke, when you approach a hummock, or convexity (such as a Volkswagen-sized mogul), instead of turning around it, you strike it head on, unweighting and setting up your next turn. The snow on impact will burst around you, you passing through it, temporarily blinded and skiing purely on balance and momentum alone. Sometimes, without the snorkel, you'll get a mouthful of crystalline powder snow that nearly chokes you.

But that is all exhilarating, because in a fraction of a second you are through it, shocked brilliantly awake, and headed for the next hummock, like a bird.

With the old equipment, boards, Alta skiers perfected a method known fondly as the *dipsy doodle*, weighting only the turning ski through the powder. Later, a new method was arrived at, where the skier weighted both skis, turning them as one in a continuous, fluid motion, appropriately named, the *double dipsy doodle*, the dipsy doodle giving birth to pure powder skiing. Likewise, mogul skiers perfected machine-gun-fast unweighting and turning techniques for skiing radically steep and bumpy slopes, and freestyle skiers, jumping, went from maneuvers like Dag's helicopters, daffys, and mulekicks, all done upright, to inverts, where the skier's body is at times upside down—front flips, backflips, back layouts, freestyle skiers finally combining the two, upright moves and inverts, to create the now-popular multiple maneuver jumps seen in Olympic competition.

Technology has helped immensely in the development of freestyle, maneuvers practiced year-round, in the summer competitors training on artificial grass and landing in pools of water. Even the landing in the pool has been improved since its introduction in training. Now, using a system of bubble aeration, the landing surface, the water in the pool, is made entirely porous. The skier no longer slaps into the water, but enters cushioning, meters-deep water bubbles.

Still, though, the sport of freestyle—with its beautifully orchestrated flips (double back and front, or even triple), helicopters, tucks, layouts, and combined flips and axial rotating maneuvers—is dangerous in competition. Freestyle skiers, tossed some forty feet into the air to land on very steep slopes, commonly tear out their anterior cruciate ligaments, or tear cartilage in general, have spinal compression problems, also suffering the usual maladies of broken forearms (silver-fork fractures), clavicle fractures, and general fractures of the legs.

But the maneuvers are pressing the very limits of what is physically possible, which has birthed the term we have now for this skiing life:

EXTREME.

And it is. Some things skiers do now seem nothing short of—and this is a former radical skier speaking—beyond imagination.

To say nothing of the moves that snowboarders—who we'll address later—have cooked up.

THE NEW CARRIERS OF THE TORCH

Take, for example, the current star in the star-studded firmament of extreme skiing, Shane McConkey, the son of Jim McConkey, who'd followed Dag in the invention of a new sport.

Shane, in this new Wild West, is the current poster boy.

Shane, as a child, was mesmerized watching the opening sequence of the James Bond film *The Spy Who Loved Me*, in which stuntman Rick Sylvester, doubling as Bond, and skiing down a mountainside, BASE-jumped from a cliff to escape his pursuers, popping a parachute after falling an eternity.

Shane knew, watching, *that* was what he wanted to do. BASE jump.

Shane, though, like most radical or extreme skiers, did not start his career jumping, but as a racer, at Squaw Valley, California, where his mother had moved him after she split with Shane's father. Shane raced. Over a dozen years of it, Shane training at Burke Mountain Academy in Vermont and entering FIS events, which he excelled at. He had aspirations of going to the Olympics, as a competitor for the U.S. Ski Team, but after years of successful racing, he switched to moguls, and from there took up freeride and skiercross, where as many as five skiers stand at the starting gate, all battling each other to the bottom.

Always, out of a field of stars, Shane rose to the top.

So, as had happened with Dag, and with Shane's father, Jim (who had made a name for himself as one of the original powder hounds at Alta—Jim's hotdog skiing with daffys, spread-eagles, mulekicks, helicopters, and flips, so inspiring locals that they named a run after him, McConkey's), ski companies and filmmakers also found Shane. And there started Shane's collaboration with Matchstick Productions—and Shane's pursuit of the "sickest" lines down impossible slopes, all to be caught on film.

Shane defines *sick* this way: "Sickest means the craziest, ballsiest, and fucking gnarliest so therefore the raddest." To which he adds, "The sickest skiers in the world are mostly dead now."

In a *Ski* magazine interview, when asked who was pushing the sport of skiing the hardest, Shane replied, "Me. 'Cuz I'm a cocky fucker." But he then amended that, saying, "No, actually, that's a hard one. There are a ton of people who are equally pushing it really hard in different ways."

Some names that come up in extreme, freeskiing circles are Rob Holmes, Jamie Pierre, Aaron McGovern, and Seth Morrison, all of them endorsing their sponsoring manufactures' "freeride" skis. All appear in ski flicks.

Leading the pack, though, Shane has formed the International Freeskiers Association, or the IFSA, which, he jokes, really stands for, I Fucking Ski Awesome.

And what is "awesome"? Most recently, Shane skied Bella Coola, in British Columbia, on a pair of Stinger water skis drilled for downhill bindings. Shane navigated the forty-five-degree top slope, and where it "got really steep," on the spine of the mountain, he threw the water skis sideways, making a two-thousand-foot slide, at the bottom of which, at nearly seventy miles per hour, he navigated a sharp right around a rock outcropping and hurled from the vertical face there, the *Bergschrund*.

Shane then plummeted down the rocky face before popping his parachute.

In making descents of this sort, Shane and his fellow extreme skiers have created a new sport, one called ski BASE jumping. (It is important to note here that ski BASE jumping is no longer considered a *stunt*, as when Rick Sylvester jumped for the Bond film.)

Again, one particularly daring individual crosses the line, does the next thing, which in this case was Frank "the Gambler" Gambalie, who had been a skydiver, and brought what he knew of that sport to skiing, parachute and all.

Shane met Frank in 1995, and was blown away by what Frank was doing, inspiring Shane to take up the sport himself.

(It is ironic that Gambalie met his end not in a BASE jump from El Capitan at Yosemite, but from drowning, when he tried to escape the park rangers who pursued him following his jump.)

Sometimes Shane embellishes his jumps, performing for the cameras a series of flips or layouts in the air.

Last May, Shane took on a pupil of sorts, J. T. Holmes, a twenty-three-year-old professional skier who had been following Shane's career, and the two and Matchstick Productions traveled to France, where Shane had scouted sites for even more radical ski BASE jumps.

J.T. suffered a severely bruised and twisted ankle on his first jump, but the two, Shane and J.T., continued on to their final destination anyway, the historic Eiger in Switzerland, a mountain that has claimed many lives through climbing accidents. Shane and J.T. had clear skies, and after a rough helicopter dismount, the two found themselves barely adhering to the side of the near-vertical Eiger.

J.T., even injured, skied the slope to the jump site, lofting a huge front flip off it, Shane right on his heels, throwing a double front flip.

Both, hanging from their parachutes, floated safely to the base of the mountain.

Shane, though, isn't just known to the latest crop of extreme skiers for his ski BASE jumps.

He is extreme all over. He has been known to appear on slopes buck naked, throwing a spread-eagle off some ramp and disappearing. In Matchstick Production's films, he's known, variously, as Cliff Huckstable, Pain McShlonkey, and the now-famous Saucerboy. This the outgrowth of a stunt suggested by MSP's director, who asked Shane to riff on a then new skiing craze, snowlerblades, Shane using a kid's saucer. The result has been an enduring character in MSP's films, one Shane re-creates, this slowlerblade-wearing, Jack Daniel's—drinking gufus. In a film on Shane titled, *There's Something About McConkey*, Shane is shown sucking a noodle into his nose until it comes out his mouth.

"Way cool" is the expression among this latest group of rap-rocking, nose and eyebrow (and nether parts) pierced, daring skiers.

And Shane isn't shy when it comes to après-ski party antics, giving a twist to an urban party trick called *shooting the boot*. At a ski resort though, a ski boot, not a street boot, is filled to the top with beer, the skier downing the volume of the boot in one long chug.

"I definitely have an issue with people being too serious," says McConkey. "I mean, look at the guys in the jib flicks making some face at the camera, trying to look tough."

McConkey, affiliated with Volant skis, has pushed the company's pure powder boards, sometimes called spatula skis, due to their extreme width and reverse camber (both ends are turned upward).

This a development only possible after the revolution in shaped skis.

Says McConkey, "I love it, because when I was preaching fat

skis to everyone back in the nineties, they were all laughing, being like, 'You guys are on glue, are you kidding me?' Then I'd head down the hill and leave them in the dust."

And what does McConkey think the next big thing will be?

"Something no one ever thought of," he says. "And I think that's totally cool. Because if you're not about the next thing and what's possible, about what you could be doing, then you're bored. And I don't like being bored."

If you enter into the subculture of extreme skiing, even to get your toes wet, you are rarely bored.

Seen from the lift, or the lodge, or even the parking lot of most resorts you will encounter, for the most part, weekend skiers, all in the latest ski clothing, this last winter orange and gray, and with the newest gear, say, Atomic Metron B5s or Völkl AC-4s, more ski than these skiers could ever use, but all headed for a specific portion of the mountain. At Park City, where I do rescue, during high season around Christmas and spring break, between seven and fifteen thousand skiers take to the slopes daily. Most, if not all, will find their comfort zone on the mountain if they don't know where it is already—on anything from First Time, just a stone's throw from the Mountain Patrol Base hut where we do assessments on injured skiers, to the Double Black Diamond chutes of Jupiter Bowl.

The weekend skier will, in the lodge, order a cocoa or coffee from a wild-haired kid behind the counter, the kid wearing a T-shirt that reads, you can see through the gap in his uniform, "*Corrosion of Conformity*" or "*Public Enemy.*"

The weekend skier will tip the waiter at the restaurant, will thank the woman ambassador at Deer Valley, never suspecting many of these characters are the Shane McConkeys of the mountain.

But simply call an independent professional instructor, or even take a ski lesson, and ask about adventures, and the whole varied skiing world will open to you, will take you on an adventure unlike any other.

But maybe even more important, a single day out, say, helicopter skiing, will introduce you to a group of people you will never forget. Who will connect you to the life of the resort, which is very *unlike* what you find in the parking lot, or the lodge restaurant.

Skiers thrive on diversity; they'll invite you in. Then they'll have you skiing down *I'm Out of My Mind* with them. And after, maybe shooting the boot at some shack of an apartment. But you won't care, because you will be so high from having survived *I'm Out of My Mind*. You'll take that boot and chug the beer right down, and later, if you're in no position to drive, those skiers will take you to your hotel room, leaving you with directions to your car.

Which you will find, right where you left it.

If you are up at Whistler, the skier who will drive you to your hotel will most likely be an Aussie. If you're at Park City, it will most likely be a Central or South American, slumming the winter away. If you're in Sun Valley, it could be anyone, even a star, as my girlfriend back then used to catch rides from Hailey to Sun Valley from Steve McQueen. Or you could catch a ride from a satellite, someone who falls temporarily into the extreme skiing subculture, as did my friend Jerry, who came to visit and stayed nearly two months, crashing on the floor of my Mint Bar apartment.

PARK CITY CHIC

At Park City, where I am on Mountain Patrol now, the entertainment business takes over the resort and town every year, roughly mid-January. Host to Robert Redford's Sundance Film Festival, Park City then crawls with stars, and those crawling the streets to sight stars.

In the space of a day, at the opening of the festival, the population of Park City multiplies tenfold, the klieg lights flashing on, stars such as Demi Moore and Ashton Kutcher, or the entire cast of *Entourage*, strolling the streets rubbing shoulders with directors such as Curtis Hanson, or Redford himself, or producers, like the Weinbergs of Miramax. (James Caan lives in Deer Valley, just up the road from Park City, Harrison Ford visits from his place in Jackson Hole.) In the mix, also, are identifiable writers like Charlie Kaufman or Alan Ball, and filmmakers who have scored a Sundance spot, yet to become identifiable.

Parked just off Munchkin Drive, in the Mountain Patrol lot, we patrollers come off shift, doff our red and black Mountain Hardwear for street clothes, and head out into the whirl of it.

My wife, who catches a ride up, meets me at the Java Cow, where we wait behind Laura Linney, me for the Mocha Moo, and my wife for her Extra-terrestial Tea.

The whole town is awash in buzz, gossip, insider sniping, and you can catch pieces of it here at the Java Cow, film biz functionaries and stars alike passing fifteen or twenty minutes until the Egyptian, just up the street, opens its doors to ticket holders. The Egyptian showing some indie flick, always indies here, Redford taking the podium at the front to address the accomplishments of the award-winning film. You settle into your lucky seat. When the film starts, big stars slip in the back, Faye Dunaway or Jack Nicholson or Annette Bening.

Before the film ends, these stars will again drift away, as if never having been there at all.

We see these stars on the mountain, too, of course. There is a Town Lift that runs from the heart of Park City to the top of Payday, where you can catch Bonanza up to Summit. When I am on patrol at Payday Lift during the festival, I end my days on the west side of town, on second sweep, models and stars doing interviews under reflective canopies to light their faces.

Models as tall and rangy as giraffes, like Kate Moss, or Claudia Schiffer, sit for interviews under the umbrellas, heaters glowing blue in the dusk, stars from television shows on the sidelines, waiting for their fifteen minutes.

There is a kind of peculiar ferocity to it all, which is entirely social and superficial, unlike the extreme skiing world.

Here, *everything* is appearance, and more than a few familiar faces, such as Ron Howard or M. Night Shyamalan, stride Main doing business, which amounts to *being seen*, a form of advertising for nominated features. Presence here is power. Traffic during the festival, as a result, is a continual snarl, Park City trolley cars navigating through walls of people, lines of cars cruising Main Street in both directions, Hummers and Rovers by the dozen, and women, à la Aspen, exiting them in overabundant fur, which still draws mixed reactions.

But there is no paint throwing here.

In the air, high over actors' heads, hang sound booms like enormous black carrots, actors and stars leading the holders of those booms like trained greyhounds—or, is it the holders of the booms leading the actors and actresses? There's a feeling of feeding frenzy, thousands of the guests of PCMR skiing days and spending nights viewing Sundance premieres, such as the wildly successful *Sideways*. Paul Giamatti, who played Miles in *Sideways*, wanders Main Street, his hands in the pockets of his navy-blue pea coat, taking in the local architecture.

Since many ski resorts in the Rockies have been built up around former ranch or mining towns, Aspen, Telluride, Park City, Alta, and Sun Valley all being stellar examples, the old town areas are small, and of a human scale, the buildings charming red brick, some with facades sporting dates, most from the 1880s to the turn of the century. Since, initially, ski resorts were *not* the mega-businesses that they are today, the original buildings were renovated wherever possible, the buildings undergoing for the most part cosmetic improvement, this earlier money-saving tactic preserving a great many lovely Victorians, these tiny resort towns in that way keeping their charm.

Sprawl, really, is the new development in resort towns, and sprawl has become rampant, some of it fueled by the new resort ethos. Since the late 1970s, when the owners of the resorts discovered their "numbers" had gone flat (a fixed number of skiers were taking to the mountain while operating costs were escalating), the resorts have radically expanded, developing the concept of the "four-season destination," which by default now includes golf, tennis, swimming, and ice skating year-round, and in certain areas, mountain biking, kayaking, river rafting, mountaineering, and even spelunking. World-class resorts, such as Aspen, Sun Valley, Park City, and Vail, cater to an endless round of conventions for upscale occupations, such as law or medicine. Think-tank focus groups for the environment, peace in the Middle East, or alternative fuels also commonly meet here, scientists, surgeons, and political pundits wandering the streets of Ketchum, or Telluride, or Breckenridge.

(Sun Valley, when I was teaching there, hosted an all–African American convention called, appropriately enough, Black America.

They were the wildest group we had that winter, the town coming alive with an infectious soul. It was nothing short of extraordinary.)

The truth is, those of us who lived year-round in towns such as Ketchum, Idaho, in the past, had the so-called off-season to ourselves, a good six months of the year. In Sun Valley, we really looked forward to the quiet, the nearly empty streets, the untrammeled mountains to the north, but all that is a thing of the past now. Whereas, before, you had to be fairly off on the fringe to live year-round in a place like Ketchum, or wealthy, or connected to the ranching or mining community, now, with the popularization of so-called extreme adventures in the media, a broader range of people find themselves out in the wild in warmer weather.

And it is these same people who have begun using their cell phones when encountering trouble in the wild, most of it the result of ill-preparedness and simple ignorance. (Cell phones give city folks the false impression that "out there" isn't really out there at all. These people should know that if they call in the rescue teams, they will be the ones paying for it: $15,000 to $30,000 being the norm for a Park Service search and rescue.)

Snow, for example, is possible at elevations over seven thousand feet anytime after September 1. Rain, at high altitudes, can knock down the temperature from eighty degrees to forty in a matter of minutes. And furthermore, that rain will soak your clothing and chill you, and will, at higher altitudes, more readily evaporate, accelerating the possible process of mild hypothermia. Experienced hikers will always have with them a breathable, waterproof shirt or jacket, or, if not that, an even simpler, cheaper solution, a large garbage bag, which can be pulled over the hiker's body in a rainstorm, making of the rain a pleasure. Summers in resort towns are pure magic.

In fact, a fair number of people only visit the resorts May to August.

Summers, in Sun Valley, when I worked Mountain Operations, for example, we had a variety of people, skiers and nonskiers alike, on our crew.

There was Tucker, a polite Tennessee kid with a drawl, Tuck just accepted into medical school and bumming for the summer where his father had skied in his youth. There was a contingent of New Yorkers, like crazy, charming, and excitable Adam Finklestein and his buddy Augie Baleowski. We had a redneck Texan, who just went by Tex, a guy so cross and ill-tempered that just to look at him was to threaten a fistfight.

And we had the older ski instructors, Austrians and Germans and Swiss, the Europeans, such as Rimon Wurtsrheiner, who became a fast friend, lending me at one time twenty or so classical albums—Beethoven, Chopin, Mozart, Liszt.

It was a Rolling Stones kind of atmosphere at most times, though, so it was good to find Rimon in it, Rimon taking a vacation from his usual summer work in Chile, where he would, again, teach ski lessons. (Rimon was fifty-seven that summer, thirty-five years older than me, still absolutely but quietly alive, and open to things, an inspiration. One day, I got up the courage to ask him if he still liked skiing. "Achhh," he said. "I love it even more now than I ever did." Rimon's father had resisted the Nazi annexation of Austria in the late thirties, and had been executed, Rimon and his mother fleeing the country—how, he never told me.)

All of us, on that mountain crew, were there for the adventure. Raw, hard work, the temperature nearly a hundred by noon, and dry. We built two new runs, Holding On, after Earl Holding, the new owner, and Hemingway, both on the north side of Baldy. We had nearly yard-long chain saws, and an old cable-operated Bucyrus Erie tractor and a smaller Muskeg for skidders. We cut the brush, and then in ankle-deep dust, felled trees so immensely heavy that we used forty-pound forged iron pry bars, ten feet in length, to lift those trees from the ground to get choker cables under and around them. Vinny, the son of the head of Mountain Operations, ran the tractor, Vinny spitting out mouthfuls of "chaw" as he did it, Vinny always in a rush, pushing the operation, so that, as I'd seen elsewhere, you would barely get a cable under a log and around it, and the plug fixed into the drag cable, before Vinny would be off. Realize that this was done on twenty-five- to forty-degree slopes. Or steeper. Sometimes the logs would threaten to roll. And if your hand was still between a log and a choker cable when it tightened?

When I worked for the U.S. Forest Service, surveying logging roads and running centerline, missing fingers were common with coworkers who ran choke cable.

In that furnace heat and dust, and roaring noise of those chain saws, we worked ten-hour days, without so much as a first-aid kit, something we discovered when one of those logs *did* roll, pinning a sixteen-year-old boy's leg under it. A large log would weigh a ton or more, and we had a few minutes of supreme terror, as the log threatened to roll farther, over the boy's chest and head.

It took the lot of us, ten, by that time, mountain-hardened hard hats to get that log off the boy (again, he was on the mountain because he was the son of one of the managers and needed a summer job), and when we did, we were relieved to find the log had not broken any bones, due to the fact that the terrible dust we were working in, the sometimes nearly foot-thick debris from cutting the scrub, had risen up over the leg, cushioning it.

But he'd been cut, and was bleeding, and it was then we discovered we did not so much as have a box of Band-Aids with us.

Nothing. So we bound the boy's leg in our neckerchiefs—we were all wearing them against not so much the dust, but the particulate matter the chain saws threw, piles of yellow, resinous chaw—and sent him down the mountain in the Muskeg.

He was back the following day. Only fourteen stitches, he told us, grinning.

One afternoon, when a cloud bank rolled in threatening lightning, Augie and Adam got into a pissing contest over whether we should knock off work. Adam had been studying meteorology, or wanted us to think that, and after some arcane explanation as to why this cloud bank would not discharge a bolt of lightning, we got out of our crew cabs, now on the north peak of Baldy, and began to set ourselves to the job of the day, putting in new post for an avalanche fence.

We got out our pry bars, as I noted earlier, a good forty pounds of forged iron, ten feet long, and had at it. Now someone would haul up a compressor and a jackhammer, but we were breaking through solid rock with those pry bars, had been at it five or ten minutes, when a deafening blast hit us.

I leaped a good fifteen feet toward our truck, out of pure reaction, the doors both hanging open and my leap so energetic that I went through the driver's door, flew across the seat and out the passenger door, to hit the mountain again, where I rolled to my feet, all ten of us there looking at each other.

We scrambled into our trucks, yard-wide bolts of lightning coming down around us in a spectacular and lethal light show.

I told Adam he was full of shit, his meteorology worse than misguided.

Adam only grinned. "Some people'll believe anything," he said.

Later that month, we had the ignoble job of reopening the slope on which Bill Janss's wife had been killed.

We put down seed for ground cover, which would mitigate, when the brush had grown up, the propensity for that slope to avalanche.

We spread hundreds of bales of straw over the seed and watered it.

The straw chaff pierced even my Mule leather gloves, leaving my hands bleeding and swollen. Daily, I came off the mountain so dusty that when I took off the neckerchief from around my mouth and nose, it produced a reverse raccoon effect, and like that, dehydrated from working ten hours in that heat and near-zero humidity, we clocked out and headed over to J.T. Haney's, a beer joint not much more than a shack, J.T. an immense Irish bear of a man, perhaps six five, and three hundred pounds. He catered to the roughnecks who worked the mountain, grabbing, now and then, one who'd gotten into a fight by the back of his shirt and hurling him out the front door into the yard, which was as much packed dirt as it was grass.

There was a sign you could turn over, inside the door. On one side it read, "*Glad We're Closed.*" On the other, "*Sorry We're Open.*"

Oftentimes we didn't bother staying inside and sat Indian style in the dirt yard, Baldy looming over us, playing backgammon, which was popular then, Little Feat, the Ramones, Dire Straits, or the Stones blasting from J.T.'s sound system.

A thirty-two-ounce schooner of beer was ninety cents, the schooner chilled in an enormous freezer, so that when the beer was poured into it, a rime of frozen beer formed on the inner wall of the glass. The schooner was J.T.-sized, the beer strong.

Anyone under two hundred pounds, having worked on the mountain those ten hours, and having eaten the equivalent of a baloney
or peanut butter sandwich for lunch, and having brought too little
water for the day, as we all did, was knocked blissfully senseless
by the first schooner. The second was just collateral damage.

Adam, the smallest, was always the first to pass out on the
grass.

Tuck, the doctor to be, would tenderly turn Adam on his side,
Tex, helping him, Tex actually a gem of a guy when he had two or
three schooners in him.

The two talked in that way of southerners, as if with their
mouths full of marbles.

"I think this here old boy aughta be set sideways so if he don't
take kindly to his drink he don't suffocate on that unkindliness,"
Tuck would say (joking, of course).

"This boy ain't goin' nowheres," Tex would say, and they'd set
Adam on his side.

Somewhere in the middle of the games of backgammon, as
portions of our wages on Fridays made the circuit of winners,
Adam would leap up, oddly bright-eyed and manic.

"Woah!" he'd say. "I needed that!"

We'd wander off to have dinner, as on one evening, when we
all forgot we'd signed on to work the following morning, Saturday, and started our evening at the then upscale Silver Creek restaurant.

We'd gotten so lubricated on J.T.'s beer, we'd forgotten ourselves, and thanks to Tuck, our patrician pal, we were informed
that we were incommoding a sleek-looking couple at an adjoin-
ing table. Adam protested. It was payday, dammit, and we were
having steak. And whiskey. (And, for Adam, his usual after-work
cannabis, his, as he called it, date with his Green-Eyed Girl.)

"Don't complain," Adam shouted over to the couple. "Join the party. It's on us."

To our amazement, Walter and his much younger wife, Lisa, joined us. Walter was an investment banker. He thought the banks were going to collapse and was looking for land to buy, where he could ride out the coming depression.

"Depression?!" Adam shouted. "Get high with us!"

Walter, in his fatal forties, blond, thinning corn-silk hair, and overserious, just then got a smile on his face. He was a bit like Jack Nicholson in *Easy Rider*. Here was this guy who'd built into his life every possible security, had bagged the trophy wife (no doubt there was an unhappy first wife out there somewhere who'd paid part of the price tag on that deal), and he was not enjoying one minute of it.

He was like a study in ticks, this fear of losing it all having overcome him, and his wife terrified, too, watching what she'd earned, in bagging this catch, just disappear in paranoia.

We left the Silver Creek in a spirit of ebullient camaraderie. Walter and Lisa sat in the bed of Tex's '49 Ford with us.

Tuck led the way in his Mercedes 220 SE. We drove to some hot pots, and Walter was, as you might expect, squeamish about disrobing, though Lisa did so with such stylish aplomb that you couldn't not watch her.

She was a redhead, and sat upright in the hot pots, instead of reclining, rightfully proud of her figure, which was a wonder and an irritating distraction, and we sang silly tunes, "Up Against the Wall You Redneck Mother," "Take This Job and Shove It," and "Your Cheatin' Heart," all with hilarity and true imbecility.

I think Walter smiled, truly smiled, for the first time in months. Enjoyed himself, some future he might want to live suddenly a possibility. We all had that. Tuck was off to medical school at the University of Virginia in September, I was headed back to microbiology at MSU. Tex was going to run his father's pavement business in El Paso. Adam and Augie were headed back to NYU.

We all had lives waiting for us elsewhere, which made it possible for us to live just then in a way we couldn't have otherwise.

Hope is the thing with feathers. Our futures were colorful, yet-to-be materialized dazzling birds.

And where was Rimon in all this? Rimon had shared a schooner with us, and had, as was always his way, gracefully retired for the evening.

When I got back to my room, I flopped spread-eagled down on my white bedspread. I know this because, when my crew chief, Wally, pounded on my door the following morning, waking me, as he did the others, I took a photo of the bed before I went out the door.

I'd left a negative of sorts, a mountain dirt body on the spread. I had forty minutes to meet Wally in the parking lot.

I ate breakfast with my then girlfriend, Carol, who'd gotten Jesus of late. She thought I needed saving.

So we were talking holiness and virtue and the will of God there at the table, and I was trying not to be sick. I excused myself, and was sick under a pine tree in front of the Challenger, and we resumed our breakfast, Carol asking me if I'd really think about all that, which, I told her I would, and got to the parking lot.

Running my chain saw on the mountain, the saw puking out clouds of oily smoke and resinous pine dust glistening with pitch, I reached for the next cut, and not paying attention, not applying sufficient pressure, the big saw skipped, throwing the cutting bar nearly into my head, the bar coming down on my leather chaps and tearing through them into my thigh.

My crew chief, Wally—imperturbable, Buddha-like Wally—was standing just off to my right.

The engine on the big saw had stalled when the teeth on the bar'd bitten into my chaps.

Wally hit the kill switch, then helped me pry the teeth of the saw out of the chaps and my jeans.

I had a hell of a welt there, but the skin was barely bleeding.

"I don't have to tell you what I think about your performance on the mountain this morning, do I?" he said, in that sometimes maddeningly flat voice of his.

I didn't need to say no.

Of course, he didn't; and it went without saying that Wally had been right where I was that morning too many times himself.

It didn't happen again; not for any us who survived that interminable day.

Though, God knew, we all had our excuses. Tuck had worked very hard and tirelessly to get into medical school. Adam, whose father was a rabbi, had bucked some very serious home pressures to be able to come west, and Augie and Tex were guys just taking a vacation from the lives that were waiting elsewhere for them—for Augie, managing his father's properties on the Lower East Side, for Tex, running uncountable, hot miles of Tarvia, cement, and asphalt.

Some of us had even yet more reason to let loose.

I had lived part of the year prior to my bailing out of my premedical studies with the knowledge that I possibly had one of two terminal illnesses, a diagnosis that turned out to be incorrect (almost criminally so).

I had become so exhausted, though, by the disease I *did* have, that I nearly died completing my YMCA scuba certification, something I'd decided I wanted to do, regardless of how I felt at the time.

When I was told that not only would I recover, entirely, and fully, but that the disease had in no way damaged me, that my family doctor's diagnosis had been wrong-headed, to the point of medical incompetence, I threw out my old life. I hadn't breathed so freely ever, as I did walking from my new doctor's office. Anything was possible; how could I go back to school and spend time in those goddamn labs? So I got a job with the U.S. Forest Service, surveying logging roads, where I hiked miles into wilderness daily; I broke things off with my then girlfriend, whom my Rocky Mountain racer friends had dubbed the Drape, for the way she hung all over me, not letting go. Had been pressing for marriage, which I was in no way ready for.

How could I *not* go crazy?

But all that is another story.

Sun Valley was my vacation from life, but as anyone knows, life always comes crawling back in. And in the strangest ways. I was rawboned, blond hair to my shoulders, wild. A woman who ran the winter program, a lovely woman, surprised me by asking if I'd work as an ambassador for the company. I had the look they wanted, if I'd clean it up a bit.

It was, in some ways, the offer of a lifetime. Of a life, really. And, I admit, I was flattered. Me? An ambassador? One of those kind of Stein Eriksen-looking guys skiing cool and fit? This amused me.

But I'd promised myself I'd finish the microbiology degree.

I'd been in the Wood River Valley well over a year. I had friends there, was connected to this very rich, in some ways unbelievably so, culture. I'd started racing again, and was having some success with it. Was teaching part-time, and was summers on Mountain Operations. But here was access to a *real life* in the company, and not just as a satellite (as so many of us were, and still are).

Here was a chance to be an *insider*.

Ski resort towns, for the satellites, are intense and wonderful, but they can be, after a time, also awful places. Over time truly bad things happened to people who were on the periphery, as happened with my friend Joe.

Late my last spring living in the Valley, Joe was kicked out of his dorm for running a gas stove in his room. Joe was a philosophical sort who had already passed through the craziness of his early twenties, and when I ran into him, it was often in the parking lot where he'd be frying trout he'd caught fly fishing in Silver Creek.

He always said a prayer, and ate with a certain quiet satisfaction. He was an Italian, from Massachusetts, had dreams of some quiet ranch, some place where he could just work and be outside. It amused me that a mule always fit into Joe's dream. Joe loved the mountains, hated the pretension of the resort life.

That night he was kicked out of the dorm—heartlessly, I thought, for where was he supposed to stay, after all?—I took him with me to a friend's. Greg was staying with two girls he'd worked with at Slavey's, a grill and bar.

When it got late, the five of us talking about movies—Greg and the girls had been extras in the film about a racer fallen on hard times, *Swan Song*, which had just been made on Baldy—and it was time to call it a night, I insisted that Joe crash on the floor of my dormitory room.

Joe refused. He'd been kicked out of his room by Ron Prohaska, who managed the dorms, was furious with him, and Joe, now, wouldn't set foot in my room. He was too proud to do it.

So, in the kitchen, I asked Ashley and Jill if Joe could spend the night on their living-room floor, where my friend Greg was sleeping.

The girls, both trust-fund kids who hadn't lifted a finger to buy the condo they were living in, refused.

Joe had body odor, they said.

It was true. But it wasn't that he was dirty. Joe was of that granola group back then who thought deodorants were unnatural. He washed his hair with Ivory soap, smelled of sage and pine smoke. And yes, BO.

The girls wouldn't have it, and they wouldn't tell Joe, either. They left that job for me to do.

Someone else would do the dirty work. Someone else would buy the house, pay the bills, clean up the messes. They (and they were *not* the beauties they pretended to be) would paint their faces, dream of being movie stars, and, in the meantime, find people to carry their burdens for them.

It put me in a furious frame of mind. Joe would not take my room, and the girls would not let him—just for six or eight hours—occupy eight square feet of their living-room carpet with Greg.

Joe, when I told him he could not stay in the condo, simply said, Sure.

We went outside. It was April, and snowing something fierce. An absolute whiteout.

Take me out to the canyons, he said, and I refused. Again I insisted he stay in my dorm, sleep there for the night. Ron would never know. But it wasn't about Ron, it was the principle of the thing, he told me.

I understood that.

So, up the canyon we went in my car. Where the road became so snow-covered that I could go no farther, I turned around, and one last time, and angrily now, told Joe he should, if not stay in my room, then use my down sleeping bag, just sleep on the front seat of my car, and we'd figure something out in the morning.

Joe refused. And like that, he got out of the car, in his parka, shouldered his pack, in it his stove and some gas, his tent, a Eureka Timberline, and a few odds and ends. He slung his rifle over his shoulder, a 30-06.

I remember him waving to me, though with his back turned, just lifting his hand, and into that heavy snow he disappeared.

He'd show up in a day or two, I told myself.

●

When the mountain closed, just a day later, and we had some interim time before construction on Baldy started, Greg, another friend, Russ, and I, left Sun Valley for what was to be a three-week trip down to Mexico.

We left in Greg's Vega, a stereo he'd stolen, as someone had stolen his, crammed into the hole in his dashboard with a shoe.

That was April 5. I didn't return from Mexico until the end of June.

My car, when I found it where'd I'd left it, was sitting on three flat tires. I got them inflated, and the thing started without hesitation (Slant 6, best engine Chrysler ever built; a dog, yes, but you couldn't kill it). I got out on the highway to Hailey, was driving with the radio on, when I heard a news report that the body of a young man had been found up a canyon by hikers. A chill ran through me.

I'd just gotten into town, so it seemed too much of a coincidence to be possible, my returning and just switching on the radio like that. The young man had no identification on him, and the police wanted anyone who thought they might know him to come in. I went to the police station and filled out a form on how I had come to drop Joe off up the canyon in April.

I was left to sit in the police ready room for nearly an hour.

When I was ushered into the morgue, I knew in a second, by the leather watch band, hand tooled, the funky knit Rasta cap.

It was Joe, all right.

From what the forensic pathologist could put together, Joe had lasted a couple months, and then, in a fit of despair, emaciated from living on nearly nothing, and rather than hiking back into town and dealing with the world he could no longer tolerate, he had put the barrel of his rifle in his mouth and blown out the back of his head.

Joe, who would offer what trout he had frying over his one burner stove to whoever (such as myself) passed by.

Joe, who'd loved the quiet, and mountain streams, and remote, snowcapped peaks of the Sawtooths.

Working for the company that summer, taking in Wally, my crew chief, who was a fair and reasonable man, but blank-eyed and through with all our youthful foolishness, this watchful tolerance in his every gesture, I decided *not* to take the job as ambassador for the company.

Becoming Wally, I realized, was my future there.

Or worse, this guy, "Rocky K2." Balding, his remaining straw-blond hair hanging to his shoulders, he was the object of much derision. He wore K2 racing gear and factory-promo racing suits, all, by then, ten years out of date and worn ragged. I don't recall his real name. After all, resort towns are full of Rocky K2s. Posers. Only, it was obvious Rocky'd been one hell of a skier, a phenomenon, until some crippling fall had brought him down. On the hill, or in the lift line, always, in Rocky K2s eyes this ultra-serious but faraway look, as if he were standing on some winners' podium, or skiing a great and prestigious race.

Which made us laugh. We thought he was a goofus, a moron, a clown, Rocky K2 and his secondhand-store castoffs.

And then we found out that Rocky K2 had been a top-ranked U.S. Ski Team competitor—an Olympic hopeful. Sponsored by K2. We didn't laugh at him after that.

When people who didn't know him got on his case, we always told them, "Leave him be. Don't ask."

Poor as he was, we sent food out to him when he sat on the deck of Elevation 9,000 or Warm Springs on sunny afternoons, which he accepted with a certain amusing magnanimity, given the star he was.

(A caution to us all.)

Then, one of our summer crew, Troy, was killed by a drunk driver.

A man who ran a mountaineering shop, and from whom I'd bought a pair of glacier glasses, went parachuting with friends. His chute did not open; he screamed all the way down, my friends told me.

I promised myself, leaving Sun Valley, that I would return, but when I did, I would stand at some distance from the craziness, be enlivened by it, but not subsumed in it. Maybe like my friend Rimon.

You can only live the way we had a short while, and when you are truly young. It was a glorious, decadent, and magnificent step out of the sometimes heaviness of the world. We'd been plugged into some Dionysian, 220-volt current, and run with it.

But the need for some balance reasserts itself.

You need quiet, as Joe had. You need to be of some use, and not just to yourself. You need to move forward, not backward.

The mountains that you love, and the life that you love, you need to give back to, or something terrible happens to you.

You become unreal. Some caricature of a person, such as Rocky K2, and all that *had* given you life becomes so much dust.

That is the dark side of the resort life, of the extreme life. The caricatures of people who live too long on the edge.

It is as if they've forgotten it isn't about the simple thrill, the adrenaline rush, the Wow! experience. Neurophysiologists want to reduce extreme sports to that. This chemical rush one inhabits in it. But they're wrong in thinking so, because core to the experience is gaining *a sense of mastery*. If even for a moment.

That March in Sun Valley, a friend of mine came down from Canada. Tom was a Canadian National Team champion, and we competed on the downhill run, on Greyhawk. Before Sun Valley, in Bozeman, Tom had always beaten me.

But that Saturday in March was different. It was the light, that high desert light. It was the snow. It was the magic of Bald Mountain, of Sun Valley. And it was the magic of my Rossignols.

That afternoon, the line I took down the course was nearly flawless. I'd never been in finer shape.

I bettered Tom in both runs by a wide margin, Tom furious with himself, so much so that, later, free skiing, when he, again, challenged me, though this time off the course, I let my skis fly, really, irresponsibly, skiing sixty, seventy miles per hour down Warm Springs, flashing by slow-skiing guests as if they were gates.

Tom was to my right, a mere twenty-five or so feet behind me, all the way to the bottom, where Tom, trying in those last few seconds to pass me, nearly took out a number of guests—we both nearly did.

Still, I'd beaten him, again. By, perhaps, thirty feet, on a run a mile and a half long.

I was exhilarated, thrilled. And I'd reached the end of something, some silly, self-deluded dream.

Tom could ski like this on his worst day. I'd started too late, had some bad habits, very difficult if not impossible to correct, had not gotten focused on the right things early on, and had spent those years I could have been navigating gates jumping, which I wouldn't have missed for the world.

It was a beautiful day, and I was thrilled, almost beside myself—but there was a sadness in it, too.

I'd won the race, but the truth of things was looking me in the face.

If I put my entire life, I thought, my every waking moment, into racing, I could, maybe, ski as well as my friend Tom did now. By nature. It was in his every cell, skiing the way he did.

I could win any number of silly, privately sponsored events, could possibly even be a competitor in FIS tournaments.

But I didn't want it badly enough (you have to literally breathe skiing to win in international circles).

What I was, was an *amateur*—a very experienced one, one who loved the sport, had lived it, been a competitor in it, had even gotten, however briefly, into the winner's circle jumping.

But beating Tom, just then, was as good as it was going to get. Racing downhill, anyway.

As a racer, I would always be just a satellite. At best on the edge, trying to work my way in.

But as a skier? There was a whole world out there to explore.

I could still scare the living bejesus out of myself, challenge myself skiing runs like Corbet's Couloir, or the ridges in Bozeman; there were helicopter skiing, and new and beautiful resorts to explore, and my powder technique to improve.

And you never exhaust a mountain like Baldy, anyway.

I bought beers, and we drank them outside on the deck with the other skiers, in the pine-smelling air, Baldy stretching miles away from us to the summit, that spring sun warming our faces.

That had been the moment I'd let go of that life, and all those adventures that came after, that spring, and that summer, were gravy, and were also a warning, and a caution.

What Hemingway said of his years in Paris turned out to be true of skiing also: it *is* a movable feast.

That's what I discovered in Sun Valley, and what allowed me to let go.

There is always more to any mountain. For any skier, from the rank beginner to Bode Miller or Hermann Maier. There are runs you can ski better, more gracefully. There are tantalizing moments when the mountain is yours and you can fly on it, and an hour later, thinking, Now you own it, the mountain will, again, surprise you, sending you flying in one direction and your equipment in another.

Skiing (and now riding, too) is about the whole package. The smell of the snow, the variety of it, corn snow, hardpack, boilerplate, powder, cold smoke, sugar snow, cement, death cookies, slab, corduroy, mush, and ice. It's about the feel of the mountains, the space, the fresh air, the sage, the pine, the fir, and if you are in the East, or the Midwest, the oaks, maple, birch, alder, tamarack.

But, having said all that, it is so very much about the people. There is this enormous range of people brought to any mountain, thrilled to be there, from guests flying in from Florida to those who have been living and teaching and working on the mountain whole lifetimes. People like Dag, the father of extreme skiing, who still run an hour a day, competing, now, once a year at Sun Peaks, who told me, when he was going to die he'd ski into the mountains, sit down on a rock, and say, "Thanks for the ride." There are movie stars, and racers, international and domestic, and wannabe racers, and people up from the South, who don't know how to ski, and don't want to learn, but want to be part of the mountain life. There are totally out there types like Shane McConkey, and grandmothers, and grandkids.

Millionaires like Earl Holding and the Duponts. Presidents like Gerald Ford or Jack Kennedy.

Arab Emirs and sheiks.

There are the biographers of the life, like Warren Miller, who, in Sun Valley, lived winters he was first there in the back of a panel van, Miller so in love with the place and skiing that he became the preeminent film biographer of the Extreme Skiing Life.

Were you to ask him if he was poor back then, he would laugh. He has said as much in interviews.

We all would.

Because if there is anything that joins all these people, the stars and instructors and racers and ski patrollers and moms and dads and kids, and those in orbit around the winter mountain sports scene and those in the red-hot center, it's this:

Life. This big, open, daring as you can make it life. Pine-scented and lived-on mountains so lovely there's something holy about them.

Something that makes us, if even for the short space of a run, truly *live*.

MOUNTAIN PATROL

A DAY IN THE LIFE . . .

A HEAD CASE

"I will *not* get in a toboggan," the man tells me.

Sixtysomething, dark, and tall, he stands in a circle of blood fifteen feet in diameter. Scalp wound.

Blood on snow is a brilliant crimson, and this guest of Park City Mountain Resort has lost a fair amount of it. (But how much *exactly?* A quarter of a pint will color a large area of snow, will look like this, alarming.)

This man's blood loss puts a sharp edge on my call. Every second now balloons as I catalog assessments, making decisions.

"Can you or can you not *stop the bleeding?*" the man demands, glaring.

This I consider the good, long space of a second.

I have already gone through my approach protocol. I surveyed the scene for safety and jammed my skis into the hardpack in the classical X, warning other skiers to steer clear. Looked for a mechanism of injury, and in this case, it obviously was a hard fall, the man's snowboard a few yards from where he stands now, where he removed it. I offered my aid, in the form specific—*My name is, I'm with the Park City Mountain Patrol. Can I help you?*—thus putting the Good Samaritan law into effect, and moved in, a friendly expression on my face.

But now I see I've got something unusual here: this is no anterior cruciate ligament call, not a simple silver-fork fracture of ulna and radius, both simple joint immobilizations and transports.

I've got a mess here, though not an unusual one for a snowboarder: for every head injury with skiers, there are five for riders. (Likewise, for every lower-leg fracture with riders, there are roughly five for skiers—this due to the ergonomics of the boots each group wears: hard shell and high for skiers, soft, pliable for riders.)

"Sir," I say. "It would help if you could sit down."

This he does not do, but I take his stubborn immobility for the opportunity it is.

While he looms over me, I glove up and check his vitals.

ABCs okay, for now—which is always a relief. Airway (he's certainly got that); breathing (sure, he's agitated, but I observe him for fifteen seconds, make pretenses of examining the cut he has over his left temple, while counting his breaths; seven in a space of fifteen seconds; not good; he's either hyperventilating from stress, or he's compensating for developing shock from the blood loss; probably both). Circulation? He's got good perfusion, his face still ruddy.

I lift a strand of hair from his forehead, as if taking in the extent of the cut on his scalp, and while doing that, I check his pupils, which should be equal and round, regular in size, and react to light (PEARRL). His pupils, I can see, are the same size. I move my hand over his face, his pupils widening, again, equally.

"Sir," I repeat, "if you could sit down, *please*." I tell him what I'm supposed to tell him next, that his sitting down would really facilitate our getting his bleeding stopped.

"I *can't* sit down," he tells me. "I've had knee operations."

Can't or won't? What I've got here, it occurs to me, is a former skier taking runs as a snowboarder due to his knees.

(Crossover riders are everywhere now, and are usually middle-aged, as is this injured guest.)

"Sir, if you could—" I begin yet again, and he launches into what is evidently Spanish invective.

"And I'm *not* getting in any fucking toboggan," he says again. "My son's going to be down here in a few minutes and he's an EMT. So stop the bleeding on my head."

Son. Terrific, I think. We can get into a three-way argument, his son throwing in his opinion. But that doesn't matter.

I hate to do it, but I'm calling this one in. It's going to be ugly, I just know it.

"Sir, were you unconscious at any time after you fell?" I ask him. "Do you remember if you—"

"I'm *fine*," he tells me. "I just need help with my head. It's just a superficial cut."

"Sir," I say in a yet more forceful tone. "If you could, *please sit.*"

"I'm *not* fucking sitting! You—" And there is more of that no-need-to-translate Spanish. "And I already told you, I had surgeries on my knees and I *cannot* sit down and I *won't*."

It occurs to me that I truly hate head injuries. Just about half of our head-injured guests become combative. It's part of the whole compensation picture. *Pull the plug on it*, I think. No response, period, no matter what he says.

"Just bandage my head, and I'll go," he tells me.

I smile and tell him that is exactly what I'm going to do, but he'll have to sign release forms.

"Release forms?" he says, staring. "I'm not signing anything!"

We're way over the protocol line here, the guest non compos mentis, and I have to do something to tip the whole situation in my favor. But I don't want to further agitate him. I reach for my radio, prepare to thumb the call button, but the guest lashes out.

"I told you, *'No fucking toboggan!'*"

"I'm *not* bringing in a toboggan," I lie. And I don't. I make what would appear to be a routine update. "Twelve twenty-eight to Summit Patrol."

"Summit Patrol," the radio barks back.

"Got a ten forty-five here on Homerun. O_2 and board. AirMed."

"Ten four."

"Twelve twenty eight clear."

"What was *that?!*" the guest wants to know.

"Just letting my superiors know what I'm doing," I tell him, "which is bandaging your head."

"All right," he says.

I have called in patrollers, oxygen, a backboard, a toboggan and a helicopter. I've thrown the red flag—we've got serious work to do here, and we're going to do it *fast*. We're flying this guy out, whether he likes it or not.

Which he doesn't. Not any of what we're doing. When I begin the task of attending to the cut on his scalp, he curses me again.

I press a blood stopper to his cut, and he is agitated to a point where I am almost certain he will try to hit me.

I am prepared to knock him down, if it comes to that.

I glance at my watch. All of three minutes have passed since I kicked off my skis, but it seems an eternity.

I have to reach up to get to this guy's head, he's got to be six two at least. Direct pressure is the best method for stopping superficial bleeding, but this guy winces when I do that. Jerks his head away. More evidence he's really hurt.

A rider in a red one-piece swoops down from above, and I can see he's aiming himself right at us.

I am, in this moment, outnumbered. The son, in his late twenties, and another crossover rider, snaps out of his board, leaving it where my skis are.

"Dad," he calls.

My guest turns. He's got this winning look on his face. But the look his son gives him is not a happy one.

"You do EMT work?" I ask.

"East L.A.," he says, coming in closer. He's seen the blood, knows what this is all about.

"I'm *not* sitting down, and I am *NOT* getting in a toboggan," the guest tells his son.

This, too, is typical. Head injured—brain traumatized—skiers repeat themselves. Endlessly. They might ask you what day it is, or where they are, or how they came to be lying on their backs in the snow ten or even fifteen times. This is not an exaggeration. And it is a sure sign of trauma.

This the guest's son knows, and when he glances at me and nods, I feel a wash of relief. We're on the same team here.

"I think he's a little disoriented," I say.

The guest glares. "I am *not* disoriented!"

"We're gonna get you some help, Dad," the son says.

"Look," the guest says, turning to his son. "I'm fine. He gets this done, we'll head down. We still have the whole day."

"Yeah," his son says. Yeah, and I'm Che Guevara.

Now, out of the trees, on the mountain above us, come Moose and Walt, Moose on his board with a fully loaded toboggan behind him.

The guest sees them and spins around to take a swing at me, which I duck, knocking his arm up over his head, his son catching him in a bum's rush behind the knees, something I can see he's done before. Not even a linebacker can overcome a bum's rush—

cops and criminals alike use it. Once your legs are shot nearly double at the knees, from behind, you can't right yourself. The son catches him, though, which is important here. (And it is *very* important that *the guest's son* initiated the bum's rush. Standard rescue procedure would have mandated getting the guest in a cervical collar and on a backboard while he was standing, something that, given the guest's combativeness, would have been impossible, or at best extremely difficult. Still, I would have had to do it. We all would have.)

But our injured rider, even taken down by his son, is not nearly finished. He rolls onto his knees and lunges up, right into Walt, who catches him in a kind of bear hug, in that big, jovial voice of his, Walt saying, "Hell-oh," Walt then easing him to the snow again, even as the guest is swinging at us.

"Goddamn you sons of bitches, I'mina sue you within an inch of your fuckin' worthless lives!" he shouts at the top of his lungs, guests stopping now to watch, taking in the free theater.

Moose runs them off. "Hey, no need to be here. It's all under control." It's an ugly scene, the guy screaming threats in English and Spanish.

We get the cervical collar on him, then logroll him onto the backboard, and strap him down (always in the same order: nipples, nuts, knees, and feet).

I get the re-breather mask on him and the O$_2$ running. Somehow, he frees one of his hands and tears off the mask.

Walt's got this unflappable, affable voice he uses with guests like this, and he uses it now, tying the guest's hands down, the guest cursing Walt, too. I'd laugh, but it isn't funny.

In reply to the guest's "You fucking *maricón!*" Walt says, "I love you, too," chuckling.

In the distance, there is the faint chutter of the copter.

"Your call," Moose says, meaning, assign a toboggan operator, and I nod, and Moose takes the handles of the toboggan, and we all head down, Walt and me clearing slope for Moose. It is a mild slope, Homerun, and we don't need the safety rope, so we make a faster go of it.

I blow my whistle, as does Walt.

"Clear the way!" we shout, weaving through skiers down near the lodge.

At the Base lot, the chopper waits. The AirMed guys spring out of it, taking our snowboarder from the toboggan on his back-board.

It is an immense relief.

Then the guest, on the backboard, is shoehorned aboard, the son climbs in after him, and the copter cuts into the air over our heads, tilting toward downtown and the University of Utah's critical care unit.

"Well, that was jolly, wasn't it?" Moose says. "Wasn't that just the bee's knees?"

"What's a *chupa cabra?*" Walt asks.

"He call you that, too?" I laugh. (Later, I will ask my friend Carmelo what this means, and he will tell me it's some superstitious nonsense, like a werewolf, or a vampire, something that sucks blood. Why did I want to know? Nothing, I tell him, and we leave it at that.)

Walt, Moose, and I stow the toboggan, then head back up to our hut assignment.

Riding the lift, I feel a number of things. A mild sense of fatigue, some relief we got the job done, and a nagging feeling I could have been . . . faster in my assessment, better with this irrational guest, more in control.

The next time I have a call on what a guest says is a superficial cut on his head, I tell myself, I will give far less credence to what the guest is telling me—will trust my judgment over his protestations.

My supervisor, Lewis, tells me up top, "You get someone that even seems he's going the direction of combative, call down help."

I want to explain that the guest seemed sharp enough when I got to him, but Lewis stops me.

"*Any* combativeness—any at all—just call other patrollers in. You got the weight of judgment on your side then, okay? You did good," he says.

I head out to my post at the top of Bonanza Lift, where I am the Happy Guy for a half hour. If a another patroller gets a call, I will take the toboggan and gear down to him. The view is beautiful. I am high and over ranges of mountains I can see in all directions. I mull over my last call. Umpteen rescues and assists on patrol, and I am still learning how to be sharper, faster, more efficient.

When guests, particularly snowboarders, fall getting off the lift (walking, much less running, with a snowboard, as I mentioned earlier, is extremely awkward), I rush in and set them moving.

Now and again, a guest will wander over to me to ask where good runs are.

There are over 106 at Park City, and more counting chutes off Jupiter and the slopes on Pinecone Ridge, if Pinecone is open and the guest wants to hike up to it.

"Intermediate, and not so crowded," the guest tells me.

I tell her, try skiing off Pioneer. Which she does, returning for lunch at the Summit restaurant.

"Good tip," she calls over.

I wave in return, and all that with the head-injured snow-boarder and what I'll make of such a situation in the future falls into place—finally. I take a deep breath and give a wobbly kid of seven or so a hand down the lift runout.

I stand back of the lift, waiting.

Out on the top of Summit, I feel ready again.

I have been up since 4:45, had roll call with the other patrollers at 7:30, was on the mountain by 8:00. Just noon, I've done one other backboard case; a guy with a torn knee; and two snowmobile assists out of Thayne's Canyon.

How many more calls could I get in one day?

LATE-AFTERNOON HOT SEAT

Surprise. I have another unusual call that afternoon.

Many afternoons may pass slowly, even allowing for patrollers, when they are off the active roster, to take runs around their hut stations, to free ski.

But not so this afternoon for me.

There at Summit, "reading" a copy of *Powder* magazine, albeit very distractedly, I glance at my watch. I am the first responder on the Summit Patrol bench, last shift of the afternoon. It's 2:45.

I am on the hot seat during the peak accident time of what is on patrol the bewitching hour. That 2:30 to 3:30 time slot when skiers from all over will push themselves for those last runs, many of them dehydrated and suffering a mild form of altitude sickness.

Fifteen more minutes on shift and I can call my day a success (that is, after sweeps are completed, temporary signs removed, the mountain shut down for the day). Fifteen more minutes and all of this is a pretty good memory. And a good lesson, which, you think now, is enough for one day.

You've learned plenty from the El Chupa Cabra guy. The crazy guest.

But no. The radio crackles across the Summit Patrol hut (hardly a "hut," it is a nearly five-thousand-square-foot structure, housing the command desk, and providing storage for critical supplies: toboggans, oxygen, C-collars, etc.).

"Twelve twenty-three to Summit Patrol."

Lewis, assistant director, looks up from behind the Summit desk, where he's been stationed all day.

"Summit Patrol," he says.

Even from the number, I know the call is from Tony, one of the youngest patrollers. He's still in high school, but he's very good, surprisingly so for someone just seventeen. We have every confidence in him, and it is merited. It is the call itself which is distressing.

"I've got a ten fifty on Double Jack. I need a backboard and O_2. Call AirMed. Got an ABC problem. Bring a KED."

I am already up off the bench, headed out the door, Lewis calling, "He's off the upper section." Behind me, a number of patrollers have rushed into the supply room. Outside, by the time I have set myself at the handles of the first toboggan in the row of them fronting Summit hut, the others have emerged, strapping the gear Tony requested onto the toboggan I've aimed toward Double Jack, not a word said.

I kick skate down an incline, and navigate a traverse, the others following.

There is comfort in knowing Mike is with us, Mike probably sixty, long Elvis-like hair and earrings, a groovy dude, but with over thirty years of experience. Chris, my team leader, is along, too. And Glenn.

We're all so serious, it seems like someone should crack a joke to cut the tension, until, after we navigate the section of moguls, we reach Tony and see what we've got.

A skier bent around an aspen in a tree well, Tony at his side.

Tony, though, has his gloved hand on the guy's *neck*, and that's what is most disturbing. Tony's pants are covered with blood. There's blood everywhere, but unlike my guy's blood in the morning, this blood has come out in jets, and is darker.

"My call," Mike says, moving in. This means it's really bad—we could have this guy die on us right here.

I swing the toboggan around, which Chris and Glenn will take care of, and dash in to kneel beside Mike. Glove up. (Latex is worse than a poor insulator, and my hands are nearly numb in seconds.) Tony is shaking from the effort of keeping the skier from falling farther into the tree well and holding his hand over his neck.

The whole thing feels like a nightmare. The volume of blood and the skier's injuries. We are moving almost slowly, because we are doing so methodically. We're acutely aware of procedure.

The skier's face is ashen, but he's breathing, though there's a wheezing with it, too. And he's conscious. It's the breathing and blood that concern us.

"Don't move, Tony," Mike says. He turns to me, "Let's put together an occlusive dressing."

I dig in my pack, get out the yard of plastic wrap I keep in it and my roll of duct tape.

"All right," Mike says, swinging me around him. I stoop on the skier's right, double, then triple, my sheet of plastic wrap. Tear a piece of tape from my roll and anchor the wrap to the right side of the skier's neck. That's when I see what the problem is. The skier has somehow not only hit a tree, but slashed his throat on one of his skis. Newly tuned skis are as sharp as knives.

Mike takes the other end of the wrap and pulls it around to the left side of the skier's neck, motions for more tape. Anchors the other end of the wrap.

We snap a cervical collar on him, dig, behind his back, Chris flying into motion with his avalanche shovel, and get the KED (Kendrick Extraction Device, which is a metal-ribbed nylon jacket) on him, and, with the straps, lift him out of the tree well. Broken femur, midshaft.

Glenn and Chris slide the traction splint into place, fix the strap on his boot. Crank on the traction.

"Logroll him, count of three!" Mike shouts, and we get him up on his side and he vomits. Vomits again, then a third time.

I can see, when the skier breathes in, the saran wrap pucker concave.

"Get those vitals," Mike says, helping with the traction splint.

Breathing: 28 a minute, dangerous. Pulse, 110. Our skier is in compensated shock. This, actually, is good. If he'd gone into decompensated shock, the prognosis here would be grim.

I stand to call Summit to give them the vitals, which they radio to the incoming helicopter.

When I turn around again, Chris, Mike, Glenn, and Tony have the skier on the backboard, in the toboggan.

Mike takes the handles. We've got a shit ride over moguls, and I take the brake rope, to keep the toboggan from swapping ends. My legs are burning something awful, and I can only imagine how Mike feels. Chris and Glenn are ahead of us, shouting for people to steer clear.

At the bottom, just off Thayne's Lift, we can hear the rattle of an approaching snowmobile.

I take our guy's pulse again. Still 110. Good. Holding at least. But his breathing is still badly elevated. The light on the snowmobile flashes in the coming dusk. Gray light. Chris has a forged carabiner out, and when the snowmobile swings around, we rush with the toboggan to the rear of it, unbolt the toboggan's handles, and fix them against the sides, Chris throwing down the bile's triangular steel hitch, and locking the toboggan to it using the carabiner.

"What're your last vitals?" Mike asks.

I tell him, and he straddles the toboggan, and the driver of the snowmobile gets the nod, and they roar off.

We stand there, in a way stupefied at it all, and Chris says, "That was a little touch and go."

In the failing light, we don't want to move just yet. No sense of triumph here. More so the feeling of fate having worked on us.

"You ever have anybody die on you?" I ask Chris.

"Yup," he says, but does not elaborate.

"And," he adds, pointing into the trees just to the right of us, "found a dead guy right about there. Frozen solid."

We hop on the lift and ride up to Summit. We will not hear for a week that our injured skier made it just fine, after all.

I would like to say it doesn't affect you, the outcome, but it does. You feel absolutely alive doing this work, and at the same time, your illusion of control is shattered, giving you the sense at times of swimming in strange waters.

No one asks if anyone other than me had foil or plastic wrap. But it was in every patroller's pack the following week.

And duct tape.

PATROLLERS, AND HOW IT'S DONE

"And how do most people see ski patrollers?" one of the instructors at the autumn Outdoor Emergency Care Refresher (a mandatory course for all patrollers) asks. "What do *skiers* on the mountain think of patrollers?"

A woman who has been a full-time patroller for years, with that seasoned been-there-done-that air about her, responds, joking, "Patrollers are a bunch of dorks!"

We all laugh. It's not true, really, since all kinds of skiers will tell you on the lift that they are more than happy to have you on the mountain, will thank you for being out there, yet . . . there *is* something dorky about patrolling in our hypermaterial culture. At Park City, where I am a patroller, there are 62 salaried full-time patrollers, working in blood and with broken bones for near minimum wage, and to cover the full-timers' days off, Saturday and Sunday, there are 141 *volunteer* patrollers, who do it for free.

Injuries are any resort management's worst nightmare, and skiers and snowboarders do not want to hear about them, either. Which is altogether as it should be. The guest should use any resort's lifts with total confidence, and should exit the lift, to signs that will direct him or her to appropriate slopes. Slopes leading to cliffs and other dangers will be roped off (another job of the patroller), signs erected there warning of dangers. Slopes that become unsafe will be closed, and traffic, to an extent, will be controlled: Again, patrollers give "blue slips" to, say, those kids who have to ski sixty on an intermediate slope, or ride crazily, which, ironically, most of us patrollers did at one time or another, and any guest knows it, from watching us—

That's why we patrollers *are* dorks sometimes. We don't want to be, but we are at times *killjoys*.

Sometimes you feel like some overprotective and meddle-some mother: No, you can't have that BB gun, Bobby. You'll put your eye out with it!

In our case, it's "Sir, that run is closed because rocks are coming up through the base. Yes, I know you wanted to get away from the crowd, but this slope is closed." Or, "What's your name? Okay, Bobby, we all love jumping, but did you think about what would have happened if there'd been someone down there on the cat track below you, someone you couldn't see? No jumping here. Okay? Otherwise, we're going to have to ask you to leave. I'll blue slip you. Understand?"

You ask for the kid's pass, write down his name and address.

"I'm not going to see you doing this again, right?" you say, handing him his pass.

The kid will nod, but he will not be looking at you. This is all humiliating. It was for you, too, kicked off the mountain more times than you can remember, and having to hike, in your horri-ble Raichle Red Hots, up the backside of, say, Lost Trail, where you skied the rest of the day, hoping that patroller Bob Dilby didn't see you again. One resort wouldn't sell you a lift ticket, after, you being a Nordic jumping competitor, leaped 150 feet from Blaster, at Trollhaugen. But it was only 150 feet, you pro-tested. And you meant it. You were taking rides three times that up in Michigan by then (though, you knew all too well, under far more controlled conditions).

"Dork asshole," the kid who was jumping says under his breath as he trudges away from you, and at a safe distance dons his board, grudgingly, and with a kind of exaggerated preciousness rides to his friend at the bottom of the hill.

Dork asshole. That's right. We are, with the exception of racers, some of the most experienced asshole riders and skiers on the mountain, and many of us, such as myself, are former asshole racers or instructors, or both.

Still, we are pointing out the obvious, which no one having this much fun wants to have pointed out: *Accidents happen.* Our presence is proof of them. And *really* awful ones, especially in a sport where anyone can strap on a pair of planks (the new hip term for skis) or a snowboard, to rip down a mountainside, until, basically, he or she hits something—other guests, a tree, a snow-cat, a rock face—and at a high rate of speed.

Tell someone, even a friend, You know, if you ride your bicycle into the back of that parked car there, you're really gonna hurt yourself, he or she will look at you as if you're a total mental case. Tell some intermediate snowboarder, Hey there, Ralph, trying to ride thirty through those trees like that isn't a good idea, and you'll, without exception, get the fuck-off look. And this is saying nothing of racers, or extreme riders, or just skilled and very fast skiers, all of whom, at some time of the day, will make an error in judging snow conditions, or the slope, or will simply screw up an edge change and be tossed on his or her head.

Just last week, I was asked to make sure Combustion, a run off King Con Ridge, was closed. I went down with another patroller, and, sure enough, a bright orange and black rope, about four and a half feet high and stretching the entire length of the opening to the run, was in place—flapping in the wind the entire length Day-Glo orange strips of plastic. Also at intervals along the rope were signs reading CLOSED. There was, however, at the north end of the sign wall, between the lift tower and the lift hut, a gap of about four feet. Something we did not see, since the sign wall was clearly in place and functioning. *Who* could miss it? Yet a skier ducked right through that gap. And if this weren't bad enough, the skier decided to navigate the closed run at a high rate of speed. Seriously, if you're going to be ducking closed ropes, this warrants exercising caution when skiing. A sign bank such as was in place on Combustion is *always* proof positive that something *really nasty* is on that run. In this case, the skier mistook the machine-made hard-as-Styrofoam hummocks for powder, charged into the first, and instead of the hummock giving, as it would have had it been powder, the hummock threw him high into the air, so high that when he came down he buried his skis in the second hummock, bodily smacking into it, perhaps doing thirty.

One patroller had actually seen the skier heading down from the lift and shouted to him, "GET OFF THE RUN. IT'S CLOSED!" A woman with this skier, but behind him, glanced up at the patroller and actually said, "IS THIS RUN CLOSED?"

They had ducked around eighty feet of orange rope and Day-Glo plastic strips, and signs reading CLOSED. Was the run *closed*?

The skier was thirty-two years old. Should he be held responsible for observing and complying with warnings such as these on the mountain?

We had, right off with this skier, broken bones. We put him in a cervical collar, got him on O_2, had him on a backboard and in a toboggan and behind a snowmobile headed for the Thayne's Canyon exit in minutes. His vitals were strange, not right for the fractures he had. Shock had come on too suddenly. And his face had gone gray, as if from significant blood loss.

That afternoon all hell broke loose over the gap in the "sign bank." Was there any way these skiers could have, as a result of that gap at the end of the wall, thought the run was open? Park City management was asking. An investigator was sent out. By that time skiers and riders had navigated onto the run through the trees bordering it, ignoring the sign bank in its entirety.

But these guests, making their way down the mountain out of bounds, did so with some measure of caution.

A week later, the director of the patrol addressed our Sunday group, all seventy of us at morning muster. He commended us on our very fast work with the skier who'd gotten onto the closed run. He had torn his ascending aorta, had had open-heart surgery, but would make a full recovery—our quick work had saved his life. This was an enormous relief. But we were asked to be even more diligent with our sign-bank work.

All of us left that meeting feeling challenged: always, we could be sharper, faster, better.

But skiers and riders challenge themselves, too. And it is always in the direction of faster, steeper, more difficult terrain. Young or old.

Once, down in Sun Valley, when Jean-Claude Killy was visiting, I was freeskiing with pals and spied him there, standing just yards from a sign, two metal legs set at the most three feet wide holding it up.

We'd seen Killy around the last couple of days doing promos for some company or another, cooler than cool in his Vuarnets, always actors, or recognizable folks, like the Duponts, with him.

Wow. Here he was, one of the greatest skiers of all time, right in front of us.

I was twenty-two, had just won some downhill competition; I was on my favorite skis, my Rossignol SMs, which I trusted entirely. We schussed the slope and of course, Killy, talking to, that day, Andre Arnold, another world-class racer, was not giving us a second's thought. And why should he have?

Well, I'd change that, I thought.

At the last nanosecond I aimed my skis right at that sign, CAUTION, DROP-OFF, saw Killy's eyes widen, and when I reached it, I pulled into my old jumping ramp (inrun) position, and, like threading the eye of a needle, whipped though the space under the sign, easily doing forty, throwing a mulekick from the cornice behind the sign, coming down in a mogul field where a ski class was being held, barely banging through and around those skiers.

Kick-ass! Thrilling!

At the bottom, as quickly as I could, I got into the lift line crowd. Sure enough, here came a patroller nosing around.

The following day, some fifteen-year-old kid freeskiing out of control struck Killy and broke Killy's arm.

I think back on that moment, my deciding to ski between the legs under that sign. And if I'd hit either of them? Or come down on a skier in the mogul field I knew was on the other side of the cornice?

Stupid. And while racing, we did things like it every day. Skiers and riders do these things, every day, all day.

Push the envelope. It's what makes the sport so thrilling. So unlike tennis or golf. Or even a game of softball.

You can kill yourself out there. Probably won't. But if you just push it that much harder—

Younger kids, especially, are always pushing their personal boundaries. But don't think for a minute that they do this out of just silly youthful rebellion. Sure, there's some of that, and especially so for the snowboarding crowed.

We patrollers know this, have experienced it ourselves.

But, no—there are other things more powerful here, too, of which we are also aware. There is, first, the *challenge*, both in skill and in nerve. And when that is sufficient, and the skier or rider is out on the edge, in the moment succeeding, say, in navigating the most chunked-up crud on earth in a radically steep bowl, or putting the spurs to a mogul field and not missing a beat, the feeling you get in that second is akin to being Master of the Universe, or Totally Hot Shit, better than the Best You Can Be.

And, in certain moments, there can be this out-of-body aspect to it also—*ecstasy*. In these moments, your body knows far more than you do—you directed it into this challenge, and it's doing what you'd wanted it to, but far better than you could do it yourself.

These moments, without any exaggeration, feel like magic— something also *beautiful*, full of soul, some *grace*.

As a patroller, you know a good half of the guests on the mountain (and at peak, in Park City, that might be well over seven thousand) are going to be pushing, from lift opening to lift closing, for these moments.

Even the poorest rider or skier, if he hangs in there, will have them.

They're what bring us all back, even for a lifetime.

But, too, there is always the flip side of this coin, and we patrollers know it well: the moment when a message from that inner athlete in nanotime tells you, Oh-oh, and then, as with Bode Miller's save on his 2002 Olympic downhill run, you try to correct the error, and, if failing that, are entirely, totally at the mercy of whatever error of judgment you've made.

Luck, now, has to be on your side. Which, on the mountain, more often than not *is* (snow can absorb a great amount of energy): Like Hermann Maier, you go into the nets, fall hard. And seconds later, shaking yourself out of it, you get up, snap on your gear, and take it easy, until you feel the need to get out on the edge again, which inevitably happens.

All this on designated runs. *Natural terrain* we patrollers watch over.

But there are man-made terrain parks now, too, on which snowboarders and twin-tip skiers can challenge themselves, on half-pipes, jumps, and rails. So the *area* on the mountain where you are stationed (and stations are taken on team rotation), will determine what kinds of injuries you work with.

A far higher percentage of terrain park injuries are upper body, wrist fractures being particularly common with snowboarders.

Being stationed at Payday at Park City, where there is a terrain park (there are three on the mountain), nearly assures you that you will have on any Sunday a number of moderate-to-severe upper-body injuries. If you are on upper rotation, on Jupiter, you will have very few boarders, no terrain park injuries, but those injuries you do have will be in extremely steep bowls, and will require steep slope extrication methods (possibly even lowering an injured skier by rope to a less steep area where he or she can be put in a toboggan).

If you are on First Time, the beginners' hill, you are bound to get the less-severe injuries: sprained wrists, and from mothers who have not gotten much exercise, ACL injuries, five women for every man.

All of this you learn in your first year, working with other patrollers more experienced than yourself.

These patrollers you are, by increments, getting to know while stopping the bleeding on someone's head; or applying a traction splint; or waiting for a 10-50 call in one of the huts. Allen, for example, who is now an emergency room medical technician, but who, you discover, spent five years crewing sailboats in Tahiti, following years living in Princeton, New Jersey, and a childhood in San Francisco. Or Jackie, our World Wrestling Entertainment Dynamite Girl. Or Dean, who did his PhD in physics and worked in high-tech semiconductors, and now runs a business buying and selling collectable weapons and aircraft. And there is Dave, a successful stockbroker, who is unflappable—a joy to work with.

It was Dave who gave you your toboggan training.

THE ART OF RUNNING A TOBOGGAN, AND A RESCUE

Even toboggan handling is not as simple as it might appear. First, we use three kinds of sleds. The Akja, for steep slope and bowl evacuation, has handles on *both* ends and is never towed down the slope, the injured skier being transferred to either a Cascade, which is fiberglass—so especially light—and has angled aluminum rudders, or a Sun Valley, which is built like the proverbial brick shithouse.

The Cascade is ideal for the box-splint case, or the ACL, or a minor injury. It is easy to maneuver, especially when empty. But when you have an injured skier in it, and you are on a very steep slope, trying to navigate moguls (with a skier in the toboggan the combined weight with the Cascade, can approach three hundred pounds), the Cascade does not bite into the slope or steer as well, which makes it feel more prone to swapping ends on you. Which, if you are the toboggan handler, even the suggestion of will put your heart right up in your throat, this *something that must never happen*—even though, on a steep slope, you will always have another patroller behind the toboggan holding the rear safety rope to prevent that. Also, the Cascade's brake chains are not as effective as the Sun Valley's.

Both the Cascade and the Sun Valley have brake chains at the front (usually stowed inside the toboggan, and about three feet long), which the patroller can lower, so the front of the toboggan, rather than gliding on the snow, will ride on these brake chains, slowing the toboggan. These brake chains are very much like those put on car tires to ascend or descend icy mountain roads. To increase or decrease braking, the patroller operating the toboggan, respectively, forces the steering handles down into the snow or lifts up on them.

The Sun Valley is the toboggan suited for all calls, with the exception of the super-steep call. It has a removable litter (a body-sized basket of heavy wire), which allows patrollers to carry an injured skier directly from the toboggan with the release of one locking bolt. Made of steel and wood, it is extremely heavy, though if the patroller has any concerns about navigating nasty terrain, this is the tool for the job.

The Sun Valley's braking chains are so effective that the operating patroller can, if he really bears down on the handles, bring the toboggan to a complete stop on the bumpiest and steepest slopes.

With an injured guest in the litter, the Sun Valley can easily weigh four hundred or more pounds.

No big deal, right? In fact, you'd think that old turning and braking method, the wedge, or snowplow, would be ideal for this kind of work.

Which would be absolutely wrong.

Imagine you are descending a slope that provides a moderate challenge. Twenty-five to thirty degrees and moguls. It is around two, and the slope which you happily navigated earlier is now, in the afternoon, "carved up"—meaning that intermediate level guests have skidded around the moguls, leaving alternating stretches of ice and hooked moguls fronted by sluff, the snow the skidding guests have forced into the moguls' front sides. (And by their very nature, snowboards cut lozenge-shaped moguls, which are harder to navigate, especially if you are on skis.)

You are called out to give first aid to a woman who has been diverted from a closed slope onto a cat track, which would have taken her to another "easier" slope, Homerun, but she decided to take a short cut onto Erica's Gold instead, a black diamond run.

Toboggan calls like this you never forget.

From the cat track you can see her, a woman in a hot pink Bogner one-piece outfit, easily weighing 225 to 250 pounds. You've taken a Sun Valley, knowing full well that Erica's Gold is oftentimes referred to by patrollers, late afternoons, as *Upper Skating Rink*.

Dean has come with you, Dean about six-five, which will help with handling this guest. Though, if anything, given it is your call, Dean will be the tail roper. The Sun Valley, heavy, around two hundred pounds, is supple and elastic behind you getting down to the 10-50. The toboggan follows, while you, using short, carved turns, lead it, trying to keep the handles near your hips, though not forcing them down, braking too much, turning around the moguls and avoiding the ice.

All is standard procedure approaching this woman now: scene safety (skiers and riders are skidding on the ice, barely in control, so you'll have to set your skis up in the usual X). Mechanism of injury (you are relieved to see nothing, but that has you wondering, maybe there is an illness here, so you shift gears, begin to think, NOI (nature of illness), which requires a fairly different approach). Airway, breathing, circulation? She's lifting her head, watching you come down with the toboggan. Good.

Both you and Dean kick off your skis, Dean setting his in an X above you, you using yours to secure the toboggan to the slope.

"Hello, I'm . . ." you tell the woman. "Can I help you?"

The woman lies on her back, staring. She's hyperventilating, but when you talk to her, in a slow, soothing voice, her breathing slacks off.

"I can't move," she tells you, and you notice she is guarding her *right* arm, holding it against her side with her left.

"Ma'am, what seems to be the problem?"

"I hurt my arm."

"Did you fall?" you ask, kneeling beside her. You have to see if there is something worse than the arm here.

"Yes." She turns her head slightly, giving you this wide-eyed look.

Well, she's alert, that's for sure. Her breathing is in the range of normal, twenty breaths a minute. When you check her pulse, it is 115, which is high, and feels a little "thready," but she is obviously agitated.

"Taking any medication?"

"Blood pressure."

"Anything else?"

She shakes her head. When you ask her how she fell, out spills this story, about her weekend of skiing, just her and her son, who lives in Amherst now, and she's all alone in the City, when she isn't in Florida, and she came over the rise there and thought, this was the easiest way to get down, she and her son got separated and they'd agreed to meet at the coffee place right at the bottom . . .

"Okay," you tell her, and Dean has his cell phone out, not his radio, and calls down to the Mountain Desk, which connects him to the coffee place. He asks them to page,

"Aaron," the woman says. "Aaron M-E-I-E-R."

"Thank you," Dean says.

When you ask if you can do a brief body survey, the woman tells you, through Dean's conversation with the son, that it's *only* her wrist. Her wrist is hurt.

You glance up at Dean and see his brows furrow. This never happens, and you think, *Oh, shit.* In half of the rescues you do there is some weirdness, some impossible thing, some complication. You can think you're prepared for this weirdness, but how can you be?

Dean gives you one of those significant looks, which, of course, you cannot read. Which freezes you in place for a second.

"Is he coming?" the woman asks Dean.

"Yes," he tells her. "He'll be up in fifteen minutes."

"Ma'am," you tell the woman, after you've finished the brief body survey, beginning with her head, and ending with her boot-encased feet, "I'm going to splint that arm of yours." The woman is nearly as stiff as a board all over.

You consider the pain—it *is* her right arm. PQRST (provocation, quality, radiation, severity, time)? Not the left, so less likely some heart problem. But still . . .

"It's just the wrist then?" you ask.

When she swings the allegedly injured arm over toward you, which you have *not* asked her to do, so you can splint it, you can see it causes her no pain. So why is she exhibiting classic guarding behavior?

You get the splint on and anchor it against her chest with a triangular bandage.

"Just a second, you tell her."

You scoot around Dean, who whispers into your ear, "Her son said she has panic attacks."

You are marginally relieved, but wary yet, hoping you know

now what is going on here, but the awkwardness of this rescue has not been diminished.

You call in a 10-45/10-17. You request O$_2$ and an AED, just to be safe. Which means, patrollers needed, situation under control. Bring oxygen and an automated external defibrillator.

When the patrollers arrive, Chris and Glenn, you are all saddled with the prospect of getting this enormous woman into the toboggan.

Part of you is darkly amused. Here's this bit of ridiculous theater. It's funny, and it's not funny at all. You don't have a problem with the woman's weight, it's the simple physical problem of moving someone who is hysterically immobilized, caught in this odd family farce that is playing itself out here. (One time, I did an assist on a very pretty young woman who'd torn her ACL. She wouldn't get into the toboggan because, as she put it, "I'm just so embarrassed, I *couldn't*. I don't want anyone to *see* me in a toboggan like that." I told her that no one would be able to see her when she was wrapped up in the toboggan, but that didn't help. "Isn't there some *other* way I could get down?" she said. "With a torn ACL?" I asked, incredulous. Fortunately for me, the boyfriend stepped in about then.)

"I want my son here," the woman tells you.

Dean glances at his watch. Then a skier comes over the lip of the cat track up the slope from you, aimed in your direction. There is an almost lazy, calm control to his skiing—he's a better-than-average skier, and dressed in a sedate navy blue. You can tell, though, he's had an entire lifetime of this sort of thing.

"Hey," he says, turning in near you. "Mom?"

"I'm not skiing down," she tells her son. "If your father was here . . ."

"Ma," the son warns. "I didn't say you should."

"If you hadn't left me back up there none of this would have happened." She glances over at you. "All I wanted was to have a day with my son, and now look at me. Will you look at me?"

Dean pats her shoulder. "We'll get you down, and you'll be fine."

"You don't treat your mother like this, do you?"

"All mothers are special," Dean tells her.

"Some more so than others," the son says, grinning.

"Humphhh!" the woman says. She glances at you now. "Do you treat your mother this way?"

"My mother passed away a couple years ago," you reply, and to this sobering bit of information, the woman responds, her eyes narrowing, "A lawyer, he thinks he knows everything. Always telling his mother what to think."

The son takes a deep, all-suffering breath.

You stoop beside the woman, say, in a calm voice, "So, we're taking you down in the toboggan, right?"

"What, I'm gonna walk down, I can't get my skis on and I hurt my arm?"

You nod the other patrollers, Glenn and Chris, over. The woman rears up, as if there is something menacing in it.

"If you could get your legs under you a little as we're lifting, and push up a bit, that would be good," you tell her.

When, on the count of three, you all lift, the woman clutches at her chest, her eyes wide.

The situation here has gone from bordering on silly to potentially lethal in a second. Or is this just more hysteria?

"What?" you say.

"It won't stop!" she cries out.

"*What* won't stop?" You have to zip it here, kick panic right out. You turn to her son. "She have any cardiac history?"

"She has panic attacks."

"Arrhythmia?"

"I don't know."

"*Yes!*" the woman says, and her face crumples in terrified defeat. (If the son had known, there would have been no ski trip, no enticement to be out with his mother in Utah for these days together.)

"Ma'am," you say to her. "You with us here?"

When she can't speak, you shoot your hand out to press on her carotid artery in her neck, feel her pulse. You've got an altogether irregular beat. You can't load and go, and things are getting worse, the look on her face more panicked. You thumb your radio. "Twelve twenty-eight to Summit Patrol."

"Summit Patrol."

"We're going to need AirMed."

"That's a ten four."

If you can get her in the toboggan, it's a five-minute scoot from here. You drop to your knees beside her. "Ma'am, if you could *breathe—*"

She tries to breathe, but she does so in ragged, shallow breaths.

You are trained, in cardiac situations, to at all times wear a face of calm. It is *very* difficult to do this now, but something in you says, *This is your job, IT'S NOT ABOUT YOU.* Again.

"*Breathe,*" you say, trying to instill some calm here.

But the son, behind you, is throwing his arms around, pulling at his chin, literally doing this all-too-common panic dance.

"She said the altitude was making her feel a little funny," he says.

You feel so horribly powerless in these situations, if you are a bystander, or family, but as care provider, you *keep moving. Procedure saves you.* You have *tools.* If she goes out, and we have a pulse, we'll jam her into the toboggan and run for the bottom. If she loses the pulse, we've got the AED and we can give CPR a go.

The woman's eyes roll back into her head, and she's out. That's it. Things are just going south here.

You check her pulse again—galloping, irregular, atrial or ventricular fibrillation.

"OKAY!" you call in a loud voice. "AED." When the son moves in, you say to him in a definite, no-nonsense voice. "Let us work here." And he backs off, struck dumb.

Glenn hands you the AED. Dean has his scissors out, runs them right down that thousand-and-some-dollar Bogner suit. You reach in, grasp the bottom of her turtleneck, and, pulling up, run your scissors bottom to top. You cut the bra away.

There is absolutely nothing remotely embarrassing in any of this. That part of you is off somewhere on Pluto. It is as if those considerations, modesty and embarrassment, are nothing.

You read the AED pads. Thank God for this technology. You peel the paper from the adhesive on the first, press it firmly just under the woman's right clavicle. You tear the paper from the second and secure it under her left armpit.

You turn on the AED.

"Analyzing pulse," it says, in a robotic man's voice, though one you seem to vaguely recognize from some documentary you've seen on PBS or a commercial for NyQuil.

"Charging," it says.

You slip back on your knees. If the charge were to carry through the woman into the melted ice under her and into you, you would receive a jolt so strong that your own heartbeat could be stopped.

"Delivering first charge," the machine says.

The woman shakes when the machine delivers the charge, which is good, but you don't move in again.

"Analyzing heartbeat," the AED says, in that robotic voice.

You're hoping it will say, "Heartbeat reestablished." But it doesn't. It says, "No heartbeat," then, "Charging."

You close your eyes for a second. Come on, DAMMIT! If this doesn't take, you have an extremely hard half hour ahead of you—desperate work, with small chance of a happy outcome.

"Delivering second charge."

There is this quiet moment, this awful stillness. Oddly, you hear birds that must have been calling through it all these last fifteen minutes. Then the woman shudders, and the machine says, "Analyzing heartbeat." And then, "Heartbeat reestablished." Now all four of you, Glenn, Dean, Chris and you, move in.

You remove the pad plugs from the AED, force the AED down into the space where her suit isn't cut.

"Call it," Dean says, all of you taking a place, you at the head, Dean and Chris torso, left and right, Glenn at her feet.

"On three," you say. "One, two—"

You all lift, Dean stepping backward over the toboggan. With four men working, you have her loaded and ready to go in seconds flat. She's opened her eyes, and you kneel, say, "We want you to do something for us now, all right?" Sometimes this really helps, letting the injured person be a part of the rescue. It takes the person's mind off what is wrong.

"*Breathe*. Think only that. Nothing else. Breathe. IN. OUT."

The woman takes a deep breath. Arrhythmia can be like this, the heart pumping like it always has, once the problem of the misfiring nodes is corrected, or it can just go bad again.

You take the handles of the Sun Valley, Dean takes the tail rope. Glenn and Chris prepare to ski outside and clear the way.

But you've got these awful moguls, on this icy, steep slope, and, you are too proud to say, your thighs are twitchy. Adrenaline is great, but when it wears off, which is about fifteen to twenty minutes after you get the first eye-opening jolt, you have a blood sugar deficit, and you can shake all over.

Here is why you love the Sun Valley. You've got this woman who might die in the toboggan behind you. You have to navigate this steep, icy, mogul-covered slope. When you kick off, leading the toboggan, you throw an immediate, braking parallel right turn, nearly a quarter ton of sled coming on behind you.

And here I return to the challenge of toboggan handling, which it is—especially given that you only do it with someone who is seriously hurt (or crazy, or belligerently drunk) in it, and it is unthinkable that you would have one of those Homer Simpson moments when YOU let your guest go end over end.

You are NOT going to have it, but every patroller has had those times when the sneaky toboggan, on a slope such as this, wants to swap ends with you.

There is no happy-going, devil-may-care moment with an injured guest in the toboggan on a steep slope.

It's hard work.

There's an absolutely wonderful few minutes, toward the bottom, headed for Base, but you aren't there yet.

You are never so aware of mass as when you've got four, five hundred pounds of it just dying to zoom over you like some eighteen-wheeler over the Road Runner in those cartoons you watched as a kid. And the damn toboggan, you discover when you first start handling them, picks up energy (force equals mass times acceleration) in—literally—the blink of an eye, or an awkward move. It comes at you from behind, but you're ready for it now.

When you first took the horns (the handles) of a toboggan, in training, you thought, Well, hell, let's just snowplow. When you did this, though, with a patroller in the toboggan, you very quickly learned something. If you double your body mass by running a toboggan, you can't revert to the safe old snowplow, which, if you could have used it, would have ensured full-time braking force against the mass behind you. No. With all that weight behind you, snowplowing, your joints and muscles aren't up to the task.

And why not? First of all, the angle that you've got to cant your legs inward to snowplow puts an unusual stress on the outer meniscus of your knees, which makes your knees hurt like hell, and furthermore does likewise with your hips. This oldest of skiing techniques you learned as child not only *doesn't* work to lead a toboggan, it threatens to make you cross-eyed with pain and mess up your sacred, must-be-cared-for, already beat-to-hell knees (one injured in a ski jumping accident that ended your career as a jumping competitor) and your already aching-at-night hip sockets.

This you were warned about in training, using the snowplow, but you had to feel it for yourself.

Because when you use braking, parallel turns, you learn something else: Yes, you have a definite mechanical advantage, being able to really use your quadriceps, in tandem (both legs), but you have to turn (unless you *sideslip* all the way down). And *when* you do, there is that motion you know so well, and use to change edges, and in that half second, when your skis are pointed *down the fall line*, and your edges are *not* set against it, that toboggan does everything it can to pick up speed, say, the sixty-five or so it would do if you weren't preventing that.

So you use quicker unweighting, hard-edge sets, and realize you've got ice, so at times your skis, even set against the fall line, skid anyway, again the toboggan coming at you from behind.

Also, in the middle of this, the lactic acid buildup in your thighs is awful. You've begun to sweat. Your heart is hammering.

You're concerned about the woman behind you. You stop, and Glenn dashes in, gives you the thumbs-up. Heart okay.

You've got another five hundred feet to cover on this steep section. A little more than a block.

You think now, God almighty, and you thought the business you did on yourself skiing gates years ago ripped up your legs.

So you have to do something strategic—you aim for the sluff on the back sides of the moguls, getting some cushioning and braking effect there. It works, scrubs off a lot of momentum. Still, the toboggan, on the glare ice section, has enormous lateral momentum. Which is why you CANNOT simply make a very high (low-angle) traverse of the slope. The toboggan will veer off sideways.

Turning left, you brake hard. Unweight, that awful moment—a fraction of a second—when the toboggan picks up momentum, making it seem to weigh a ton, which, given the acceleration, it possibly does. And turn right, braking again.

Here, now, the slope levels off. Your thighs are burning. Your hair, under your Park City Mountain Resort hat, is sopping wet.

"Good job," Dean calls from behind you, stowing the tail rope, and skating out with Glenn and Dave.

Here, on Homerun, you can skate, and you do, picking up speed, reaching around the left horn and tearing your jacket zipper down.

The cool air feels wonderful. You're moving, the helicopter swinging in below you, and when you take your last skate, you slide through the gap in the snowbank surrounding Base hut, and, with enormous relief, hand the toboggan off to the AirMed EMTs.

There is that rush of activity in front of you, which you watch with a certain narcotized exhaustion.

Mel, your buddy, approaches you, having come down with another toboggan, an injury from Payday.

The two of you watch the AirMed guys load the woman onto the helicopter. Mel jabs you.

"Well, you did it," he says. "Won't get much worse than that. *Ever*. Think of it."

I nod. Something in me limbers up. Stretches. Yeah. That was about the limit—just minus . . . but I don't want to think about that. The limit.

The helicopter lifts, then slides off toward downtown. The son calls, "Thanks," and gets into a cab.

We patrollers at Base pause a second, then cheerfully reload the toboggan with a fresh blanket, a pillow, throw in the box splint, padding, and secure the burrito to the toboggan with the straps.

I ride Eagle Lift to the top of King Con Ridge, making small talk with a guy from Rhode Island.

In the King Con hut I stash the new O_2 pack I've brought up. Fresh green cylinder. Dean's handing off the snowmobile he used to bring up the Sun Valley.

The radio coughs.

"Summit to King Con."

"Con here," you reply.

SWEEPS, DAY IS DONE

On sweeps, you close the mountain, making sure you've left no injured skier or rider unaccounted for. Sometimes you are so shot by the time you have sweep meeting at 3:30, you have to focus to get it all right. Sweeps are complicated. In the space of an hour, on two sweeps, one starting at 4:00, the second at 5:00, you have to cover 106 runs.

On first sweep, you have to put up long sections of rope like the China Wall, and with it CLOSED signs, to divert skiers onto Park City's front-side slopes. Then, on second sweep, you pull all those temporary signs and ropes you just erected, for the cat drivers who will groom all night, and clear the other half of the mountain. Sweeps usually turn up nothing. Which is a good thing. But that single time you are on a sweep when something *does* happen makes all the others worthwhile. Or, really, *critical*.

Like tonight now. The end of this long, difficult day early in December.

You are headed down Homerun in the near dark. It is after five.

Skiing now, on second sweep, is part joy, part torment. Below you, the lights of Park City have come on, jewel-like, inviting. Just this twenty or so minutes of sweep, and you are done. Here is joy in having the mountain to yourself, and in the prospect of skiing, in minutes, untracked powder.

Skiing down, you stop to call into the trees, "THE RESORT IS CLOSED!"

You are doing this, hat pulled up so your ears are exposed, listening for some cry for help. This is the torment part. It is around ten degrees, and your ears are cold; in fact, your whole body is a chilly husk in damp ski clothes.

But you focus on this task at hand, second sweep, having already radioed to Summit Patrol, "Down and clear," on your first.

Guests have been found on closing sweeps, those who have gone deep into the trees and injured themselves. So it is *not* a race to the bottom, *not* a leisurely run down the mountain.

And your legs are rubber. They burn when you really put your spurs to the skis, which you have to do to navigate these slopes, they're steep SOBs here, making of this run a challenge.

But the whole day has been a challenge since snow has been late in coming. There were rocks standing out on many runs, and you have tied ropes with bits of fluorescent orange plastic across openings to those closed runs a good part of the day. And when young hotshots like you once were ducked under those ropes, calling out, "WOAH! COWABUNGA, DUDE! LIKE, UN-TRACKED POWDER!" you went after them and, if they mouthed off, you pulled their passes, and if not, you took their names and addresses and pass numbers, turning these names over to the Park City Patrol director. Then you hiked, in your newly "tuned" Tecnica boots (in no way made for hiking), back up the slope you chased these errant riders down. The boots are . . . *better* than they were before, the toe boxes so blown out now you actually get enough circulation to prevent your neuromas from killing you, but just that. And the new heel cups you put in to make the boots perform more accurately take some of the skin off the bony parts of the backs of your feet. They're raw in spots.

Skiing now, and calling into the trees, you're mulling over your error on first sweep. You pulled the China Wall, the dividing ropes between the west side of the Homerun Ridge and the east, which required, again, hiking in sometimes nearly waist-deep snow in your heavy downhill gear. You and Doug, a fireman in his other life, got the China Wall up, from the top of Silverlode Lift all the way around to the opening of Mel's and Hidden Splendor, a distance of about six or seven hundred feet. Done with the wall, you took Mel's alley farther down, which you were to work with Hidden Splendor and Prospector sweepers, waving each other off (all clear, no injured guests) through stands of trees at Larson Park, Newport, Lost Prospector, and Dynamite.

This you did flawlessly.

You pulled a CLOSED sign and rope from the bottom on Prospector, and in doing this had to, again, hike a good distance up the mountain (standard procedure) to place the rope and sign in the trees.

Bliss and glory, you got to ski the last half of the run, which had been closed all day. Absolutely fresh powder, untouched but for one single set of tracks, your excuse for skiing here, rather than cutting over one run.

If there is a set of tracks, there might be a skier out there.

At the bottom you met up with your group of Summit sweepers. Someone having called and given the all clear on your first sweep, you then hopped on the lift, and luxuriating in the sensation of those turns in that famous Utah powder, turned creamy, and swooping, and effortless, you rode to the top, where, again, you had to doff your skis and hike to the Summit hut from Silver King Lift.

But coming through the front door of Summit hut, Lewis waved you and Ted, your sweep partner, over.

"You forget something?" he said.

You got that icy feeling in the back of your head. *Forget something?* You hate screwups. Which you, and every other patroller, have had, never with injured skiers, but with complicated sweeps and routine maintenance procedure. When it's some minor screwup, being called on it, teased, is called . . . *being gooned.* But you're not being gooned here, this is serious.

"Where's your Prospector sweeper?" Lewis asks.

You do a quick head count from memory. There were at the base of Silverlode Lift, you, Ted, Walt, Walt's shadow, the new patroller from Pennsylvania, Nancy, and—

You think again. Shit! You are exhausted, almost beyond bearing it. Cold. Run ragged up and down the mountain. A hard day.

"All right," Lewis says. "Here's what you did. Ed and Dave were pulling ropes on Upper Prospector, and since they had to hike up, it took 'em a long time. You guys, all of you, got to the bottom, gave the lifties the all clear, and they were shutting down the lift when Ed and Dave, your Prospector sweepers, got there. See? They were really pissed."

Lewis gives you both a serious look. You, yourself, didn't call the all clear, but you didn't see this coming, either.

"*Don't* leave anybody behind," Lewis says. "I'm not pissed, but this is serious. This is just between you and me. But you have to be sure all your sweepers are down before you call all clear."

"Okay," you say, and you mean it. It's sobering. Each patrol hut has its sweeps, and each sweep has its little booby traps, those things where, at least once a season, when you get to the top, and someone says, Did you remember to take down that slow sign at the intersection of Single Jack and Lower Single Jack? you have to say, Got me—the cat drivers'll do it.

There are so many things to watch for on sweep, you write them down before, and make mental notes. So now, even though you are truly exhausted, you rouse yourself to make sure that *here*, on second sweep, there will be no mistakes.

But, already, because of the earlier snafu, you're late, making this darkest time of second sweep even darker.

Here you are, on Homerun, and you take the exit to King Con Ridge, off of it Erica's, your powder day sweep. You, Mel, and Ted blaze down the cat track, heading north. Erica's is a steep run, but it is blissfully covered in deep powder, which is a joy to navigate, but for your legs, which are burning badly and refusing to give you full power.

Mel swoops to the right and down and you follow him. Here the snow is especially deep, the run particularly steep.

On the steepest section, you try to just let the skis run, and they do, which is bliss, until you nail a hummock, something you could not see in the dark, and, in a way that never happens, your skis go off in opposite directions, due to the compression, and you do a full-out flip, an endo, popping out of one ski, and the other coming around 360 degrees with you. You sit in the powder, stunned. When you look through your goggles (which you were not wearing, but have gotten jammed down on your face), everything beyond the snow in them looks a mighty bit foggy.

Did you injure your head? Is this a concussion? You're not thinking too clearly just now.

That's the way wrecks always are. There's this time of disorientation.

And then of feeling your arms, legs, neck, blinking, a sharpness returning, as it does now, you pulling the goggles from your face, and—

You've lost your glasses. (All right, I'm not Mr. Coke Bottle Bottoms. But without glasses I'm badly myopic, nearsighted—which, if you don't know, actually means I can't see things some distance from me.)

So, now, add losing your glasses to the darkness. This fills you with a moment of near panic.

"Son of a bitch!" you shout.

"You injure yourself?" Ted calls.

"No," you call back, Ted just a hundred feet or so from you. "Lost my glasses."

This, in all your years of skiing, has never happened. In the old days, racing, you had a tie on your glasses—or wore contacts.

Here is four feet of freshly fallen snow. You've been tossed into the air, doing a somersault, landing here. What are the chances you'll find your glasses? In all this powder? And *in the dark?* About nil. You begin to dig, around where you sit. Still, there's this despair about it (and the damn things cost $300, courtesy of LensCrafters). Goddammit. But then you spy something there, a line of black, and, you reach for it. Holy Lord, thank you! Here are your glasses—and *not even broken!* You zip down your jacket, yank the corner of your cotton turtleneck from your skiing pants, and clean your glasses.

Then you're all put back together, and you and Mel and Ted head down again.

But it is even darker, and the lights of Park City below you lovely, and you and Mel continue off a cat track after Ted tucks over the Men's Slalom course. It is absolutely gorgeous out, and if you were cross-country skiing, and taking your time, and had a bottle of wine along, say, some merlot, this would be paradise. But you are looking for skiers who might be dying in the trees.

All you have to do is cut over to the Women's Slalom course, which has been closed all day, and sweep it. And you're done.

"Be careful," Lewis warned. "Some rocks are coming through the snow. Shouldn't be anybody out there, with the ropes up all day."

But no, you've come down the cat access and—here is a track running out and beyond the Woman's Slalom course opening, a snowboarder's. That track means pure hell to you. You'll have to follow it, making sure this rider hasn't been injured, isn't in the dark and trees out in front of you.

"Oh, man," Mel says. "I am so glad you're with me."

Which you give assent to. Yup. For a truly shitty job, it is a bit of grace to have someone along. A friend.

You ski to the boundary of the run, preparing to do what you have to do. All you want now is to get off the mountain. Your legs are mush and burn when you really demand anything from them; you're cold and clammy, and whacked right through; your feet, which don't get cold in these boots, are starting to get cold. Frozen.

You ask yourself, *Why* am I out here? At least, *now, here?* In the dark, and when you are just about 100 percent shot.

You've done these sweeps umpteen times, and you have—happily—never turned anyone up. Though you know of sweeps that have. In fact, a patroller you all knew was found on a sweep at another resort—critically injured, having hit a tree, and the rescuers saved his life. (Weekly, from his wheelchair, he works at Base, a very knowledgeable person to have around.)

So there's no choice but to go on.

You follow the cat access, and where the opening in the trees to the Women's Slalom run ends, where you hoped to see the snowboarder's track veer down and onto the slalom course, it doesn't. It continues on into the dark.

Ah, *wonderful.*

Down you go, and now you actually ride the exact track of this boarder who ducked your closed ropes, the track suddenly veering right, Mel skirting over the lip of the cat access. You follow him, in the perpetual blue dark, down, where the rider's track again veers, directly into a thick stand of aspen.

Instantly, you have a spike of adrenaline. You look for a runout track, but there isn't one.

You both ski into the widely spaced trees. You are doing this by starlight.

And there you've got it. A body. Somebody, by God, *is* out here.

"Hey!" Mel shouts.

You jet forward, snap out of your bindings. Mel, whose sweep this is, makes the call.

"Twelve sixty-one to Summit Patrol."

"Summit Patrol."

"Ten fifty off Women's Slalom access."

While he's telling them how to find you, and to call in AirMed, you kneel. It's a girl, in some boarder's rad gear.

A very pretty girl, maybe fifteen or sixteen.

When you touch her neck, to feel for a pulse, she turns her head up. Blinks, and starts to cry.

That's all she can do. She's got hypothermia, and got it bad. She's conscious, but not very. You do a rapid body survey. Broken tib fib down at the top of her left boot, which she's managed to get free of her board.

The hood of her jacket is glazed with tears. This was one terrifying stretch of time for this girl. An eternity.

You dig the snow out from around her leg. The pants zip from the bottom. Oh, thank you for luxuries! You run the zipper to her knee. Bad break, you can see that in the dark, swelling—she must have hit the tree here. But the bones have not punctured her skin.

If you have an open break, you have to use a blood stopper and pressure.

Mel, bighearted to a fault, takes off his jacket and wraps it around the girl. Mel does amazing things at times. When we were in the OEC class together, he rescued a man thrown from a jeep, and, not having a CPR barrier, knew he had a choice. Save the man and risk himself, or . . . let the man die. Mel gave the man mouth-to-mouth in a wash of blood.

And here he is now, slapping his arms.

"Vitals?"

"Breaths are at ten. Pulse sixty."

Mel makes a face. It hadn't occurred to you until then that given the amount of time she's been out here, even if she pulls through, she could lose some of her toes, or even fingers. But now, you think happily, she's got her hands under her armpits. That's a plus.

You hear the roar of snowmobiles in the distance.

Throwing up clouds of powder where you just skied in, their lights cut cones of blue-white in all that dark. They pull up to the lip of the cat access where the girl, and you and Mel, went over, spin the biles (snowmobiles) around 180 degrees, ready to head back out.

Vince comes down the slope, the toboggan, a Cascade, beside him. When he reaches you, he says, "What do we got?"

You give him the vitals, the results of your rapid body survey, then, using the gear in the toboggan, you box splint the girl's leg. Lewis, up top, radios in the information.

"Safe to lift," you tell Vince.

He turns the toboggan the length of the girl. Mel is with you now.

"On three?" he says.

You lift, and have her in. Mel hooks up the oxygen, turns the valve open. You toss Mel his jacket, and even as he's putting his arms through the sleeves, Vince is securing the girl's board to the toboggan, then guiding the toboggan around the slope, angled to meet the cat access, you at the rear as safety, your skis stashed on the side. Then, with a bump, the toboggan is over the lip.

Mel is right behind you. It's been hell climbing in the downhill boots, and you think, Maybe I should carry snowshoes on sweeps?

Vince and Lewis get on the biles, Lewis waving you over. You try to force your mid-fat skis into the carrier at the rear, but they won't go in.

"Just hold 'em!" Lewis calls over the engine.

You sling your skis over your thighs, the seat of the snowmobile icy and hard. Lewis gives a wave, Mel hopping on the back of Vince's bile, and you head out, the engines pulling hard and sharp, the cold wind in your face, the crystalline snow abrasive. You feel like nothing but a husk, hollowed out.

At Base, the helicopter waits. As if in a dream, you pass the girl off to the AirMed technicians. Yet again.

Always, there is this tremendous relief as the helicopter, as if magically, lifts, your part in this drama over.

Minutes later, in the Patrol locker room, you sit on the bench in front of number 132, almost too tired to get out of your suit. Your feet are burning so badly you can barely think.

Your glasses are cockeyed on your face. You have mild hypothermia yourself. You ache all over.

Dressed in your street clothes, you head down Highway 241 with Mel, Mel chatting on the cell as he does, catching up with business. He gets you a coffee at the 7-Eleven, the usual Mountain Dew for himself.

"Well, don't believe me," he says, and hands the phone to you. "Tell Cindy about our rider girl."

You give her the one-sentence version. "Found one on sweep, just like Mel said."

You chitchat. Cindy's been cleaning all day.

You sip at your coffee. You are so happy to be inside. With this warm drink. And only your feet raw, and this tendon stretched to hell in your groin from the bad fall. "Yeah, we'll get together," you tell her, and you mean it.

At home, in the house, you take a long and very hot shower. When you come out, your wife has made you some southwestern smoked-chicken dish, which you eat in front of the TV.

"How was it?" she asks, your lovely wife.

"Well, a little rough."

Rosemary & Thyme is on PBS. It's a bit saccharine, but right now that seems wonderful. Warm, fuzzy.

You are pretty zero on Monday. Tuesday, you begin to feel you have your old energy back. By the end of the week, Saturday, almost perversely, you have this insane itch to get back out there. On rotation, at King Con hut, Sunday morning, while you are checking out the toboggans, Glen taps your shoulder.

"That woman over there wants to talk to you."

"Who is she?"

"Wouldn't say."

When you walk over, the woman puts out her hand and introduces herself. She asks your name, if she has the right person, and when you tell her yes, she tells you she is the mother of Ashley, the girl, the one that was in the trees.

You do not dare ask—she make it?

And when she tells you that the girl's fine, and she came up herself to thank you, she just can't say how much, you feel your throat swell.

"You're welcome," you tell her, all that you can manage to get out, and pressing her hand, you head back to work.

RIDERS, THE NEW KIDS ON THE BLOCK

AIRDOGS, ARCTIC COUGARS,
C3POs, GANGSTARS, HOEDADS,
BETTYS, AND BEAVERS

RIDIN' AND TWEAKIN' THE MELON

A bluebird day, you are perched heel-side on your Burton at the top of Pick 'n' Shovel, a Park City Lower Mountain Terrain Park run, on it a number of gnarly jumps, the largest of which you are about to hit, though with some trepidation. X-tra Big (or is it Rapper 2 Kool?) is blaring from the speakers at base, something about blowing up the world or killing cops, the lines, "Explode and kill, a real chill," repeating endlessly, a whole contingent of Jesses, Bettys, and beavers on the slope behind you, waiting for the jon at the front to shred, which he does, barging suddenly downhill. The jon boosts a superhit, busts big air, tosses a 360, and, on landing, pulls switch, rides goofy, then pulls switch again to the bottom.

"*Sick!*" the kid behind you says.

"*Awesomeness,*" says his pal. "He *ripped* that one."

"Well, he should have," says the first, "that booter tweaks my melon, dude! It is *way* burnt!"

The Betty just to his right gives him a hard look. "Easy to say for a frenchie crip like you, Justin."

"F'in' McGookin," the kid says.

The friend laughs, jabbing Justin with his elbow. "Hot for the Arctic Cougar, are ya?"

"That is so beige," Justin says, but his face reddens. "Hey, Gray on a tray," he adds, addressing you, "You takin the hit, or you playin' roadkill?"

"Yeah, punter, you gonna go or what?" a kid at the back of the line says.

You give the jump a last look. Today you're riding goofy on a rental board, just to see how it goes. It was something you did waterskiing slalom in your teens. Which snowboarding is, at least a bit reminiscent of. Especially the toe-side, heel-side moves, though blasting a dookie on boilerplate's nothing like taking a pitch on water. And there's your student on your mind, Matt, who, on a jump not unlike this one, caught way sick air, and on landing broke his back, paralyzing him from the waist down.

Matt, a handsome, once nationally ranked snowboard competitor, both a warning and an inspiration. Twice a week in class you see him, Matt another Minnesota boy transplanted to the Rockies.

Only three weeks on the board, you shouldn't be jumping, but here you are once again. The chatter behind you is an amusement, an irritation, and reminder of your age. You are tempted to roll your eyes over the hyperbolic chatter at times, but resist.

"Yo, *bitchboy!*" a kid, conveniently hidden in the line, shouts down. "You goin' or not?!"

Bitchboy—a kid who is everybody's patsy. Which you are not. Nor are you quite in a rational state of mind right now.

"Killin' and chillin, it's real thrillin'," blares X-tra Big from the sound system below.

Focus, you tell yourself, and you—really—hear nothing, it's all just so much white noise around you.

You know this moment from fortysome years of it, racing and competing, and ski patrol. The moment at the gate, where, if you can get inside it, the world disappears, and it's just you, flying.

You release your heel edge, and leading with your right hip sail downslope, cocking your arms to your right, and at the jump, you squat slightly and tighten your legs, which causes you to catch way big air, and fifteen feet over the hill, legs fully extended again, looking flat out at the mountains on the horizon, *not* down, by instinct (using a decades-old gymnastics move), you glance sharply over your left shoulder, throw your arms left, and while in the air, as if some corkscrew, turning, it seems forever, your body follows, hips, legs, and the board, two rotations, the whole enchilada, and you, luckily, land your 720 nose grab poke, leading goofy again, though (partially) catching an edge, your heart in your throat, you turning heel-side to absorb your minor mistake, then turning radically again toe-side to the bottom, where, exhilarated, and feeling almost preternaturally lucky, you look up the hill at the kids who were behind you.

You're too old to be that stupid, throwing a jump like that on a board, but the bitchboy remark didn't sit right, and all the hip-hop jargon just finally got to you. And you had that one winter, an eternity ago, when you gave Snurfers and Monoskis a go, tired of your Austrian coach shouting at you. So, technically, you were riding before these kids were a saucy twinkle in their folks' eyes.

Justin hits big air now, but trying for a 360, doesn't lead with his head, which makes his rotation short, and he lands edgewise to the hill and falls hard, lying on his back in a heap.

"Yo, Justin!" his pal yells. "You pull a digger!?"

Justin gets to his feet and brushes the snow from his pants.

"Just a fly-swatter!"

Justin has skidded to a stop beside you when the friend heads down, the rap coming on all that more ferociously, because the speakers are only yards back of you now. "Burn it up, learn it up, hip-hop high, the time is nigh."

"Bleah!" Justin shouts. "Bomb it!"

The friend nearly hits a kid snowboarder who has taken this poor occasion to cross the hill, then disappears behind the jump, is hurled into the air, and pulls a 180 nose grab, but landing too far on the backside of the board, he jets off to his left, trying for a save, but goes end over end, too.

"Yokay?!" Justin calls to him.

He's up, waves. "Just a bip!"

When you turn to get to the lift, Justin is grinning at you.

"That was *spiff-u-licious!*" he says. "Totally *bonus.*"

"Just lucky," you tell him. And stupid, you add to yourself.

"Awww, get off." When Justin's friend stops beside you, Justin says to him, "That bizatch beef your hit?"

The friend shrugs. "At least I didn't hit the weasel." Giving you a once-over, he says, "I thought you were a gaffer, but that was *phat.* Way huge. You bagged our game, man. You do inverted?"

"Only on a trampoline," you tell him, and to Justin, you add, "Give a hard look over your shoulder first, *then* follow with your arms."

"Killa guy," Justin says, and he and the friend take the lift, and you soak in the sun, listening to the music, enjoying the moment (but also quietly wondering if you've just used up another of your, possibly, diminishing nine lives).

THE SCHEE-WANK SPORT, EPIC X-TREME

If anything is presently *extreme* in the world of mountains and ski resorts and snow, it is snowboarding. From the time of its explosion onto the scene, snowboarding, which actually shares a great deal in common with skiing, distinguished itself as a new sport.

Snowboarders are the New Kids on the Block, this difference as much something cultural as one of ergonomics and necessarily different technique from skiing. Initially a young male phenomenon, snowboarding crossed over from skateboarding in the early eighties. The typical snowboarder of the eighties and even into the nineties was in his late teens to early twenties, listened to the then still very edgy urban rap music, wore sag gear (pants so low that a belt around the pants' waist held the waist around the upper thighs), shirts sporting slogans (such as *Subvert the Dominant Paradigm*, *Public Enemy*, or the much less subtle, *FUCK YOU*), and spent a great deal of time adapting skateboarding tricks to ski slopes (such as *the grab*, where the rider, catching air, reaches down and grabs the edge of his board). All of which, to skiers, looked nothing short of ungainly if not preposterous.

Antagonism between boarders and skiers was so fierce initially that the bulk of resorts banned them.

On a lift this winter, talking with a man from Colorado, I was told that a group of snowboarders at Copper Peak were actually mugging skiers, threatening violence and taking wallets. Whether this was true or not, it was a typical kind of story older skiers passed around about riders, and still do. (Skiers have a whole repertoire of jokes about snowboarders, as do riders about skiers. Such as: Question, from a skier: If you have a car with three snowboarders in the back, what do you call the driver? Answer: A policeman. Or this: What do you call a snowboarder without a boyfriend/girlfriend? Answer: Homeless. Or: What is the difference between a snowboard instructor and a snowboard student? Answer: Three days.

Riders, of course, have their own jokes. Question, from a rider: How many ski instructors does it take to change a lightbulb. Answer? One; the mountain revolves around him. What's white, magenta, and screams? Answer: A tour bus of Groovy Dudes going over a cliff. Or this: What day of the week did God create skiers? Answer: The day apes took their first dump.

Coloration in these jokes is, of course, representative of the gap between the opposed camps. Riders' jokes tend to be scatological; skiers' jokes have embedded in them references to old-world order and hierarchy.)

And radical snowboarders did, and still do, draw a heavy line between themselves and skiers, skiers being uncool "fancy-pants two-plankers."

To riders, skiers are old, crusty, frozen, petrified, way, way uncool, unhip, unwised-up squares.

Which can, in part anyway, be true of skiers—this petrification. Theirs is a nearly five-millenia-old sport, and carries along with it a rich, and sometimes heavy, history.

Snowboarders, on the other hand, when the sport took hold in the nineties, could afford a ferocious antiauthoritarian, antihistorical stance, given that the style and a good portion of the technology of the sport was, in their thinking, radically new (though not really).

Skiers, conversely, if they cared to get anywhere in racing, or jumping, or freestyle, had to perfect old moves, adding new twists or improvements to them, as well as deal with the old and hidebound politics of the United States Ski Association (USSA), The Fédération Internationale de Ski (FIS), and, worst and most conservative, the International Olympic Committee (IOC).

Snowboarding, though, had no *established* old school, no authoritarian old Austrians, and from the first it reveled in that freedom. Even in creating its own language, a large part of it hip-hop/rap, skateboard, surfing, and street slang applied to the hill or mountain, the very terms for navigating a slope on a snowboard being themselves creations: A snowboarder *"rides,"* is a *rider*. To make a run is to *"shred"* it.

Snowboarding, at least up until now, when pundits are claiming the sport has become completely mainstream (which, for serious riders, it definitely has *not*), had at its core an urban spirit of hard-edged, rough-talking rebellion. And rap, as was for skateboarders, was the new riders' song.

Everywhere, in extreme boarding, rap language influence is evident: to tell a friend, "killa guy" means they just landed a sweet move; a "frenchie crip" is someone who pretends to be a hot rider, but who is actually terrible; a "board bro" is a male boarder; "freezin the coopa" is when you get snow down your pants from falling and sliding downhill headfirst; "gangbaginit" is when your "homeys" leave you at the lodge to go "shred"; "chillax" means to chill out and relax; "ghetto" is a term for something gross or crusty; a "hoedad" is a person who poses with his board in the parking lot, but is never seen on the mountain. And a "mofo" is a ski instructor, "sno-hoes" a group of girls who ride together.

One snowboard company even markets hip-hop/rap boards, its top seller the BRO, in the advertisement, behind the board, five gangster rappers in do-rags.

But other influences in the snowboarding lingo are also evident, language taken directly from skateboarding and its predecessor, surfing: there are the expressions "beige," meaning poor, or inferior; "boost," catching air; the eponymous "dude," for anyone, male or female; "jib," meaning riding on anything other than snow, things such as rails, trees, garbage can lids, foldable tabletops; "krunked," for being knocked senseless. And "hang ten," which, to snowboarders, means wait up, or "stoked," a term for being psyched or revved up.

Yet even given those sources, a great deal of snowboard lingo is pure fabrication, having in much of it an ironic, playful humor.

Which is pure fun, riffing on old themes to the tune of riding.

For example, an "Arctic Cougar" is "an old lady who goes for young guys on the slopes or in the lodge." An "airdog" is a rider who spends most of his time jumping. A C3PO (the gold, human-like robot from the *Star Wars* films), is someone wearing hardshell boots, a person one doesn't want to be kicked by in a fight. A "gangstar" is a "rider so on form that it is considered illegal to shame his fellow riders in such a fashion." A "horndog" is some rider who crashes because he's showing off for the Bettys. All female boarders, incidentally, are "Bettys" (accomplished boarders), "Snow Angels" (good looking but not such great riders), or "Sarahs" ("snowboarding chicks who can't do anything, but think they can"). Kids on boards are "Beavers," or "Knee rockets," or "Weasels."

Acronyms abound, such as ADIDAS, though here, this not meaning a shoe, but "All day I dream about sex."

There are the cartoonish, technical terms for snowboarder "moves," such as an "Andrecht": A rear-handed backside hand plant with a front-handed grab; or an "alley oop," any maneuver in a half-pipe with a rotation of 180 degrees. A "fakie," or "cab" move, for example, means riding backward.

And blends and whole-cloth coinages are common too: "Awesomeness," or "bodaciousness," meaning great, or the best; "craptastic" for something that "sucks."

A "ganjala ride," for example, is a ride one takes to the top in a gondola, on the way sharing, as riders put it, some kind of "bud"—say, some Blueberry, or L-13, or AK-47, hybrid stuff ten times more potent than that old Acapulco Gold or Thai Stix popular in the late sixties and seventies.

And a snowboarder name for a character such as myself? A late-in-the-day (temporary) switchover? Anyone over thirty on a snowboard is a "Gray on a tray."

All of which—the recent appearance of snowboarders on the mountain, the hip-hop music and newly coined slang, the skateboarder moves, and the typical contempt of the snowboarder for anything "old school"—could give one the impression that snowboarding, or "riding," came fully formed from some urban skateboarder's imagining in the early 1980s, which would be grossly incorrect.

A (VERY) BRIEF HISTORY OF THE SPORT

Legend goes, in 1929, M. J. Burchett cut out a "plank" from a sheet of plywood, secured his feet to it with clothesline and some horse reins, and on a hill near his home went "riding" on the first snowboard.

Burchett cut enough of a figure that he was remembered for his "snowboard" and his attempts to steer it, standing, while sliding down hills. (And, of course, he was remembered for the falls he took, curiously, often on his head.) Others fashioned "boards" such as Burchett's for years following, but these boards remained mere amusements, or novelties, in the skiing world. That is, until Sherman Poppen, a chemical gases engineer, in Muskegon, Michigan, built a board for his daughter to use on local hills thirtysome years later, though, with this important difference: Poppen fashioned his toy for his daughter by binding two skis together and running a rope from the tip for her to hang on to, making her sliding toy more stable. Poppen's wife named the device, which in her thinking was a snow surfer; so—*Snurfer*. In no time at all, so many of Pop-

pen's daughter's friends wanted a Snurfer that Poppen licensed his idea to a manufacturer who built and sold them all over the Midwest. Nearly a half million Snurfers were sold by the end of the sixties, though, even given the competitions that sprung up for Snurfers, they were still only seen as toys for children.

Children such as Jake Burton Carpenter, who competed in Snurfing events, even though he was a fairly accomplished skier.

The Jake BURTON Carpenter of the best-selling snowboards in the world, BURTON BOARDS.

Jake had wanted to surf, but his parents wouldn't buy him a surfboard, so Jake took Snurfing as an opportunity to do so on snow. From the first, Jake was impressed with the Snurfer, loved it, in fact, though he imagined Snurfers with ski-like qualities, steel edges for example, which would make them carve more effectively. Jake had just begun thinking about building his own, improved snow surfers, when he was involved in a car accident that so badly broke his collarbone that he could not ski for a season. The following autumn he went off to school at NYU, where he studied economics, and his dreams of radical snow surfing, just then, died.

Enter Dimitrije Milovich, who was the first to build snowboards as we know them now. In college, Dimitrije, sliding down hills on boosted cafeteria trays, invented front-side/back-side turning techniques, Dimitrije also developing the classic wider, double-tipped shape of the contemporary snowboard. Dimitrije's invention, which he called the "winter stick," fused the properties of downhill skis and Snurfers: it would turn in powder like downhill skis, but it was ridden like a surfboard. Amazing! Especially given how crude Dimitrije's boards were.

Such interest and furor was created by Dimitrije's "snowboard" in the skiing world that he and his invention were featured

in *Newsweek*, *Playboy*, and *Powder* magazines, among others, gaining for this budding sport a certain visibility.

Still, though, snowboarding did *not* take off—even though *everywhere* skiers of all sorts were giving Snurfers, Wintersticks, and other single riding surfaces, such as Jack Marchant's "Monoski," a whirl. For nearly two decades, beginning to expert skiers spent days to weeks goofing on these early boards.

Even die-hard skiers such as myself, all of us wondering, What was this fixation of ours with two planks buying us, anyway?

THE MAN WHO FIRED THE REVOLUTION

And that was exactly what Jake Burton Carpenter thought, moving from NYU to Vermont's Green Mountains, long healed from his life-changing car crash and having finished his economics degree.

Why pick up skiing again? Why not *ride* the snow, as he had on the Snurfer, but now on a sharper, higher performance one? One *he* would build?

Realize that this was in 1977, more than ten years after the appearance of the first Snurfer.

Races were regularly held for Snurfers by this time, but the boards had not changed much at all.

Riders skidded down courses, standing on their boards sans bindings.

And the surfing connection was by this time worse than, as riders would put it, *lame*. Brian Wilson, of the Beach Boys, had fallen off the face of the planet in a seemingly permanent drugged stupor, his music dismissed as infantile fluff, surf riffs by then about as edgy as Elvis in his Las Vegas glam gear. Fake, bloated, and riding on momentum alone.

Carpenter dumped the whole surfing business by mounting bindings on his "snowboard," in doing so committing a kind of Snurfing sacrilege.

With this board (and it *was* still a board, had been fashioned from laminated hardwood), Carpenter gave himself a tremendous advantage, easily beating others in "snow surfing" contests, and shocking the snow-surfing world.

Almost overnight, the term *snowboard* came to be de rigueur.

Carpenter began to build boards such as the ones he won races on for others, his only competition at the time Tom Sims, whose snowboard was a piece of wood with carpet glued to the top (to give purchase on it), a sheet of metal screwed onto the bottom (what would have been an important modification, had Sim's board been used for something other than "goofing" on terrain).

But it was Burton who created the first snowboard as we know it now, adding to his board, in addition to the bindings, metal edges and a P-tex base, as all skis had had since the middle sixties.

Burton then gave his board a side cut and experimented with carving, which he found the snowboard excelled at.

Suddenly, a whole world opened up for snowboarders. And they were still "snowboarders." With Burton's new "plank," snowboarders could accurately navigate mountains slopes as did skiers, carving turns, skiing gates closely, and floating powder—in fact, carving snowboards excelled in powder, unlike carving the skis of the time. Yet, even by 1982, at the first national competitions held at Suicide Six, outside Woodstock, Vermont—which was more a survival test on "the Face," a steep, icy run, than a conventional "race"—snowboarding still hadn't distinguished itself as something revolutionary, something truly new.

Snowboarding was thought by the majority in the skiing world to be derivative, and inferior to, its true progenitor: skiing.

Realize that between the years 1977, when Carpenter first began manufacturing his snowboards, and 1982, nothing short of a cultural revolution had taken place in the United States, particularly in sunny Southern California. Punk rock had hit, speaking for a whole generation of angry dispossessed youth, and on its heels had followed rap, an even more specifically vocal form of protestation. Teenagers, but for the most part teenage boys, adopted the violent and sometimes fatalistic rap posture, imitating rappers in dress and behavior, slinging rap jargon, and physically working out their rage on skateboards, "jibbing" on stair rails, and working out moves taken from rap dancing in empty swimming pools, in effect creating a cohesive and white-hot subculture.

This skateboarder pose was to the eighties what black leather jackets and motorcycles were to the late fifties and sixties.

As Oscar Wilde put it, "The first duty in life is to assume a pose. What the second is, no one has discovered."

Skateboarders adopted this gangsta pose with a vengeance.

And add to this the technology of being seen: the affordable and ubiquitous handheld video cam. Kids by the thousands got hold of their parents' camcorders, skateboarders then making movies of themselves, further driving this tendency toward very self-styled poses.

But true athletes and masters of the form rose from these skateboarders, here a new and complicated blend of music, dance, and sport, a thing unto itself, some moves in the terrain parks that sprang up stunning and beautiful.

And strangely, to outsiders. It caught our attention.

There were the easy moves, like the grab (jumping and reaching for the board), skating backward and forward, and riding on the rear of the board. But there were masters who ripped up sides of swimming pools, shot into the air and off their boards, and, falling, caught their boards under their feet again, swooping to do the same across the pool, aces also pulling switch (turning 180 degrees in the air), "corking" (rotating), and jibbing on (sliding on top of) anything narrow and off the ground.

And it was *this* group of skateboarders, wearing do-rags, sag pants, and miming rap lyrics, who hit the slopes.

It was akin to an atomic explosion, putting the old-world skiers and these talented skateboard rappers together. Some critical mass resulted.

Skiers *hated* the snowboarders and their sag pants, *Eat Shit* T-shirts, do-rags, and rap music.

The New Kids on the Block *hated* the skiers, with their stretch pants, goggles, long pencil skis, and fossilized old-world pretenses of sophistication.

So violent was this clash that the majority of ski resorts *banned* snowboarding.

Yet, oddly enough, the epicenter of this explosion was not in the California Sierras, or the Sun Valley Sawtooths, or even Colorado's Rockies, but in staid, conservative Vermont's Green Mountains, old-school skiing country, where Jake Carpenter was cranking out his snowboards.

Burton boards, from this middle name. The best snowboards in the world then, as now.

In a recent interview with Gene Sloan of *USA Today*, Carpenter remarked, "I remember the manager at Stratton saying to me, 'You guys make one mistake and you're out of here forever.' I would lie in bed thinking, 'If just one person does one stupid thing, it could shut down snowboarding.' I should have had more confidence in the sport."

Carpenter was right. Snowboarding was a newly recognized

way of riding snow that would only grow more popular, and would develop its own specializations, as did skiing. But it was the spirit that the skateboarders brought to it that made it take off, that still distinguishes it from skiing.

That in-your-face, on-the-edge; hip-hop/rap; happenin', new-flamboyant grit. That self-referential, posturing, X-treme attitude.

Recently, a former roommate and good friend of mine from Kashmir came to visit with his two boys, Arjun and Kunal, ages ten and eight.

I had promised Vikas I would get him on a ski slope from the time we'd met, when I was in graduate school. He'd love skiing, I'd told him, and his boys would, too. Utah was the perfect place for them to learn.

But when I brought up skiing that first evening of their visit, neither Arjun nor Kunal was the least bit interested. It was *snowboarding* they wanted to try. And *only* snowboarding.

When I asked them *why* snowboarding, and not skiing, they only shrugged.

"Skiing's not cool, Uncle Wayne," the philosopher of the two, Kunal, told me.

"Really," I said. This surprised me, given Vik and his family live in Chicago, and neither of the boys had any direct contact with snowboarders, or snowboarding magazines, or promotional materials (which are everywhere in ski towns—posters, films, the riders themselves talking tough).

Kunal shrugged again. His brother, Arjun, a bright, sunny boy, the diplomat, gave me a winning smile.

"Riding's where it's at!" he said.

So, out to Brighton we went, one of this continent's premier snowboarding sites. I'd just fractured my ribs skiing with my old (insane) friend Oakie, and was in a mood to take it easy with Vik,

Vik picking up skiing quickly enough to be a danger to himself—
but having a great time.

The boys were thrilled with their day, having made an entry
into the way cool world they'd obviously seen on TV.

They even slung a little rap lingo around. I teased them that
they had to be very clear about what they'd become.

"And what's that, Uncle Wayne?" they asked.

"*Riders,*" I told them, not without a good measure of irony
in it.

Currently, nearly 29 percent of visits to ski areas nationwide
are made by riders. One study even puts the number of riders
ahead of skiers for the first time, resorts such as Keystone and
Breckenridge, the two areas most embraced by riders, specifically
catering to the sport with multiple and varied terrain parks.

And though the tension between skiers and riders persists, no
one can deny the influence that riding/snowboarding has had on
skiing.

For one thing, skiers dress differently now. Those loose-fitting
sag pants and bulky jackets riders favor have found their way into
ski clothing style. Gone are skiers' stretch pants, now replaced by
Gore-Tex baggies, which actually afford more mobility than their
stretch predecessors. Gone are the slick-look black or blue jackets. Skiers now wear colors they wouldn't have been seen dead in
just ten years ago, camo, or orange, or army green, and on their
heads are weird hats with spikes, or dragonlike crests, or cartoon
figures—especially for younger skiers—such as Bart Simpson.

And those younger snow sports fans who have, after all,
stayed on two planks, now ride the terrain parks on twin-tip skis,
on which they can jib rails, ride half-pipes, and pull stunts, all *bor-
rowed from snowboarding.*

Which numbers are currently *annually* growing, according to a recent American Sports Data Superstudy, by 50 percent, as opposed to skiing's nearly moribund 6 percent.

Snowboarding, then, is on the crest of some cultural wave, a veritable explosion, which will soon (by some estimates), eclipse the old skiing world, this fierce attachment to snowboarding by the current generation of American riders fueled by the excitement of discovery, and the *ownership of something new and edgy*.

Something *distinctly American*, its Afro-centric qualities putting a new spin on a very old, and very white, game.

Snowboarding, as did jazz and the blues, burst onto the scene out of nearly volcanic cultural influences (though now co-opted by marketing, watered down, and pitched to a broader, less-edgy audience).

And skiing, up until very recently, and with the exception of such bright lights as Steve and Phil Mahre, Picabo Street, and Bode Miller, has always looked to Europe, the home of not only most world-class stars, but also the home of ski development, testing, and manufacturing.

To old money, to the Old World.

Such is *not* the case with snowboarding. Kids don't want Old World. (As the lyrics to a once popular R.E.M. tune go: "It's the end of the world as we know it, and I feel fine.") The best-known, and most prestigious, snowboard event in the world now, the U.S. Open, is held at Stratton Mountain Resort in Vermont. Sonnenburg Ski Hill, also in Vermont, was the first resort to give riders a Snowboard Park, a run of their own—along with a supply of hay bales and picnic tables they could use to make jumps, paving the way for the creation of more sophisticated terrain parks, which nearly all larger resorts in the United States now have.

The best-selling snowboards in the world, Burton boards, are an American product. Burton distributes goods to more than thirty countries and three thousand specialty shops, operating factories in Vermont, Austria, and Japan. (Most high-profile boards are American, with names to equal those of snowboarding itself, such as Funky, Crazy Banana, Aggression, and Checker Pig.)

And board graphics (a snowboard is a fairly large palette for artists), including skulls, slogans, rap lyrics, beer company advertisements, and facsimile graffiti, are driven by American pop culture.

But given all this—the skateboarder/hip-hop/rap/surfer influences; the terrain parks and the skateboarder moves; the posturing and hype—are snowboards *really* that unlike skis?

Is there that great a difference?

X-TREME STICKS, AND HOW THEY WORK

Day one: Riding, you jump on the chairlift, with the board attached to *one* foot, the leading one. If that happens to be your *right* foot, you're riding "goofy;" if the *left* foot, "normal." When the chairlift reaches the top and the ramp, where beginning skiers are, albeit awkwardly, gleefully snowplowing down to the run, you are hobbling free foot, then snowboard, free foot, then snowboard, like some Louisiana convict in ball and chain. The hounds are baying in the distance, which makes you rush, so that you catch your edge and fall on your face.

What fun snowboarding is! you think. This is just for starters. (You can, as the other beginning boarders are doing, take a couple steps off to the side, out of the way, and from there make your hobbled way to the slope.)

On the slope, you snap your other foot, your back foot, into the binding. You have decided to ride "normal," so it is your right foot in the back binding.

Fixed to this immovable board, you cannot, as you can with skis, sidestep, herringbone, or snowplow. You can, though, make little bunny hops until the board threatens to jet out from under you, at which point you squat, thus picking up yet more speed, you heading down the hill, your instructor shouting from behind you, "TOE-SIDE!" as you head for a stand of pines on your left, any of which could shatter your head like a pumpkin.

Toe-side?! you, the onetime skier, think. *What the fuck is that?*

And just before you impale yourself on a branch, as did some poor sod you rescued on Mountain Patrol, fate being kind, so that this skier had not lost his eye, but had only had a portion of his scalp torn free of his head, you think again—

Toe-side?

You glance down at your feet, this molten freeze going on in your head. Am I *normal* or *goofy?*

Left is right, right is wrong. Okay. I'm *normal* (sometimes).

And turning toe-side while riding *normal* is? A *RIGHT* TURN! YEEEEE-HAAAA! To make a toe-side turn, you lift your heels up, press your toes down, and move your knee over the top of your leading foot. Your back boot will follow. A toe-side turn, if you're riding normal, will send you to the right, the board carving, you leaning radically into the turn, this maneuver reminding you of days skiing on near-death hangovers. (A toe-side turn is the same as walking forward, you've been told.) But you don't want to hit those trees, which remind you now of those creepy, evil trees in *The Wizard of Oz* here, and you throw in a little extra body English, thinking for a second, *Gee, this IS fun,* until you've gone too far, and . . . *bang!* Down you come on your knees, the snow here hard enough so that you get that nauseated feeling you've had from banging your shin or kneecap into some immoveable object in your house, say, the corner of a desk or bed frame.

But it passes. And you've traversed most of the slope at a fairly high angle, so, lucky you, you've got nearly all your vertical still. Great.

Off you go again, squatting over the board (suddenly recalling, too, the night your Snurfer nearly killed you), and trying a heel-side turn, because those same *Wizard of Oz* trees are waiting for you on the right side of the slope, too, but instead of wielding apples, they've got broken branches sticking out like daggers, these *Wizard of Oz* trees of a darker, more urban sort. Ghetto trees. Knives and chains and AKs for these snowboard trees.

Your coach—no, *hired instructor*, you correct yourself—behind you is shouting again.

"Heel-side! *HEEEEEL-SIDE!*"

Again, that brain blank. Normal or goofy? Normal! So heel-side is, gee, *left*, since Coach—whoops, Chase, my instructor—wants me back for more lessons and more filthy lucre.

You lift your toes up, press your heels down, roll your hips backward, and—voilà! You are arcing around to the left. And picking up speed, and more speed, you applying yet again more body English, and . . . *WHAM!* Down you go again, catching yourself with your *fists*. Never an open hand (most snowboarding injuries are wrist fractures, a large percentage of serious snowboarding accidents taking place on the would-be rider's *first day*). Which hurts like hell anyway. So when you bump back up onto the board, getting pissed now, you pull another heel-side turn, enjoying the arcing, until you overdo it a second time, and *WHAM*, you come down backward again, saving your hands and wrists this time by taking it square on the rear, which jolt runs directly up your spine and into your head.

But you've gotten a taste of carving, left and right, toe-side, heel-side, and that same spirit that had you jumping off Suicide in Michigan tells you this is nothing, goddamn snowboard, you'll show it.

And for a whole day, you battle. You carve a nice heel-side arc, and just when you're really feeling *burnt, sick, way rad*, you crash on your rear again. Your ski racer pal's warning from his three days learning to snowboard echo in your mind: "Best to strap a pillow on your ass."

The first day isn't even a draw. The snowboard has won twelve rounds of the fifteen you duked it out, this on a run so bogus you haven't skied such since your first week on those terrible Holiday Discount Store skis you started on. Your knees are swollen, your backside black-and-blue, your wrists and forearms tenderized to the point where massaging them makes your eyes water.

Day two: Arms in front for balance, with almost all of your weight on your front, left, foot. You have discovered, as most first-time riders do, that *the toe-side turn is easier*, as you are facing the direction of travel.

Heel-side, with your back facing forward, still feels unnatural, and even a little dangerous. But you switch back and forth now, catching yourself before you fall by squatting, thus making the falls you do take also not as harsh. The board now is not so much your enemy as a difficult friend. It trips you up time and again, but intrigues you more than it pisses you off. You even pull a switch move when you catch a foot of air on a little hummock.

Day three: You're cockier now, arms held out moderately, and not as shakily as before. You've begun to trust the board, have found that when you are leaning into a carving turn that the board will not skip out from under you, that you can really lean into your turns, and it feels terrific. You're not skidding now, as you did on the Snurfer, you're riding a flexible rail, and it is truly exciting.

You even find a nice jump, and, quite easily, getting a few feet of air, do a grab. You land flat and, heading into another rise, jump again, fooling with variations of the grab: If you grab the board on the toe-side edge between your feet, you've done an "indy." If you grab the board by the tail, toe-side, you've done a "tindy." With some "big" air, you can grab the front of the board, doing a "nose grab," or at the rear of the board a "tail grab." If, in the air, you cock the board up and behind your rear end, you have grabbed "method."

When you tire of this, you decide to try some rotation. There are two choices when spinning: front-side spins, where the front of the body turns to the fall line in the first stage of the spin, or back-side, where the rider's back turns to the fall line in the first stage.

The back-side spin is easier.

With a 180 back-side, for example, when you thrust off from the jump, you glance up the hill, your upper body, then waist, legs, and board, following. When the board has reversed itself, you look for your landing space.

This 180-degree move changes your leading leg, so, the "normal" rider in a 180 "pulls switch," continuing downhill from his jump "goofy."

A 360, or even 720, just requires more of what you've just "boosted": you need more air (height, and with it time), and more rotation (the rider more forcefully tossing his head and arms).

With a 360 or 720, you have the advantage of landing "normal" in relation to your takeoff stance.

But you fall hard when you fall, because a 360 or 720 requires time (so height) for all that rotation.

And there it is. By the end of your third day you are navigating the hill, doing grabs, rotations, and pulling switch.

To do this on skis would take you months, if even that. For a beginner, thirty to fifty days. A year, maybe. More for the less co-ordinated. (So, skiers' attitudes about riders come in good part out of resentment: riders are having a great deal of fun, without paying the same price.)

Still, you're far from accomplished, are struggling with your heel-side moves, which remain problematic.

Which brings me to addressing one of the worst, and most corrosive misunderstandings skiers and riders had early on. Riders, when carving heel-side, whether normal or goofy, *are turning against the slope with their backs to the inside of the turn*—that is to say, *they are basically blind to any and everything uphill and to the inside of the arc they are cutting heel-side.*

Which, if you think about it, creates a certain danger. (Which can, with a preturn glance over the shoulder, as with skiers, be corrected.)

But early riders weren't doing that, exercising caution. Nor were they just pulling skateboard moves off any pimple they could jump from on the mountain—performing grabs, tail rides, switches. No. They were cutting skiers off, and a lot of them, especially ones skiing fast. You guessed it, older skiers, racers, world-class wannabes. (Realize that skiers *down the hill* always have the right of way.)

Those early riders, looking for terrain on which to jump, and pulling skateboard moves, were skiing fifteen to twenty miles per hour, and, with their backs to the top of the mountain, and moving that slowly, pulled hard, very short radius turns, ones that were surprising to fast skiers, who were long accustomed to navigating mountains around slow *skiers.*

Any *skier* doing fifteen to twenty on a big slope is a rank be-ginner, or a cautious weekend skier, and their movements are (usually) so predictable you can ski around them like gates in a racecourse.

Riders made essentially blind turns in front of fast skiers, who hated the riders in the first place.

And when such collisions and near collisions were discussed, neither side was the least bit rational about it. A suggestion from a skier to a rider in those early days went something like this:

"Hey, ASSWIPE, you got rocks in your head?! Look before you cut people off like that, got it?!"

And the rider's typical response went like this:

"Fuckin' tool. Dincha see me? Are you like, some brain-damaged dildo, or what's your fuckin' beef?" (*tool* and *dildo* were synonymous words at this time and used interchangeably.)

To the rider, the skier looked like some species of irritating, fossilized Stein Eriksen wannabe. Nauseating (back then) neon one-piece snowsuit, in aquamarine and hot pink, neon pencil skis, in colors to match the suit (which gave rise to, for the riders, chicken or the egg jokes: Did the hideous Bogner ski suit come first, or the hideous aquamarine and pink pencil skis?), and, always, the skier had this look of ownership and entitlement on his or her face.

To the skier, the rider looked like those pimpled teenagers seen loitering around libraries and public offices, making nui-sances of themselves, hair died orange or green, dog collars around their necks, the skateboarders posing like oversized, badly coordinated simians as they slid down stair rails on their boards, making a spectacle of themselves, arms akimbo over their heads and shouting things like "I am ONE MEAN MO'FO' BRO! CHECK OUT MY RAD STYLE!"

These near collisions happened very frequently, which gave skiers cause to ban riders from resorts.

And collision's really *are* dangerous. One afternoon, when I was skiing Bridger Bowl, an out-of-control teenage rider (I was only twenty-three at the time myself) hit me from behind, the kid striking me in the side of the head with his shoulder so violently I was knocked senseless. When I got to my feet and gave the kid a very hostile look—about to lecture him on the downhill skier's rights—he simply darted off and away. About then, I realized I had something floating in my mouth—sharp-edged, with a strangely irregular shape. I spit it into my gloved hand, surprised to see something there that looked like a bit of whitish stone.

Which, on closer inspection, turned out to be a tooth—or part of one.

When the kid had hit me, I'd bitten down hard, and the kid's shoulder had shifted my lower jaw over, breaking off the outside half of my rearmost, right-side molar.

As much as it angered me, I realized I was lucky the kid hadn't, after all, broken my neck.

So the threat of collisions, which posed a real danger, became the battle cry of skiers trying to prevent riders from overtaking their mountains. But the riders just kept coming, and more of them each year, all paying the same lift fees as skiers. The management of the resorts couldn't help but see the boon to them in this new population of snow sports enthusiasts, so they worked out a smart compromise: The riders would have access to the mountain, though riders wanting to build jumps, ride rails, jib on odds and ends, would do so on *resort-built* terrain parks. The remainder of riders *off the parks* would observe all the rules skiers did.

Who could argue with that?

So the problem of slow-traffic riders was mitigated, and riders were cautioned about traversing slopes blindside.

It worked. And snowboarding, still coming on like gangbusters, branched out into three distinctly different groups, all of which have their own areas of competition now, as do skiers.

FREESTYLE

Of snowboarding's many talented and various riders, *freestylers* are the current crown princes and princesses.

And why wouldn't they be? These riders continue to modify and perfect the very moves that most distinguished snowboarding from skiing in the years it emerged as a new sport. All of freestyle's jumps, tricks, and rail slides were, very early on, derived from skateboarding, and remain today the white-hot center of snowboarding, but most so the halfpipe.

A halfpipe is a riding surface literally the shape of a pipe cut in half, first designed by skateboarders who made their halfpipes out of wood. Natural gullies served as the first "halfpipes" for snowboarders, until riders began hand digging/forming their own U-shaped trenches. Now a machine called a "pipe dragon" forms near-perfect halfpipes without the need for a team of people using shovels.

The 2002 Olympic halfpipe in Salt Lake City (now called the Superpipe), had 15-foot walls, and was 450 feet long. Halfpipes have three parts, which riders exploit for tricks: the *wall* is that section of the halfpipe that slopes up from the bottom, tossing the rider into the air. Also important here is the *transition* (the section of the halfpipe where it "transitions" from the flat bottom to the vertical wall—the transition's size being a standard measure from a given circle's radius); and the *lip* (the upper edge of the half-pipe, where the wall ends). The *deck* is the flat area on either side where judges and the audience can stand and watch.

Each time a rider takes a run in a halfpipe, he or she "drops in." "Front-side wall and back-side wall" describe the way a rider is facing when going up the wall of a halfpipe. "Front-side spin and back-side spin" refer to the direction of spin. In front-side spins, a rider turns his *chest* into the spin first; in back-sides, he leads with his *back*—so, it's a "blindside" spin. "Corked" describes a rider spinning off axis, as in a corkscrew, the rider's body horizontal. An "inverted" trick is any move where the rider's head is below his feet. One common move called a McTwist is an inverted 540 or a backflip with a twist.

From here it is all invention, a good deal of it specific to each competitor.

As you would expect, world-class competitors have continued to create new moves and perfect old ones on the halfpipe.

All this, even in competition, done to rap and hip-hop music spun by a DJ who may also "mix" tunes, this "mixing" a further influence on the composition of snowboarding routines, which are "mixed."

As in freestyle skiing (and gymnastics), there are basic moves all competitors can do with ease, the "A" moves.

Again, here the mixing, new-coined, hip-hop influence is evident in the very names of these moves, most of them almost (comically to outsiders) colorful.

Standard moves in the halfpipe include poking or boning (straightening one of your legs to lift the board in the air, or used to give a move like a 360 nose grab a different, more complicated look), performing ollies (springing into the air from the tail of the board), or nollies (springing from the nose of the board), pulling air-to-fakies (an aerial nollie in which the rider and board turn 180 degrees) or shifties (the rider making it seem as though she is turning her body 180 degrees when she isn't, the rider at the last moment counterrotating), or alley oops (where the rider, jumping from the pipe, rotates 180 degrees or more in an uphill direction).

Any kind of jumping is "catching air" or "taking a hit," though there are a nearly infinite variety of "airs" or "hits," each distinguished by how the rider gets into it, and what he or she does there, including landing from it. So there is slob air (grabbing the edge at the nose of the board), crail air, indy air, mute air, and melancholy air, for example.

Once simple moves like the grab also have numerous variants, such as the "stale fish," where the rider grabs the heel-side of his snowboard between his bindings with his hand around the back of his leg. Likewise with "pokes," there's a new variant called a "melon poke."

All such moves as these, "air," "poking," and "grabs," are, for world class riders, simply linking ones to "signature" tricks honed for competitions. Ross Powers, for example, who took gold at the 2002 Olympics, did so primarily on the strength of his "Cab Seven Indy" and "Switch McTwist Golden," both big-air moves, full of complex rotation. Gretchen Bleiler, a 2006 U.S. Snowboarding Team member, is famous for her "Crippler," where she approaches the halfpipe wall riding forward, becomes airborne, rotates 90 degrees, flips over, rotates another 90 degrees and lands riding forward. Bleiler had wanted to be an Olympic diver, then an Olympic Women's Hockey Team member, both of these sports, diving and skating, contributing to her unique halfpipe style.

Todd Richards, another world-class competitor, is known for his "Wet Cat."

But the "10" of halfpipe moves this last Olympics was the "Big-Air 1080."

At the 2002 Olympics, in Salt Lake City, it was throwing a 900 that separated the medal winners from the others, a 900 being two and a half revolutions. But the 2006 winners added further rotation to that, for three full revolutions, or 1,080 degrees. Some riders performed their 1080s in a more vertical posture, while others turned horizontal, spinning like human corkscrews, always in this move the greatest difficulty being the rider maintaining his or her orientation to the landing surface.

Current speculation is that riders in the 2010 Olympics will be pulling 1260s.

And the 2006 Games results only solidified the American stronghold on its creation, Shaun White, the colorful and ebullient "Flying Tomato" (so named for his red hair), taking the men's gold medal in the halfpipe, and Gretchen Bleiler and Hannah Teter, likewise rad characters, the gold and silver in women's, all wowing the judges.

And wowing audiences worldwide as well, these halfpipe events (men's and women's) being the most heralded and watched of our last Winter Games, so new, and surprising, and controversial were they.

As is freestyle's less-known specialization, *slopestyle*, also. Which, though not an Olympic event, garners world media coverage at competitions such as the X Games. In slopestyle, riders one at a time navigate complex courses, on them a series of rails, jumps, and other obstacles (such as tabletops and quarterpipes), riders performing tricks on flat snow between elements of "terrain," such standard and bridging moves as pokes, ollies or nollies, and fakies. As with all snowboarding lingo, slopestyle's is colorful, these Gen X, Gen Y, and No Namers putting a pop-cultural spin on moves and mistakes. To "flail" is to ride badly and out of control. To go horizontal on a jump, and land it that way, is called a "max air plummet." The rail, which snowboarders jump onto and ride in a number of postures, is a veritable magnet for injuries, some slight, such as an "ass grind," "crunching nacho," or "revert to anal sex," wherein the rider slips off the rail, sliding the length of the rail on his backside. "Hucking" this trick would be "butter," landing on your face from it would be "Jar Jar" (after George Lucas's doofus character Jar Jar Binks in *Star Wars, Episode I: The Phantom Menace*). A leap off the rail, an air-to-fakie, but "pulling switch to regular," is called a "pop tart." Any one run is a sashion (say-she-on), or session. Some terms bring up amusing images, such as "rollin' down the windows," which a slopestyle rider does when he takes too big air and flails his arms, trying not to "bail" (fall).

Realize that rails come in a variety of heights and shapes. A "Sex Change Rail," for example, is any rail four feet or higher off the ground, so that if you fall on it, "you'll be talkin' like your little sister."

Given the number of falls riders take, the injuries large and small incurred from riding rails and tabletops, or garbage can lids, or anything the promoter of a competition can think to put on the mountain for the slopestyler, the range is too broad for a nod from the FIS (International Federation of Skiers) or IOC (International Olympic Committee). But filmmakers have made slopestyle, and its cousin, freeriding, lucrative to the point where hot riders sought out by filmmakers can earn a (subsistence) living from it, in those years when riders are most X-treme.

And freeriders, who do dabble on terrain parks, take it the furthest on the mountain.

FREERIDERS

Freeriding is the most general style of snowboarding, encompassing all aspects of the sport: jumping, terrain parks, and rails, but also skiing in trees, in bowls, and on open runs carving turns.

Freeriding's image, more than any other form of riding, is driven by independent film. Companies such as Matchstick Productions, employing freeriders like world champion Terje Haakonsen, set up film shoots wherein riders jump from unimaginably high precipices, turn big in shoulder-deep powder, or throw "spicey corks" from quarterpipes, wowing film audiences. The impact of these independent films, which are shown (and have been since the fifties) by company reps making the circuit of the major resorts, is vast. One such film, *Apocalypse Snow*, starring a French snowboarder, generated so much interest and awe in Europe that it did nothing short of spawning an entire generation of European riders. So fierce was the interest in Europe that by 1994, the International Olympic Committee made snowboarding an Olympic sport, though the first inclusion in Olympic competition did not occur until 1998, in Nagano, Japan. Oddly enough, soon after the IOC voted to include snowboarding in its competitions, many world-class riders, such as Norway's Terje Haakonsen, then considered to be the world's best snowboarder, eschewed World Cup and Olympic competitions, instead continuing to earn their livings through making appearances in films and endorsing sponsors' equipment and spin-off gear, everything from hats to whole lines of T-shirts, which, not surprisingly, given the present cult status of hot riders, are fantastically popular. (And the antiauthoritarian, Live Free or Die sentiments blazoned over those T-shirts certainly don't hurt sales.)

Now world-class freeriders appear in mainstream magazine

ads, such as in *Ski*, *Skiing*, *Powder*, and *Rider*, endorsing helmets, gloves, and yes, already hot boards such as Jake Burton Carpenter's boards.

Among which are not-so-well known boards for freecarve/race riders.

FREECARVE/RACE

Freecarve snowboarding, even though it has appeared as an event in three consecutive Olympics, has garnered the least attention of all the riding disciplines. But then how could it compete with the Superpipe? Or slopestyle with its free-for-all wackadoo say-she-ons on radical (and strange) terrain, or even freestyle's caught-on-film heroics? And all this set to recorded, or live, hard-driving, pounding rap, hip-hop, or rock sound scores. Here, in freecarve/race, snowboarding is most like skiing, competitors navigating courses akin to skiing's giant slalom. Freecarvers do just that: carve runs down mountainsides through gates at very high speeds, though speeds significantly lower than those for skiing.

Here there are no signature Boxslag Fruitspin McQuarter-Cheese moves, no DJs mixing rap tunes, no sag gear.

Just freecarvers, men and women, battling it out for the fastest run down the mountain, in the Olympics, on a giant slalom course. Silent, precise, carving big, swooping arcs around breakaway gates.

So how could freecarving compete with the colorful circus that is freestyle, or the death-defying (though not always) stunts caught on film in freeriding?

And, anyway, there were, and still are, all those human Ferraris and Lamborghinis out there on skis, the Picabo Streets, the

Bode Millers, and the Hermann Maiers. Those way square, way unhip two plankers. Which no self-respecting (younger) rider wants to be associated with. (That'd be *Ghet-to*, man!)

Fast, in the world of snowboarding, is *not* where it is at, even though these riders show extraordinary skill and verve. In fact, for a time, pure carving boards were such a threat to skiing that engineers created parabolic, or pure carving, skis to combat their lure.

In the 2006 Olympic games, though America's Rosey Fletcher, one the world's best freecarve snowboarders, won a bronze, it was Switzerland's Daniela Meuli who took the gold, thus further identifying freecarve/race boarding with skiing—spectators clanging cowbells as they do for skiing events. In the men's event, Americans took home no medals, regardless of how fast they got down the course.

But even then, given the world-class talent of these freecarvers and the ferocity of their sport, in the world of *riding*—

Tricks, pipes, rails, and parks are da bomb, dude! They are *way sheeewang*, the always controversial, radical core of snowboarding.

MORE FUEL FOR THE FIRE

Controversy—or, I suppose more accurately, rebellion against the old—has from the first been a part of riding. The ethos, language, and style all invite and sometimes provoke sanctions against riders, all of which, of course, makes for good media. Riders are masters of media. There is a self-referential, self-conscious posture to it all, which, at this point, has not yet exceeded itself and become self-parody and camp.

Controversy has from the first fueled public interest in riding.

Riders jumped closed ropes, "poaching runs," built "terrain" on skier's slopes, creating traffic jams and injuring themselves performing stunts with names never heard of before, smoked bud in public bars, and fought with police and resort officials in a lingo at first incomprehensible, that language changing each season (as it is doing now), riders riffing on the very sound of their sport, drawing from every pop-culture influence.

So it is no surprise that from the first, riding has been a problem child for the International Olympic Committee. At the time the IOC decided to include snowboarding in the Olympics, it also decided to turn the jurisdiction of the snowboarding event over to the International Ski Federation (Fédération Internationale de Ski, or FIS). This, of course, sparked great controversy, since, in so doing, the IOC snubbed the International Snowboarding Federation (ISF), an organization by and for riders that had been sanctioning snowboard competitions—including the most prestigious snowboarding competition of all, the U.S. Open—since the early 1990s. The fur flew as riders and skiers duked it out, the best riders in the world, such as Terje Haakonsen, declaring they would not compete in the 1998 Olympics, nor would they ever do so. Which made the X Games all that more important for world-class boarders.

All of this might have escaped public notice (and the potential to generate more visibility) had it not been for the sport's first gold medal winner, Canadian Ross Rebagliati. Three days following his climb to the top of the Olympic podium, and into the greatest public exposure yet to grace a rider, Rebagliati tested positive for marijuana and his gold medal was stripped from him by the (hated) IOC. This again caused a furor in the snowboarding world, Rebagliati's coaches and a contingent of attorneys doing the unprecedented.

They fought the IOC. The IOC's decision to pull Rebagliati's medal was heard by an appeals court, Rebagliati's supporters arguing that he was a victim of secondhand smoke at a going-away party in Canada, and that the trace amounts of marijuana in his system would not have affected the outcome of the race. In fact, they argued, if anything, the drug in his system would have *impaired* his performance.

While the media had a field day interviewing competitors and working up the image of riders for worldwide public consumption (skiers joking that the new Canadian anthem was "Oh, Cannabis, Oh, Cannabis!"), the Court of Arbitration for Sport concluded that the original decision had been based on an International Ski Federation (FIS) drug policy, but under the IOC's rules, marijuana was considered a *restricted* substance, not a *banned* one.

Rebagliati emerged from his battle with the evil IOC an Olympic gold medalist *and* a pot-smoking, way-rad rider!

He'd beaten the old bastard two-plankers! How more *snowboarding* could it get than that?!

The hot-rider core was thrilled. Riding got its fifteen minutes and then some. And, secretly, any of us who'd been in the stranglehold of the international ski bureaucracy sighed a sigh of relief.

And for skiers, a sigh not without a fair portion of resentment and, yes, *envy*.

Those uncouth, in-your-face, upstart kids who hadn't suffered at the hands of those old Austrians and Germans, those dope-smoking, hip-hop, rap-riffing, sag-gear-wearing whackos who'd earlier got in your way, bunged up slopes, and had spent hours sliding over, say, discarded manhole covers or Trojan seconds sent from the company for an early 1980s slopestyle competition had just become the new media darlings on the mountain.

And it has been that way since, riders continuing to push the envelope. In the 2006 Winter Olympics the ISF lobbied to have included in competition a new event, boardercross, not unlike skicross, where four riders at the same time navigate an Alpine racecourse of moguls, waves, and jumps, an attention-grabbing, chaotic, accident-filled event that thrilled crowds.

So riders have tremendous cachet in popular youth culture. They're noteworthy. Kids know who Tara Dakides, "the Queen of Snowboarding," is, that David Letterman is "her greatest fan," that Tara, along with Hannah Teter and Molly Aguirre, is doing provocative bikini spreads in magazines such as *FHM*.

And riders like Ross Powers, Gian Simmen, and Caroline Beliard are featured in fashion magazines.

They're HOT, as teenage kids say, and there is big money in snowboarding now—for events such as Nokia's Whistler FIS World Circuit event, purses as high as $160,000—some of these riders wading in "swag," as they call it. The good stuff. World-famous rider Shaun White at nineteen a millionaire, a recent high school graduate who earned class credits for doing the refinancing on his $600,000 home.

And it all started on a Snurfer, this worldwide phenomenon of the New Kids on the Block and snowboarding.

POWDERBIRDS

STEEP AND DEEP,
THE FINAL FRONTIER

You are called to a "50" on King's Crown, the terrain park at the north end of Payday. Asked to bring a backboard and o$_2$, you navigate your toboggan, a Sun Valley, over bumps, parallel turning to scrub off speed, using shallow traverses to let the toboggan run as much as possible.

The call for AirMed—the helicopter—you tell yourself, just means you've got a midshaft femur or an open fracture.

And with that thought, you sail down the park, happy associations here now, you having learned to ride and jump this winter. You have gained a cheerful respect for terrain parks, and that Yo-Daddy, rider's hip-hop slang is percolating in your mind, along with it a bit of attitude. Snowboarding, you've landed an inverted now and are thinking of pulling off other sick moves.

How about a layout/roundoff? A trick that was a breeze for you on the trampoline back when the trampoline was still an "exercise" in gymnastic competition.

But here is your injured boarder. You're expecting . . . a badly displaced, open silver-fork fracture (a common snowboarder injury of the wrist)? Or a compound fracture to a humerus (upper arm)? Or . . . ?

You see, though, as you swing hard right around your fellow patroller, Dave, in his red and black patrol gear, that something else is going on. The injured boarder in his camo sags and jacket is a big kid, well-built. Handsome. His hands are shaking but his lower body is still. *Not* good. You park the toboggan just inches below the boarder and kick out of your skis.

"What do you have here?" you ask. Your heart is sinking, but you're going to get this done, and done right.

When Dave doesn't answer you feel yourself shift away from it all.

Procedure kicks in.

"I'm going to get vitals on him," Dave says. "Why don't you help me with his jacket."

You doff your pack, get your scissors out, and cut right up the left sleeve of this boarder's expensive jacket, a Mountain Hardwear. Like yours. This kid's an expert. There's been a halfpipe competition, the Flying Tomato, Olympic gold medalist Shaun White himself, here in Park City for it.

"Alec, this is our second responder," Dave tells the boarder. "He's going to be working with us."

"Hey, Alec," you say.

Dave gets the BP and pulse, 160/78, 120 per/m.

One great thing about handling 50s with Dave is he's unflappable. But then, fifteen years of this sort of work might have that effect on you. You've seen your share of trauma in your years on Mountain Patrol too, now, though this one's got you down. You hope Dave doesn't put you in the position of doing what has to be done here, but you feel it coming anyway. All the signs are present. In Alec's shaking hands, his elevated systolic pressure and pulse. But the most telling feature, his inert lower body.

"I'm gonna check something here, Alec," Dave says.

"All right," Alec replies.

Dave taps sharply on the bottoms of Alec's boots and you inwardly cringe. Alec hasn't said, Ouch, or Stop, that hurts, or, even, What are you doing? All typical responses to this test.

"Feel that?"

"No."

"Check his pupils," Dave tells you, and you do that, though there is no question about Alec's pupils. Dave has already checked them. But you do that, stoop over him and ask the usual questions. Did you hit your head when you fell? ("Maybe.") How did you fall? ("I was throwing an inverted, and didn't land it.") Were you unconscious at any time, do you think? ("Yeah. I must've been. I can't remember getting down the hill.")

Your attention is split. You are looking right into Alec's face, a hot pressure behind your eyes. Here is another of the brotherhood of snow, of the extreme skiing life, only this one's number has come up. Big time.

And you're watching Dave pinch up the length of Alec's lower body, until he nearly reaches Alec's waist.

"Ouch!" Alec says, suddenly, trying to raise himself to see what's going on down there.

You feel your eyes glass up and you have to look away. *This kid is paralyzed from the waist down.*

The helicopter crew radios in:

"Do you have a BP, pulse, and resp for us?"

They're landing down at Base, Base Patrol setting off flares, the red smoke swirling and lifting over the roof. Dave gives the vitals, then adds,

"Zero CMS below L 3."

There is a pause, then the radio barks out, "We copy." Code for: We read you, *paralysis.*

Talking in code, we try to hold off that horrible moment when Alec enters that other world, one he never imagined was reserved for him. You think back to your moment of glory, hanging upside down over Pick 'n' Shovel, that wonderful, stupid moment. But here Alec has this set to his jaw: he knows anyway.

Another patroller arrives, and you get Alec secured to the backboard you brought down, the O_2 on him, and you lift Alec, backboard and all, onto the toboggan, then secure the o_2 between his knees. Dave takes another set of vitals: stable, which is good, though as second responder, it's up to you to get him to base now.

You press his shoulder and look into his face. You don't say, Everything is going to be all right. You don't say, You're fine. You don't say, It's just . . . *whatever*, you'll be back on the slopes in no time. Those things you usually say.

You say, "We've got some serious help waiting for you at Base. Dave here is going to ski alongside us. If you start feeling sick, you have to let us know. *Immediately*. All right?"

Alec gives you this three-hundred-yard stare. Looks right through you.

It's Game Over, just now. (And, getting into the horns of the toboggan, you send up a prayer—even though you're not sure you believe in any of that—for Alec. *Heal this kid.*)

And like that, you take him down.

WAY UP THERE AND BEYOND

Either it is because of Alec (never inverts, or *any* big jumps for you now, jumping for you is over), or because it is time (a warning courtesy of Bill Johnson about skiing blisteringly fast into your forties), you no longer view hiking mountain peaks in deep snow as insane, some twisted, masochistic activity.

You're . . . *intrigued*, wondering if maybe there *is* something really special in all that mountaineering malarkey with its weird gear, some secret pleasure.

Back when you were racing, hiking a couple thousand feet to ski virgin snow seemed some terrible waste of energy. Why exhaust yourself climbing a few thousand feet with that junk festooned to you just to get a five-minute run? (And could you do seventy in powder? NOT!) And those Steep and Deep skiers always looked crazy: they were either guys with hearts like diesel truck engines who ran triathlons, bearded, distant-eyed guys with nicknames like Killer, or Binky, or girls who put plugs of Red Man in their cheeks and were rumored to be having sex with who knew how many of these guys in hot tubs and thermal pools, girls with hair knotted into complex braids who wore granola clothing and Birkies. Or the Steep and Deepers you ran into were those once-demented-seeming guys who did avalanche control, who you just happen to know now—folks like Jackie, Dynamite Girl.

Those backcountry skiers, when they clunked by you in their gear at the end of the day, didn't seem to so much as *see* you. Much less *recognize* you. Decade after decade. You in your downhill gear, dressed for speed and sporting the latest ski god's colors. But what irritated you most was this: that certain smug, superior look on their faces, that look of knowing *something* you didn't, and most likely never would, contemptible Alpine racing freak and fashion whore that you were.

Still, they made you wonder. What *was* that secret thing they had? What gave them that superior attitude? You had no idea. And they didn't want you to know back then, nor do they now.

Consider this: even in a place as beautiful as Yosemite, a high 90 percent of its visitors never leave the valley floor with its Coke machines, shops selling kitsch, and thousands of milling, bored sightseers. Once, when I was motorcycling through West Yellowstone, headed for Boulder, Colorado, I stopped on Highway 89 at the south end of the park to stretch my legs. A middle-aged couple in an RV pulled up behind me, and proceeded to, with great discomfort, make their way to the scenic overlook where I was standing.

"Well, Terry," the man said to his wife. "This is a *real* disappointment." He glanced at his watch. "We've seen all of Yellowstone in about two hours and I don't know what all the fuss is about."

Realize that Yellowstone is the largest national park in the lower forty-eight states. It would take you a lifetime, and then some, to really "see" the park. These two had just driven right down 89, a four-lane, divided highway, only stopping at the scenic overlook where I had, which, they were right, was nothing spectacular—this overlook wasn't anywhere near lovely Firehole Canyon, or spectacular Yellowstone Falls. Or, even, overphotographed Old Faithful, behind it Yellowstone Lodge, the largest log lodge in the world.

As at Yellowstone, so at Yosemite.

A hike of a thousand feet up to Vernal Falls and a short distance from that and Yosemite belongs to *just you* and a handful of others. (The last time I hiked up to Vernal Falls, a model I recognized from the cover of *Glamour* magazine was posing at a stream for a camera-laden photographer. "Hello," she said, in her *altogether*, as the Brits put it. "Hello," I said in return, striding by.)

Here is what no *Steep and Deeper* (as they are now called, given that snowboarders have joined the ranks) will tell you: At higher altitudes, over nine thousand feet, there is, progressively, less water content in snow. Which means it's *lighter*. A *lot* lighter. At even seven thousand feet, powder can be heavy enough to "grab" at your skis, making this a very difficult environment for skiers of boilerplate and hardpack (anyone accustomed to skiing outside of the American or Canadian Rockies on this continent).

Powder at ten or eleven thousand feet can be *so* light as to be compared to smoke. In fact, some high altitude skiers call it that: "cold smoke." Cold smoke is like nothing else on earth. A good pair of powder skis, or snowboard, will literally "float" in it, and the sensation of coming down a mountainside in uncut, high-altitude powder, is only akin to flying.

You are a bird, dipping, swooping, darting, through pines, over rock outcroppings, down narrow chutes, alert at all times for terrain dangers, because up here, there are many.

But the feeling is akin to the purest ecstasy.

That's the secret.

And there's no fashion show at altitude. There's no splitting of hairs over course times. No barking coaches, Austrian or other.

That's what those roughneck, bearded men and wild, adventurous women weren't telling you. *How absolutely glorious it was up there.* Because as long as they were the only ones who knew what the reward was, there wouldn't be many who bothered. Only those who were serious enough.

So *Steep and Deep* is a world as peculiar as that of impassioned anglers. The Powder Hound will return from a day on the mountain sporting a "reverse raccoon" tan—white around the eyes where his or her goggles have been, the remainder of the face, if not bearded, burned a bright red. (That's right: high-altitude sunlight really burns, even when you're wearing sunscreen, SPF 50.)

"Have a good day?" you'll ask.

"Skied some pow."

"Yeah? Where?"

"Oh," he'll tell you. "Up there."

Certain areas become legendary for powder "caches." Alta

being one of the most any Powder Hound/Back Country rider will tell you. But where *exactly* is that snow? you might ask. "Oh, see—if you cross that saddle . . ." The Steep and Deeper will wave his arm around, as if batting at a fly. Sure enough, you can make out a peak, and beneath it a labyrinth of trees, all of which would make getting down such a slope impossible—*unless* you knew where to enter the trees. Which, since you don't, and since you don't like the idea of a compound femur fracture in trees at eleven thousand feet, you regard as a red flag. Won't go there, won't do that. These runs (powder caches), then, are guarded in the way fishing holes are.

Where did you catch that six-pound brown? you might ask a fly fisherman in Idaho's Sawtooths, and he'll tell you, "Well, you take the road there, go in a few miles, and there's this yellow van with a cow pie on the roof, and there's all sorts of spots just in from there."

At Park City, for example, to get to the West Face requires a moderate hike from Jupiter Lift. Once you are at the top, on a ridge so narrow that a helicopter couldn't land on it, you can go over the Backside, or down the West Face. On powder days, if you get there before noon, you are guaranteed runs in virgin snow.

Ten minutes of pure bliss. Even *one* such run can make an entire day (or even week) worthwhile.

So here you are scaling the track to the West Face: you have strapped to your backpack a pair of Völkl Mantras, magical powder boards. (If you're a woman, you might have K2 Phat Luvs, Völkl Queen Attivas, or Head Sweet Fat Thangs on your back. Or, if you're a rider, a Burton Fish, one of the "new-school" powder-sticks.) Your heart is in your throat from having hiked up the ridge in near-waist-deep powder. The sun is out of the clouds now, you having just beat the closing of I-80 due to the snow that was coming down. You doff your pack and you and your pal, Walt, from Patrol, take sips of the heavily sugared coffee you have in your thermos.

Your legs are twitching, your lungs burning, your heart hammering in your neck, but you will recover in minutes, so take the time to turn your face to the sun, rainbow dogs around it.

You are surprised to see not one but *three* patrollers scaling the last of the ridge to you. Jared, Chris, and Dean, your Sunday jabronis.

"Hey," you call over to them, "What're you doin' playing hooky on a workday!"

It is, after all, a Wednesday, which makes for all the better pow skiing, as there are even fewer Steep and Deepers out midweek.

"Got our priorities straight," Dean shouts back, grinning. "Fresh pow, baby! This is it!"

There is an almost inexpressible joy in the day. Truly, this time, you *are* on the top of the mountain. Here, you *can't get any higher*, you think, though you find out later that, yes, you *can* get higher than this—and not with the help of drugs, pharmaceutical or other.

Bearded Chris waves to you. "Skiin' the West Face or Back?"

"West Face."

Jared shakes his head. "Lightweights!"

The wind has been blowing from the north-northeast, so the Backside will have deeper snow, but will also be more prone to avalanches. And, anyway, the West Face has on its entire length only three sets of tracks.

Jared, the last in the group, and always affable, breaks away from Dean and Chris, coming around the ridge.

"You free all day?" you ask.

Jared tells you he's got to visit a friend who's just found out he has stage four cancer, lymphoma, and can only take this one run. Then it's down to Salt Lake City to visit the friend at the University of Utah Hospital. Which becomes a more sobering consideration, given Jared adds, "Well, you know him." Which it turns out you do, a very charming Afro-Caribbean guy who runs a catering business.

The sun seems, just then, all that much brighter.

You stow your thermos in your pack, get on your skis, and you, Walt, and Jared fan out along the high line.

There are serious slabs of stone coming through the snow on the south end (it nearly makes you cringe to think of hitting one), and you push to the north.

Jared, without any further discussion, drops in.

You drop in behind him, yards back. The first thing you think, as your skis cut this snow, is *Oh—my—God! Nothing* can be *this good*, there are those slabs of stone, which you will surely hit somewhere on the way down, but you see no more of them, the snow deeper now, you having no contact with the ridge.

You are literally *floating*, cutting arcing zippers in nothing so much as air: because that is what this snow is up here, mostly air.

This snow does not catch, grab, or deflect your skis.

You dart a thousand feet down, down, but flying, weightless, and each hummock that would pound your legs in hard snow bursts into nothing under you, you now in the trees, widely spaced and lovely, and even on a slope this steep, forty degrees, you can easily navigate these pines, effortlessly, arcing around them, the trees seventy feet tall, their limbs laden in snow, and always under your skis this smooth, frictionless, three-dimensional air.

All of you—you, Walt, and Jared—flying down this slope,

sing out to each other. In it this surprise. That's right. It is *so* wonderful that you call to each other. Later, you could never say what.

But there is this—since you spend most of your time on hard-pack—pure joy here, in this moment.

Snow is not this *soft*, this *forgiving*, this *buoyant*—but here, it *is*. And this powder, now, is *especially* so. At altitude. And then, as quickly as it started, it's over. Powder like this you can never get enough of. Mountaineering, you eat up your vertical in minutes.

And so up you go again, paying with legwork and with quick, temporary exhaustion, salt sweat stinging your eyes, for that oh-so-ephemeral flight.

Or, as Shane Maixner did, you can take a quicker, though far less satisfying, route to the soft stuff.

POACHING

Lower-altitude powder caches are not only comprised of heavier snow, but that snow also tends to be less stable, since it is often-times found on runs that have been closed due to avalanche danger, the primary reason they are not skied out.

Avalanches kill. As with the slab avalanche that broke loose at the Canyons (what was formerly Park City West) your first day on avalanche control with Dynamite Girl, Jackie.

Arriving late at the scene of the avalanche, you were not needed, after all, as some 150 rescue workers were already on Dutch's Draw. And helicopters with ground-penetrating radar were soon to arrive.

You stood at the toe of the avalanche, while nearly hysterical family members paced around you waiting for news of their loved ones. Initially there were over forty potential victims, then fifteen, and finally just one.

Shane Maixner. Who, with his buddy, Erin Brannigan, had ducked the warning signs at the entrance to Dutch's Draw. The skull and crossbones sign there something they certainly saw, as well as another to its left, that read: ATTENTION BACKCOUNTRY SKIERS! KNOW HOW TO USE AVALANCHE BEACONS, PROBES, AND SHOVELS, CARRY THEM AT ALL TIMES. NEVER TRAVEL IN THE BACKCOUNTRY ALONE. YOU ARE RESPONSIBLE FOR YOUR OWN ACTIONS, YOUR OWN RESCUE, THE COST OF YOUR RESCUE, AND WAIVE ALL CLAIMS FOR INJURY.

A rescue by the BLM or Forest Service, or a private company, as mentioned earlier, can run as high as $30,000 dollars.

The print on the skull and crossbones sign should have nixed Shane's poaching this low-altitude powder cache: YOU CAN DIE / THIS IS YOUR DECISION.

So, Shane was a rookie snowboarder?

No. Shane Maixner, it should be mentioned, was an expert outdoorsman, an avid kayaker and backcountry guide. Raised in North Dakota, he moved to Idaho, where he became an emergency medical technician and firefighter. Just before he was caught in the avalanche he'd finished a degree at the University of Montana, in Missoula, where he was also working as a physical therapist for St. Patricks Hospital. He was in Utah to check out graduate programs.

Said his good friend, Mathew Jones, "He *wasn't* a thrill seeker, but he was willing to try anything that sounded fun."

So, why did Shane and his friends (who were fortunate to have succeeded in veering out from in front of the slide) disregard the signs at the entrance to Dutch's Draw?

Powder. Pow. The soft stuff. For the thrill, here, of *a two-minute ride* in virgin, uncut snow.

Jones, who'd taught Shane how to surf in his native California, said of Shane, "There's a phrase in the surfing world that reminds me of Shane. When you're looking at big surf and trying to decide whether to try it, people say, 'Eddie would go.' Eddie being the late Eddie Aikau, a famous surfer from Hawaii. That's the mood you got with Shane. Shane would go."

And that was what you were thinking, standing at the toe of the avalanche: to get to the pow, *you've got to go.* You, like Shane, were once a serious poacher and tree skier.

But Mountain Patrol has taught you now, and all too many times, how hard those trees you dodged poaching powder really are (and how deadly). Racing has taught you about velocity and mass and collisions—racers like Bill Johnson warning there *is* a time to back off, or find another way. Another *kind* of adventure, which, you've discovered late in the game, turns out to be Steep and Deep, though, to your good fortune, avalanche control has taught you things you'd never imagined about that old white stuff and its dangers, especially snowpack and powder.

About *pow—the ultimate.* And the *joy* of it.

But in the coming dark the mood at the toe of the avalanche was worse than somber. Being at the site of an avalanche recovery while it is in progress really makes you wonder.

First of all, at your own (earlier, boyhood) luck. And then at your earlier lack of concern. When you ducked signs, such as that at the entrance to Dutch's Draw, you were invincible. Now, though, after avalanche control work, and racing, and taking care of injured skiers and boarders, and . . . living in the mountains, and having had your own close calls, you are more calculating.

On pow days you are up long before dawn, devour whatever works for breakfast, cram candy bars, and a peanut butter and jelly sandwich triple-wrapped in plastic—soon to become a peanut butter and jelly lump—in your jacket and head out the door. If you are stepping outside into a blizzard—a *whiteout*—you are ecstatic. You'll either rip the pow practically blind, or you'll get some measure of sunshine, which will be nearly divine. But before that, you have to drive on skating-rink-slippery roads to get to Alta or Snowbird (or elsewhere) from Salt Lake. Oftentimes it is a wrestling match with your vehicle not to go into the ditch or off the edge into the great beyond. Now, after forty years and more of counting yourself lucky, you are finally taking some educated precautions, which, at first, seem to signal the end of your lifelong skiing adventure as you know it. You have to remind yourself: Keep the speed down. No jumping cornices or ridges. No bombing couloirs or chutes.

So when you do take to the high country, even hiking there, at first worse than grudgingly, up slopes you wouldn't have so much as imagined hiking earlier—and that with gear on your back now—you are rewarded with a profound discovery: high country, away from the lifts, away from the—sometimes—comical fashion show of ski outfits and pricey gear, inflated movie stars and wannabe racers and tetchy weekend guests, is a kind of nirvana.

The views are spectacular, the snow so much better than on a run like Dutch's Draw, you become an overnight convert of sorts.

You begin to think in terms of *vertical*.

On one especially heavy powder day at Park City, when Pinecone Ridge was open, I watched, from the patrol hut where I was stationed, a backcountry skier descend and climb a roughly seven-hundred-foot-slope *eight times*.

A Steep and Deeper will call that a fifty-six-hundred-foot day.

To climb that much vertical you have to have a leather heart and leather lungs. And going down eats up energy, too. Lot's of it.

This is the way you begin to think, though, sitting at the top of the world and eating lunch in preternaturally bright, fresh snow. Vertical is *it*. Realize the fresh snow after a whiteout will have a near 90 percent index of reflection. So, not only does it *seem* preternaturally bright up there, it *is* preternaturally bright, old snow (even twenty-four-hours "old") having about half that reflective index.

And there is the pleasure of doing ridge climbs right, the technical thrill of it.

You take precautions, wear a beacon, and know, now, how to run an efficient beacon search, and so do your powder pals. (Though, as you have seen, avalanches can kill, and not just through suffocation. Shane Maixner, after all, died *not* from being buried under the snow, but from being broken in half when the avalanche swept him into a tree.)

You don't scrimp on the gear, there being no doubt that at altitude, in the Steep and Deep, gear is not just the right stuff for the job, but your sole assurance against disaster. You've got the REI Alpine pack, which set you back plenty, skins for your skis, the helmet (a Giro 9), and even those special powder skis, the Völkl Mantras. You've got the whole kit.

You get a little hirsute, rubbing shoulders with the anointed, and the door into the so-called backcountry world yawns wide— and it's a very big world.

Awesome. And that is *not* hyperbole.

There are fields of virgin snow at altitude you couldn't have dreamed of until you saw them for yourself.

What you once called Steep and Deep, six inches to a foot or two of the fresh stuff, in the trees, or off where the average weekend skier wouldn't get to it, now seems like nothing. You're plunging down chutes where the stuff is *armpit deep. Over your head deep. Ten, fifteen feet deep.*

Your eyes get a little weird, like that guy you met at that party, the legendary Ed Newland, who'd been a pro patroller for twenty-five years. Who, you thought back then, was one dangerous-looking character.

Who you've come to resemble—just a bit.

Remember, as long as you're wearing the glam gear, these Steep and Deepers will not show you where the magic is.

You have to don the requisite Pow Wizard's cloak, festooned with the arcane symbols of the Brother/Sisterhood of Pow (carabiners, nine-mil rope, glacier glasses, etc.), let that uncivilized facial hair grow, or, if you're a woman, bind your hair in those braids, pee in the trees, drink that offered Knob Creek in one long pull.

Fuck, yeah, that's good, you'll say.

Your jacket gets frayed from climbing over rocks. Your gloves are chewed up, the Thinsulate escaping like bits of popcorn from the holes. Everything fades from the brilliant sunshine, your reds turning to oranges, blues to periwinkle, blacks to grays.

You have that reverse raccoon tan. You stink like smoke and industrial strength sunscreen.

When you smile, there's that something in it that wasn't there before, a We're here! *This* is the place! exuberance.

And then—you drop over a ridge with your pals, your beacon set at high, and soar like an eagle.

Free again. Alive just now as nowhere else on earth, high on a mountaintop and everything miraculously *new* again, in *pow!*

HELI-SKIING (OR, BEAM ME UP, SCOTTY!)

Imagine riding a lift chair, and at the top of the mountain, where you would usually step down onto hardpack, letting your chair carry you beyond that last lift tower, up the mountainside thousands of feet, away from it all, then—suddenly—having the chair clear a ridge, the mountainside itself dropping out from under you.

You are truly *flying* now, in a helicopter, courtesy of Wasatch Powderbird Guides.

You wonder if the pilot is taking a bit of perverse pleasure in zooming over this ridge, the whole world dropping away, making your heart balloon with both joyful anticipation and a kind of anxious dread.

You've *really* done it this time—gotten a ride to the Beyond.

Up here there are no other Pow Hounds, Steep and Deepers, or backcountry nuts, just you, the pilot, the guide, and a family of three. The helicopter lunges up canyons, drops over ridges, veers around peaks. The guide points to the highest, and the pilot lands, here ending your magic carpet ride, and you and your group explode out of the helicopter into the freshest, whitest stuff you've *ever* seen.

Here this vertical a *gift*—you haven't bought this altitude with a heart-banging, leg-exhausting climb (though, granted, you *have* paid for this day, during regular season, $840).

From where you are standing on this mountaintop, you can see an infinite number of chutes you could rip, paths through trees, lines down meadows, all of which excite you no end. The Powderbird Guides, though, have identified the runs you *will* take—even covered with three feet of fresh pow, an avalanche expert having assessed the terrain before the pilot took you out.

Which feels a bit like parachuting to you, relying on some expert's opinion in avalanche country. But that's part of the package—the danger—and, as you already know, Powderbird Guides' safety record is excellent.

So, you're thinking about *vertical*. In this full day, you will take a minimum of seven runs, possibly more, for a guaranteed total of more than 20,000 feet. Something that would be impossible if you were climbing, where a stellar day would be around five thousand feet. Will your heart be all right at this altitude, you wonder, ripping the ultimate Steep and Deep? (Realize that altitude sickness is no respecter of conditioning—and its effects can be lethal, the onset a kind of pulmonary edema that makes you dopey at first, so you can't recognize it, then incapacitates or kills you.)

And if the helicopter cuts out? Or a freak storm blows in, keeping the pilot from getting back to you? From any helicopter getting back to you?

What if one of the others gets sick—the doctor from Tallahassee, his wife, and his daughter, who's on a Burton today?

To get to this peak you're on now, the easternmost of the American Fork Twin Peaks, in inclement weather, would take the better part of a day for even expert climbers. You are *miles* east of Salt Lake into the Wasatch (which, just now, sounds menacingly like *Sasquatch*) mountains.

Standing in all that open space, on this remote peak, you wonder if heli-skiing (which is an inclusive term now, also including snowboarders) is such a bright idea after all. You ask yourself, Who would have thought of such a thing in the first place, putting helicopter travel and skiing together?

The answer? Hans Gmoser, of Canadian Mountain Holidays.

Gmoser, an avid backcountry skier, realized in the early 1960s that the new generation of smaller, maneuverable helicopters would make great ski lifts where lifts hadn't been, and never would be built. Especially near rock spires, glacial cirques, avalanche paths, and river drainages, all of which form the backdrop of helicopter skiing terrain, such as you're seeing here. Spectacular terrain. Unnavigable by cat, snowmobile, and—in some places—even by experienced climbers.

So popular was Gmoser's helicopter expeditions that others in the United States followed suit, not surprisingly, Sun Valley's owner, Bill Janss, who established Sun Valley Heli-Ski Guides in 1966. SVHSG currently holds the longest-standing operations permit in the United States, such permits issued yearly by the United States Forest Service. SVHSG has access to 750 square miles in three ranges of the Sawtooth National Recreation Area, one of the largest permit areas on the continent. This last winter it celebrated its fortieth year of service.

The company you've hooked up with, Wasatch Powderbird Guides, based up in Little Cottonwood Canyon east of Salt Lake City, near Snowbird, has been in operation since 1973, making it the second-oldest continuously operated heli-skiing company.

Helicopter skiing, or touring, though, can be found at most major ski resorts now, whether in Canada, the United States, or Europe.

But it is *Utah* that boasts the "Greatest Snow on Earth." In the 2004–2005 season, Snowbird/Alta recorded over *seven hundred inches* of it. And that at their resort *base* elevation.

You are thousands of feet higher now, in snow even deeper.

And, in addition to that, there is, some meteorologists claim, an effect from the Great Salt Lake itself, which causes heavier snow to fall on the west side of the Wasatch Range, leaving the light, miraculous stuff to fall east of the Front Range, making for the *lightest snow anywhere* (having the least water content).

Alta and Snowbird, up in Little Cottonwood Canyon, on the *average* receive over five hundred inches.

Sun Valley receives on Bald Mountain around 160, though in the Sawtooths to the north, annual average snowfall can easily be double or, in some places, triple that.

Powderbird guides like Sun Valley Heli-Ski Guides, boasts an inventory of runs: over three hundred of them, some near Snowbird, some as far as thirty miles to the north or south. Its permit covers eighty thousand acres, an area roughly *four times* the combined total area of Utah's twelve major ski resorts.

Powderbird is how you've come to be standing on a peak at nearly twelve thousand feet—just now a seemingly impossible distance from civilization.

At Powderbird, you arrive early to complete paperwork (waivers, releasing the company from liability in the event you are killed out in the Steep and Deep), have a light breakfast, and attend two orientations. The first covers basic backcountry safety, avalanche transceiver orientation, and rescue procedure; the second basic safety procedures in and around the copter. (The tail rotor, especially, can make nice sliced salami of the careless skier.)

Toward the end of your orientation, you noticed the snow outside had stopped falling. Which thrilled you. This your third try at a day out heli-skiing. The first was too windy, the second the peaks were socked in by clouds. So three here *is* the charm. (On the average, Powderbird Guides makes only 40 to 50 percent of its scheduled flights.)

Rusty Dassing, the president of the company, monitoring the weather from his office, green-lighted the day, and your pilot, a taciturn guy in Ray-Bans named Steve, went out and fired up the bird.

You, the doctor and his wife and daughter, and your guide, Tyson Bradley, headed for the chopper.

Ty has carved turns as high as twenty-three thousand feet and led expeditions all over the world, which is humbling. But then, your life of adventure pales in comparison to that of Powderbird's guides': All have been on expeditions to locations such as Chile, Peru, Tibet, and Nepal. One guide, Spencer Wheatley, won the World Extreme Skiing Championship in 2000 and was featured in the Warren Miller movie *Cold Fusion*.

But here was the copter, and you got in.

Wasatch Powderbird Guides uses the Aerospatiale Star, or A-Star 350 B3 Ecureuil chopper. The B3 has the comfort of a BMW and the performance of a Ferrari, the 850-horsepower engine making it possible for the B3 to cruise at a speed of 120 knots (about 140 miles per hour) while carrying up to 2,300 pounds. It can also climb at 1,800 feet per minute, and operate at altitudes as high as 23,000 feet. In Alaska, B3s are commonly used for firefighting, and in the lower forty-eight states for law enforcement, news coverage, and—of course—heli-skiing. (A new B3 costs about $1.1 million, which, when financed, still runs the heli-ski outfitter about $235,000 each year. With insurance, about 8 percent of the copter's value per annum, that comes to $323,000, and there are maintenance and fuel costs, too. An A-Star B3 burns about 10.5 gallons per hour. So figure all that into the cost of your ride.)

The copter coughs, then chutters. The rotors gather speed, the copter rocks, then suddenly lifts from the helipad, the pad and building, then canyon, shrinking as if under some trick lens.

The copter tilts forward now, as if hunting. Your destination this morning is the American Fork Canyon, which, as of 9:00 a.m., has received three feet of new snow at the top, the route manager told you—that snow having a *5 to 7 percent water content*.

(You recall, from your avalanche training, that heavy white stuff in your driveway may have as much as 25 percent water content.) So you have spectacularly dry, light snow this day.

Minutes from the helipad at Snowbird you're in deep mountain country, skimming over purple mountain majesties, rugged cirques, and deeply fissured canyons, the pilot swinging around to land on that eastern American Fork peak.

And here you are now, your gear at your feet in the snow, the helicopter rising overhead (which, just then, reminds you of your work with injured skiers—all of which you dismiss).

It's so blindingly bright out you put on your goggles, standing in the copter prop wash (which is akin to being inside one of those paperweight snow scenes you loved as a boy), which subsides, finally, leaving you a bit breathless. From this peak, you can see forever.

Now, about to leap down this snowy mountainside, your guide's admonitions come to you, the first of which, down below, you'd thought absurd:

Remember to breathe. It's surprisingly easy to forget, especially on the first exhilarating run.

And there were the others:

Ski within the area your guide specifies. Stop where he stops. Do not ski below your guide unless instructed to do so.

Do not ski over something when you cannot see the other side. It may look like a breakover, but you could encounter a cliff or dangerous obstacle.

Avoid cornices. Strong winds cause overhanging crests of snow to be formed along ridgelines. When conditions are sensitive, a skier's added weight can cause these cornices to break.

If you do fall, immediately try to stop sliding by getting your skis to your downhill side and pushing the edges into the slope. With your feet downhill you can stop yourself with or without skis.

Ty makes sure the group is ready, then sidesteps to the north-facing ridge, over it a steep hollow.

Our first descent will be down this open cirque. The pitch is radical, a good place to start, and Ty drops off the ridge first.

You follow, your heart in your throat, and the first thing you realize is this: cutting turns in virgin, 5 percent pow is like *nothing* you've ever experienced.

At first you're simply stunned at it. After all that struggling to carve the cleanest turn, find the fastest (and quickest) line, buy the best tuck you've got in you, after all that banging around, charging down hardpacked slopes, and staying focused, after a lifetime of holding a line while your legs are taking a nearly 4 g pounding, this snow *can't* be believed.

This snow is *so* light, to turn in it you only have to *think* of turning and, effortlessly, you swoop left, then right again, in some avian rhythm. *This*, truly, is what flying feels like. You've had moments of it ripping backcountry runs, as on the West Face, but this goes on, and on, and on. Over two thousand feet of it, you skiing like some dream, through pines and firs higher up, then stands of quaking aspen below, you singing some nonsense song that just bubbles up out of you, out of this ecstasy.

Here, unlike ever before, this *grace*.

You have not bought this grace through climbing some ridge to make a thousand-foot descent, or by skiing within a fraction of your very life on some downhill course, that pure, in-the-bubble concentration necessary to do it making you live like nowhere else in those seconds.

This is a God's-honest *freebie*. Sure, you've paid for this thing in dollars, but up here, who cares?

Steep and Deepers having this extreme, top-of-the-mountain experience are vocal about it, exclaiming: "I have discovered my

true purpose in life. How can I go back to my real job after this?".
(Tim Byrd, skiing with Valdez Heli-Camps.) Or "I've been to
heaven." Or "Every single run was the best run of my life." Or
"You can laugh yourself breathless with joy."

You make it to the bottom, swing to a stop beside Ty, and
catch your breath. Run *number one of seven* down, and the *next*, he
assures you, will be steeper, deeper, and longer. This was just for
starters. Starters?

You race? Ty asks you.

You tell him, Yes, years ago, but you just ski Mountain Patrol
now at Park City.

If you like *this*, he says, you should try our heli-touring in
Greenland.

Greenland?

You file this away, too ecstatic to think about it now. The remainder of your group, Thom, Deborah, and Taylor, are down
now, stopping alongside you.

All they have to say is this: *WOW! Oh—my—God! That was . . . fantastic!*

And here is the helicopter, landing, and you stride to it, having
one of the best days of your life.

You are lifted, again, effortlessly, to an awe-inspiring peak,
and true to Ty's word, the second run *is* steeper, the snow deeper,
so deep that you seem to as much as float down through the trees
as ski through them, the snow so deep you have to keep your
speed up, faster than you'd ever ski through trees at resort altitudes, the snow having a cushioning, speed-limiting effect. Your
skis skim the top few inches, floating as if on some preternaturally
light, three-dimensional water. Which our atmosphere—air—is. A
kind of rarefied liquid.

You stop for lunch. Peanut butter tastes like caviar at eleven thousand feet on a Powderbird day. Coffee is the elixir of life. Here, Snickers candy bars are hands down superior to the best New York cheesecake, no competition. Private charters, Ty tells you, include a catered lunch. Catered like *what?* Oh, crab legs, clams, asparagus tips with hollandaise sauce, prime rib, rosemary potatoes, petits fours, or truffles, snifters of Courvoisier, or a glass of fine Pinot or Chard. Sound good?

Hmmm, you say, chasing down your lunch with a slug of Knob Creek. It burns going down, just right. You do a little dance to signal you are ready for more pow. Though not one of you here is under thirty, you feel like you are ten. You guard against saying something truly silly.

I just love you all so very much! Or *Isn't life wonderful?!*

You feel compelled to say these things, buoyed up with some clownish exuberance, as if you were oxygen deprived, or narco-tized. The sun does that, the altitude, the mountains, the pitch-smelling firs, but most of all the *pow*. The pow has lit you up like a small sun. And it *is* bright out here. A bluebird day. You chew forcefully, swallowing the last of your lunch, wanting more of that eiderdown pow, that Utah champagne pow, that cold smoke.

You can't wait to get back onto/into it, to let your boards run, to fly.

Which you do, all that joyful afternoon.

●

And then, too quickly, it's all over. Handshakes, exhausted amaze-ment, and you trudge to your car, parked up access road number 4, Snowbird in sight. Your gear hanging from you, you study the Snow-bird tram, which has been in operation since the early 1970s, two counterbalanced, opposed cars, each capable of packing in seventy or more skiers, the blue car now just leaving the loading area at base.

You've ridden those things umpteen times, packed in shoulder to shoulder with your compadres, especially on fresh snow days. Those days you rushed from whichever car it was you took to the top, first on the mountain (with the exception of the AC crew, out just after six), skiing away from the others as quickly as possible to find those astounding caches of untouched pow—hundreds of vertical in out-of-the-way places, or, if you were willing to climb, a thousand feet.

You regard all that now—the scores of brightly clad skiers on Snowbird's front-side slopes zooming left and right, jockeying for position, the fierce spurts of speed by some skiers, some visibly better carvers, others having stopped to natter here or there—at some distance.

Watching, your skis—your Völkl Mantras, true powder skis—slung over your shoulder, you pause. You are reminded of that time when your father seemed not to want you to ski that weekend at Vail, when you were in your early teens—your father telling you, this man who'd flown all over the Pacific after the Big War, *it would ruin Minnesota skiing for you.*

So you didn't make it to Vail that first time, but you came here: to Snowbird.

Though now you are a *true* snowbird, having skied twenty-three thousand vertical feet of pow in *one day*, away from the rush, away from the echo of those old Austrians and the pressure to look fast, *be* fast, carve clean.

Perhaps it is just age, you having to let go of some things—for one, that old demon friend of yours, speed. And throwing dynamite to get a thousand-foot corn snow run seems a bit much now.

Every day you drive to Park City to Patrol, you pass the Olympic jumping center, the 90- and 120-meter ramps there, built into the mountainside, austere and calling to you, where Simon Ammann made magic in 2002. There is a senior-level competition. You *could* ski in it. If you *really* wanted to.

And you've had your time on the snowboard, even throwing a back layout on Pick 'n' Shovel.

Skiing, you have broken your ribs three times. You were nearly impaled on a pole at Whistler. You crashed, terribly, off the Bush Lake Olympic Training Center seventy, in Minneapolis. You have no sensation in your toes, your knees ache (some days very badly, after a gratifying day of moguls), and in a seventy mile per hour crash, in Sun Valley, you tore the muscles across your midsection, so that when you stand suddenly something like a bolt of electricity runs from your lower left quadrant clear to your right shoulder.

Some days you feel like some animatronic skeleton in one of those old films, like *Jason and the Argonauts*.

Is it time to hang it up, your lifelong skiing life on the edge?

You study the mountains, here at Snowbird/Alta, jagged and magisterial and beautiful, and that old Tennyson poem, "Ulysses," comes to you.

It is never far from you now, all this time later, you having used up a number of your nine lives.

You, who cringed at the raw sentiment of Tennyson's poem in daylight, who hated it when you were a boy, now, alone, think on it and get glassy-eyed. You who have memorized without trying a few lines:

> *Come, my friends*
> *'Tis not too late to seek a newer world.*
> *Push off, and sitting well in order smite*
> *The sounding furrows; for my purpose holds*

To sail beyond the sunset, and the baths
Of all the western stars, until I die.

And with that thought, you drop your skis into your "coffin," the Thule hardshell container on the roof of your fifteen-year-old car. Who has money for a new car when that next pair of magic skis is calling?

You get in and, behind the wheel, the mountains turning purple in the coming dusk, you ask yourself, What would Dag Aabye say?

Fuck it, that's what he'd say, you think.

And you pull out onto the road, driving down Little Cottonwood Canyon, and in your mind is this: *Greenland*.

Green. Land.

You skied two thousand plus vertical runs today, but Ty told you, in Greenland, the big runs have as much as five thousand vertical *on the average.*

And Powderbird arranges trips to Alaska, New Zealand, and Nepal, too.

You have a friend who just finished building a house at the base of Warm Springs in Sun Valley, who, it amuses you to think, just discovered the same thing you did. The Outback, the Steep and Deep, the Remote and Inaccessible. Your friend didn't even buy a pass this last year, but instead made mountain ascents to peaks in the Sawtooths you've never even heard of, in a place called, of all things, the *Frank Church-River of No Return Wilderness Area*. Got the glacier glasses and the whole deal. He's been talking about the Chugach now, in Alaska, a place you've wanted to visit since reading Jack London's *The Call of the Wild*. And in Colorado there's Telluride, which you've never skied, Telluride Helitrax there. High Mountain Heli-Skiing in Wyoming. Mica Heli-Skiing in the Monashees in Canada. Canadian Mountain Holidays in the Bugaboos. There's snowcat skiing at Mount Bailey in Oregon and at Banff, right near beautiful Lake Louise, which you've never seen in winter (this a place where, in your late teens, out backpacking, you were chased by a grizzly).

Why, there's even kite skiing in Minnesota, on old Lake Minnetonka, where you fished for bass and northerns as a boy. You could get hold of a Burton powder board, try riding in the Steep and Deep.

And, why, you've never tasted yak butter, as good a reason as any to make the trip to Nepal. Right?

Why, what if you wrote a book about it? You could (possibly) even swing such a trip, the expenses part of your book deal! Or, if not that, well, you're resourceful, you'll think of *something* (the lottery, Publishers Clearing House sweepstakes, Vegas). Sure, your car has two hundred thousand miles on it and you could use a new this, that, and the other thing. Sure, the house needs a new roof, the toilet leaks, and the stove is due for replacement.

But what the hell. *When* have things been different?

You, steering your crappy car down Little Cottonwood Canyon, feel a smile as bright as a sunrise on your face. You're humming something, thinking of Dag, of your new Steep and Deep buddies, of the engineering student who didn't have so much as a few months one winter to live out a dream.

Alaska! Yeah, *that's* what you'll do! (And, hey, your Oxford-educated sweetheart has it in her head that running a bobsled team of dogs would be lovely, so there's a definite selling point for her.)

A few lines about the Steep and Deep powder experience from a Valdez, Alaska, heli-skiing advertisement come to you: *You dance. Space, time, and form disappear and are replaced with a life-energy that can only be described as pure, real, CORE. This is life, this is peace.*

Your eyes are ablaze and your soul is alight.

That's the ticket! Alaska first!

Guaranteed, *eighty thousand feet vertical in six days!* And it's only $5,845! And if you can talk your Sun Valley friend Charles into going, $5,285 for double occupancy.

That's the thing! Alaska. Then Greenland. And then Nepal.

You glance down at your speedometer, you doing, thinking about all this, nearly double the speed limit.

And what about Tibet?

You settle in, this bright light in you. You've got your last day on patrol on Sunday. Maybe you'll sign on for another year of that, too? That's exciting. And you can visit Charles in Sun Valley and take a trek into the Sawtooths. And some school in Auckland, New Zealand, has invited you to teach for a semester. Powderbird has deals in New Zealand. It would be a cinch talking your wife into visiting New Zealand, world traveler that she is. You could climb those glaciers there. Shear sheep. Drive on the left. Get to know some Kiwis.

And while your wife was taking in the culture you could, of course, *ski.*

You'd be right there.

Just a hop, skip, and a jump to adventure. Big, exciting as you can make it adventure, skiing.

When you think of it, there's a whole world of peaks waiting for you.

And all you have to do is—

Say, *Yes!*

ACKNOWLEDGEMENTS

How can I possibly thank all those people who have helped make skiing the joy it has been for me? So, I'll say thanks to my father, Wayne, and my mother, Nathalie, who got me on those wooden skis with cable bindings in the first place. I thank my jumping coach, Rudi, and my downhill coaches, Roger, Andreas, and Rimon. I thank my skiing buddies, racer pals, and partners in adventure: Chris, Greg, Jerry, Wendy, Suzy, Deb, and Tom. I thank, from the bottom of my heart, my jabronis on the Park City Ski Patrol—the best bunch of men and women you could get to know anywhere, bar none.

I thank my agent, Tracy Brown, for suggesting, when I was relating a tale about rescue on the mountain, what I had had going around in my head already: Why not write a book about it? And for finding a home for that book in Peter Borland's Atria imprint at Simon & Schuster, Peter and Nick Simonds, at Atria, providing invaluable editorial commentary.

My neighbor, Jared Stoddard, I thank for keeping my cantankerous computer running.

I thank my wife, for understanding my need to be off on

mountaintops. For making me those hot dinners, especially at the end of patrol days.

I thank the snow gods, and ski gods, and off-piste and après-ski gods for, somehow, giving me safe passage.

I thank my lucky stars, and wish you, reader, the same.

Blessings in adventures, and in snow!